The Bicentennial History of Greenville, Illinois
Volume 1

A reprint of *Historical Souvenir of Greenville, Illinois
by Will C. Carson*

Published by:

Greenville Illinois Bicentennial Board
200 W. College Ave.
Greenville, IL 62246

Publications Committee:
John S. Coleman, Chair; Sharon Grimes; Lester Harnetiaux; Kevin Kaegy;
William Johnson; Sherry Schaefer

Scanning of Original Work by: 3-Point Ink, Greenville, IL

Photo Index by: Kevin Kaegy

Cover Design and Layout by: Elizabeth Kaegy

ISBN: **978-0692313602**

First Printing: January, 2015

Table of Contents

Will C. Carson

INTRODUCTION

This book is a reprint of the *Historical Souvenir of Greenville, Illinois* by Will C. Carson, first printed in 1905. It is a unique book in many ways. It begins with a decade by decade chronicle of the town's first 90 years; from its founding by George Davidson in 1815 on a bluff overlooking Little Shoal Creek, to a vibrant community at the turn of the 20th Century. It then follows with a closer look at Greenville in 1905. It surveys the community's businesses, schools, churches, factories, and prominent people of the time. Within these pages is a rare glimpse of life when telephones, electricity, and running water were still new; and paved roads, automobiles, and airplanes were yet to be known.

Perhaps the rarest element of this work is its photographs. There are hundreds of pictures of people, homes, buildings, and events around Greenville. In 1905 it was difficult and expensive to include photos in books. However this one provides a large number of them giving a valuable visual record that many small communities don't have today.

The author, Will C. Carson, was born in Macoupin County in 1874 and grew up in Woodburn, Illinois. Carson, whose mother was from Greenville, started his own newspaper at age 14. In 1895 he got a job as a reporter for the *Greenville Advocate*, quickly moved to editor, and bought the paper in 1916. Under his guidance it won several awards and became an influential paper in Southern Illinois.

Carson was known for his strong opinions shared in his editorials and weekly column, *Carson's Caustic Comments*. But, he was also known for his strong interest in history. He published many photos and articles of Bond County's past, and printed the eyewitness accounts of many survivors of important events. Along with this book, his huge *Advocate* special editions in 1915, 1928, and 1934 are still referenced by historians today. He died on Memorial Day weekend in 1942 shortly after taking ill while working at his desk.

When our Publications Committee considered projects to mark Greenville's Bicentennial, it was soon realized that this book is a major source for the town's early history. We would simply be trying to rewrite what was already written here. Also, since many of the original photos have long been lost, there is no other source for the images printed within. So, it was decided to reprint this book and give newer readers a chance to see it in its entirety.

A newly created index appears at the end of this book with addresses of the buildings in the photos so readers can see first hand where structures either once stood, or what they look like now. Also, a name index created for a 1982 reprint by Greenville College has been included as well.

We hope that you enjoy this reprint as *The Bicentennial History of Greenville, Illinois Volume I*. Our committee will soon release *Volume II* to update Greenville's history from 1905. We hope it becomes as valued as this book has been.

Greenville Bicentennial Publications Committee
October, 2014

1

HISTORICAL SOUVENIR

——— OF ———

GREENVILLE, ILLINOIS.

Being a Brief Review of the City from the
Time of its Founding to Date

COMPILED AND EDITED
BY

WILL C. CARSON

ILLUSTRATED

PRICE, ONE DOLLAR.

PUBLISHED BY
THE LECRONE PRESS, EFFINGHAM, ILL.
1905

FOREWORD

IN presenting this little volume to the critical gaze of the people of Greenville, the author fully realizes that there are many of her citizens who are better equipped by tenure of years and by ripe experience to lay bare the story of her life and growth.

The task of assembling the historical data has been a great one, but when once assembled, the work of confining it to a volume the size of this, without losing sight of the essential facts, was even greater. In order to confine the story of Greenville to a volume of this size it became necessary to treat the subject in a general way. This was never intended to be a biographical record, but a history of Greenville could not be written without frequent illusions to many of her citizens who have contributed materially to her growth. Perhaps mention of some of these has been omitted. If so, it is unintentional.

The illustrating of this book has been conducted by Mr. Byron K. LeCrone, of Effingham, and Mr. Lon S. Matherly, of Vandalia. The people of Greenville have responded most generously in many ways to make this work a success. To single out any one individual, or, for that matter, any dozen individuals, as having given valuable assistance in this work, would be to overlook scores of others, who have done equally as much. Of course there have been some who have contributed vastly more than others in its compilation, but to the whole people we are indebted for whatever measure of success this little book attains and to them we wish to express our sincere appreciation.

Will C. Carson.

Greenville, Illinois, December 15, 1905.

ILLINOIS, AS IT APPEARED IN 1905

GREENVILLE'S CARNEGIE LIBRARY
Erected in the year 1905 at a cost of $11,000.

BOND COUNTY SOLDIERS' MONUMENT
Unveiled September 19, 1903.

A Condensed History of Greenville, Illinois

BY WILL C. CARSON.

COUNTLESS changes have taken place in the ninety years that have elapsed since a lone log cabin, on the brow of the hill at the west end of present Main Avenue, constituted the whole of Greenville. In those good old days of 1815, when Greenville was young, the public road ran past the cabin, and down the hill, and, crossing the creek at the Alton ford, was swallowed up by the forest.

Truthfully to relate how Greenville, from that rudely constructed log cabin, steadily advanced through the years and has earned her place on the map, and how she has been evolved from the forest primeval into a bustling city of twentieth century attainments, is to tell again the story of the unspeakable hardships of the pioneers, and of the determination of the settlers, who followed them.

It was ninety years ago that a sturdy pioneer, by name George Davidson, attracted by the rolling hills and clear spring water, set about to clear the forest and make himself a home, and, camping on the edge of the big ravine that yawns about the western confines of the town, he paved the way for a "Greater Greenville."

The history of Greenville, the third and present county seat of Bond county, is so closely interwoven with the history of the county itself, that a slight digression is here and now pardonable, that we may, at the outset, note the beginnings of the then new country of the Northwest Territory, of which Bond county, and by inference, Greenville, formed no insignificant part.

Wrested from the clutches of Great Britain by the indomitable will of George Rogers Clark, to whom we of today owe a mighty debt of gratitude, the Illinois country became a county of Virginia in 1778 and so remained until the deed of session of 1784, and from that time on the great territory of Illinois was pared down until it reached its present dimensions, and the great, overgrown county of Bond, that then extended to the shores of Lake Michigan, the fifteenth county to be formed, gave generously of its territory to the formation of Montgomery, Fayette and Clinton counties; in fact so liberally that it was finally compelled to borrow from Madison, in sheer self-defense, finding itself shaved down to its present

Old Brick House which, until recently stood at the corner of Main and Sixth. It was the home of Samuel White and the first postoffice was kept therein. One of the first houses built in Greenville.

unpretentious dimensions. Beyond a doubt the spirit of broad-mindedness and liberality that now characterizes the county and city was born of that period.

Bond county was organized in 1816 and was named for Shadrach Bond, the first governor of Illinois. It was one of the original fifteen counties represented in the Consti-

CYRUS BIRGE, *Deceased,*
Greenville Merchant in 1824.

tutional Convention of 1818. Thos. Kirkpatrick and Samuel G. Morse represented the county in the convention that formed the first state constitution. At this election for conventioners there were three candidates, Morse, Kirkpatrick and Martin, although but two were to be elected. The issue was slavery or no slavery. Morse and Kirkpatrick were against slavery but Martin was non-committal. Some lively Tennesseeans concocted a scheme to ascertain Martin's views. They called him to one side and told him that they, as well as some of their friends in Tennessee, wanted slavery admitted so that they might bring their slaves here. Their plan was successful, for Martin said, "Boys, don't say anything, but I am for slavery."

The boys did say something, however, and Martin was defeated. George Davidson, founder of Greenville, was one of the clerks at this election.

In giving of her territory and in being represented at the first constitutional convention, Bond county is justly entitled to be denominated one of the corner stones on which has been laid the superstructure of present day prosperity of the great northwest.

Early Settlements.

PERMANENT settlement of Bond county was made prior to 1811, but the exact date is not fixed. Mrs. Elizabeth Harbour, who lived at Chatham, Illinois in 1890, declared that her family settled near Greenville in 1808, and that there had been white settlers before them. The lady named Isaac Hill, Tom Ratan, Billy Jones, John Finley and Henry Cox as having been here at that time. It is an established fact that settlement was made at Hill's Fort in the summer 1811. This fort covered an acre of ground and was situated on the present farm of John O'Byrne, eight miles southwest of present Greenville. The mother of James H. White, of Greenville, was an inmate of this fort, her father having taken her there for safety.

In early days the Indians made annual incursions into the country in and around Greenville. They usually came in the autumn, because they then could get game and corn on which to subsist. A mile and a half south of Hill's Fort was Jones'

Fort, built about the same time. These two feeble bands of settlers, at that time, composed the entire population of Bond county. These forts were not only a place of defense but the residence of the families belonging to the neighborhood. The stockades, bastions, cabins and block house walls had port holes at proper heights and distances. The whole of the outside was made absolutely bullet proof and the fort was built without the use of a single nail or spike.

Some families were so attached to their farms that they remained on them as much as possible, despite the constant danger of an Indian attack. In the event of the approach of Indians, an "express" from the fort was sent out to arouse the settlers, who at once hastened to the stockade and thus it often happened that the whole number of families belonging to a fort, who were in the evening at their homes, were all in the fortress before dawn the next morning. During the succeeding day their household effects were brought in by parties of armed men sent out for that purpose. Some families were more foolhardy or adventurous than others and in spite of every remonstrance they would remain on their farms, or, if in the stockade, would return prematurely to their property, thus endangering their lives.

The Cox Massacre.

THE Cox massacre is frequently confused with the killing of Henry Cox and his son, south of Greenville, by the Indians. Henry Cox and his son were killed and by Indians, but the Cox massacre, which is commemorated by a monument in the country west of Greenville, was the occasion of the death of another Cox, and the taking into captivity of a young woman.

The Cox family moved from near Alton and settled north of Pocahontas a distance of two miles. They had been there two or three years and were building a horse mill at the time of the murder, which was on June 2, 1811. Several Indians of the Pottawattomie tribe, having heard a considerable amount of money was in possession of the family went to the cabin while the father and mother were away. They killed the son, cutting out his heart and placing it on his head. They then threatened his sister, Rebecca Cox, who had been a witness of the terrible deed, with a like vengeance, unless she revealed the hiding place of the money. The girl went to a chest, and fumbling around in it, in order to conceal the principal packages, handed them a small parcel, which they accepted. The Indians then stole the horses and taking the girl prisoner, started north

up the Shoal Creek timber. Rebecca was shrewd enough to tear strips from her apron and drop them along the trail as a guide for her rescuers.

As soon as the family returned and found the mutilated corpse of their son lying in the cabin, and the daughter gone, they went to Hill's Station, sent messengers to alarm the settlers in Bond and Madison counties and as soon as possible Captain Pruett, Davy White and seven others went in pursuit. The Indians, having had several days start, were overtaken near where Springfield now stands. The girl was tied on a pony. At sight of her rescuers, she loosed her bands, jumped from the pony and started to meet them. An Indian threw a tomahawk. It stuck squarely in her back and thus her saviours found her. The girl afterward recovered, married and moved to Arkansas, where her husband was killed by Indians. Three miles north of Pocahontas is the grave of Cox and above it stands a monument erected by the people of that community a few years ago.

The killing of Henry Cox by the Indians is an entirely different story. Cox was an inmate of Hill's Fort but had built a cabin nearly a mile south of where Dudleyville now stands. One morning in August, 1815, Cox took his son, aged 15,

Scene at the dedication of the Cox monument, west of Greenville, October 9, 1900. The monument commemorated the massacre of Mr. Cox, by the Indians, in 1811.

and went, each on horseback, to his cabin. All appeared quiet when they rode up to the cabin. Cox told his son to ride down to the creek and water the horses, while, rifle in hand, he went to the door of the cabin. Pushing the door open, he saw an Indian in the house. Quick as a flash he raised his rifle and fired. He missed the Indian and his ball sunk in the log over the fireplace. At the same instant another Indian, concealed behind a tree, fired at Cox, the ball passing through his body and killing him instantly. Spattering the blood of Cox all over the door, the bullet imbedded itself in the wood. The Indians then ran to catch the boy with the horses and keep him from giving the alarm at the fort. In their attempt to capture him they became alarmed at the delay and finally shot him and buried him without going back to the body of his father. The boy was not found and it was believed that he was taken prisoner until after peace was made, when the Indians revealed the fate of the boy. The bullet holes and the splotch of Cox's blood on the cabin door were seen years afterward, when the property was owned by Abraham McCurley.

There is a tradition, handed down by James Mc. Gillespie, who came to Bond county in 1816, and who, in 1860, made written report of his reminiscenses to the Old Settlers' Association, that one Benjamin Henson came to Bond sometime before the war of 1812. Living in a hollow sycamore tree in Shoal Creek bottom, he feared no man and was content. It is related that at one time during the war of 1812, the

SETH BLANCHARD, *Deceased.*
Who came to Greenville in 1820, after selling the land where the St. Louis court house now stands.

forts were all abandoned on account of the Indian hostilities and Henson alone was left in his 8 by 10 sycamore tree, the only white inhabitant of the county. When the hostilities were over the settlers returned to find Henson unmolested. Henson is said to have piloted people across Shoal Creek at the foot of Mill Hill, Greenville, until the state, in 1824, gave $200 for a bridge to be placed across the stream at that point.

Near Jones' fort, in those early days, an Indian concealed himself in the dense foliage of a tree and picked off five men before he was discovered and shot. In August 1814, Major Journey, in command of Hill's Fort, flung open the gates and marched forth to look for Indians, leaving the garrison absolutely defenseless and the women milking the cows. The Indians surprised them, killed the Major and three of his men, and wounded the fifth, Thomas Higgins, whose escape was almost miraculous.

These are some of the scenes that went toward the making of Greenville, and, though the graves of the heroes, who fell at Hill's Fort and Jones' Fort, less than a hundred years ago, now go unmarked, the memory of their valorous deeds sticks deep in our minds, for they blazed the way for the founding, only a few miles to the northward, of the puny settlement, out of which our own fair city of Greenville has been evolved.

At the close of our last war with England, a treaty of peace was made with the Indians, the forts in Bond county were abandoned and straggling settlements began to form. The settlers came but slowly however, and in 1816 Bond county numbered but twenty-five cabins.

WILLARD TWISS. *Deceased.*
A Greenville Merchant of the Twenties, who employed John A. Logan as a jockey on the farm now known as the A. J Sherburne farm.

MRS MILLICENT CLAY BIRGE, *Dec'd,*
Wife of Ansel Birge, Greenville's first postmaster, who lived in and near Greenville for 69 years. She died July 12, 1896.

GEORGE DONNELL, *Deceased,*
Who came to Greenville in 1818, and who was one of the pioneer residents.

MRS. GEORGE DONNELL, *Deceased,*

SAMUEL WHITE, *Deceased,*
Who came to Greenville in 1818, and built one of the first houses here.

When Greenville Was Young.

HISTORY bears evidence that great achievements are wrought through much tribulation, and so it was in the founding of Greenville, for be it known that milk-sickness in Madison county caused George Davidson to sell his farm there and move to Bond county in 1815. The records show that he entered 160 acres of land, where Greenville now stands, September 27, 1816. He obtained the patent from His Excellency James Monroe, President of the United States, April 29, 1825. This land is described as the southeast quarter of Section No. 10, Township 5, north, Range 3, west of the third principal meridian.

Mr. Davidson's cabin was built on the primitive style of logs with weight poles to hold the clap-board roof in place. The puncheon floor was made of slabs, split and hewn, and the carpenter had no use for nails, glass, putty, nor plaster. Mr. Davidson's cabin was located in the extreme western part of town, near the present residence of H. H. Staub. His family consisted of his wife, Jannet, two sons and two daughters. One son, Samuel, died of consumption, soon after coming here. One daughter, Mrs. Elizabeth Caroline Blundell, lived at Healdsburg, California in 1876, and in a letter to one of the Greenville papers stated that her brother and the Reverend Green P. Rice, who followed George Davidson here, laid out some lots in the western part of Greenville. This plat of the old town was never recorded and there is a story to the effect that George Davidson, one day, in a fit of anger, tore the plat up and watched it burn to ashes in the fireplace.

The existence of this plat afterwards made trouble for the people who purchased lots, when the town was finally laid out. This part of the town, then laid out, as the original town, is now Davidson's addition.

Not long after he built his first cabin, George Davidson moved to the lot at the southwest corner of Sixth Street and Main Avenue (as it is to 'ay) directly across the street south of the John Baumberger, Sr., homestead, and opened a tavern. In opening the first tavern in Greenville, Mr. Davidson again proved himself a public benefactor, for it was for many years a mecca for the wayfaring man, as well as a most convenient loafing place for those of the early gentry, who were wont to whittle and spit through the long winter evenings.

About this time the Reverend

JOHN GREENWOOD, *Deceased.*
Came to Greenville in 1838, and a few years later laid out Greenwood's Addition.

SETH FULLER, *Deceased,*
Who came to Greenville in the thirties; an early surveyor and trustee of Almira College.

JAMES ENLOE, *Deceased,*
Who came to Greenville with his father, Asahel Enloe, in 1818, and helped clear off the land where the court house now stands.

MRS. JANE WILLIFORD, *Deceased,*
Who was born in Greenville March 17, 1822, and who resided here all her life. Died May 14, 1905, the oldest native born resident of Greenville at that time.

ISAAC ENLOE, *Deceased.*
Came to Greenville soon after the town was laid out and helped clear the land where the court house now stands.

Green P. Rice arrived from Kentucky. He bought a part of George Davidson's land and, together with Samuel Davidson, opened the first store in Greenville. It is said that this store was only large enough to hold comfortably one wagon load of goods. The store was located on what is now Main Avenue and Sixth Street. Mrs. Blundell, in her letter, stated that Mr. Rice became involved in some trouble about some slaves he brought from Kentucky, and, selling his interests to Cyrus Birge, left the country.

James, Ansel and Cyrus Birge, three brothers, came to Greenville from Poultney, Vermont. Cyrus kept the store until 1824, when he sold his stock to his brother, Ansel.

who carried on the business for eight years. Ansel Birge, during this time, married Miss Millicent Clay Twiss, a sister of Willard Twiss, to whom he sold the store in 1833, and moved to his farm one mile south of Greenville. This store was the chief public institution of the town, when Greenville became the county seat in 1821.

Seth, Samuel and Elisha Blanchard came to Greenville in 1820 and entered 1600 acres of land, a part of which is the farm now owned by Mrs. L. K. King, a mile east of town,

at the top of "Blanchard's Hill," which derives its name from them. They built a cabin in town and opened a store. Seth managed the farm, Elisha conducted the store and Samuel traded to New Orleans, and they prospered. Soon after Mr. Blanchard opened the store, travel became more general and a tavern was opened in connection. A huge pair of antlers, erected over a sign made of a hewn board, printed with a coal from the hearth, announced the welcome news that here was the "Buck and Horn Tavern." This in-

DR. J. B. DRAKE, *Deceased,*
One of the earliest Greenville Physicians.

THE DRAKE HOUSE.
Built by Dr. J. B. Drake in the early thirties, and dismantled in 1905.

MAJ. WILLIAM DAVIS, *Deceased.*
Who came to Greenville in 1831 and opened a tavern. He died in Greenville.

MRS. LUCY DAVIS, *nee* MAYO,
Wife of Major Wm. Davis. Died in Greenville in 1891.

JUDGE ENRICO GASKINS, *Deceased.*
Twenty years county clerk, eight years county judge of Bond. Came here in 1835. Died in 1879.

stitution with a few other log cabins formed the original town of Greenville. David Berry later became owner of the tavern and then it passed into the hands of Thomas Dakin, who owned it many years.

There were no saloons in Greenville in those days, but the merchants all kept whiskey and treated the customers, who called for it.

In the summer of 1818, many families, including Samuel White and George Donnell, moved here from North Carolina and Kentucky. The principal families in Greenville then were, in addition to those already mentioned, the Kirkpatricks, Camps, Goss, Rutherfords, Fergusons and old Father Elam, who lived where the old graveyard is now located. At his home were held the religious meetings, which always ended with the minister shaking hands with everybody during the singing of the last song.

Good Old Father Asahel Enloe was the singing school teacher and the school master, and many a time in early days, did the youngsters of Greenville willingly obey his dictum, as he stood in the doorway of the school house and cried, "Books, books, come to books." His copies were equal to Spencer's best copper plate and his chirography is still well preserved in the county records.

In a letter dated at Paola, Kansas, June 20, 1876, Mrs. Almira Morse, one of the best known women the city has produced, and for whom Almira College was named, stated that the first school house in Greenville was on the northeast corner of the public square. The square was laid out in 1821, and Samuel Blanchard assisted John Russell in

making the survey. Mrs. Morse says:

"Once a year came 'Parade Day,' when Colonel Stout, accoutered in regimentals, epaulets and white cockade, mounted on a charger, was marshal of the motley company.

"There was one colored family in the place. Old Aunt Fanny, with her three children, bought her freedom of her master in Kentucky, and in Greenville earned a good living by washing and nursing. One day while she was washing at Mr. Blanchard's two men suddenly rode up on horseback, and demanded Aunt Fanny and her children, as runaway slaves. She declared she had her free papers at home, and with prayers and tears, besought them to leave her, but her entreaties were unheeded and Aunt Fanny was bound to a horse and with her children behind them, the men rode away. They were armed with rifles, pistols and knives and no one dared to interfere. When part way to St. Louis, however, a party from Reno overtook them. The family was rescued and returned home.

"Our town once had a visit from Lorenzo Dow, who stopped at the tavern, and old Mr. Twiss went over 'to argue him out of his religion,' but the eccentric old saint got the better of him. He preached upon the hill north of town. He sat in his chair, while preaching, for two hours or more."

Greenville Becomes the County Seat.

WHEN in 1817, Bond county, which previous to that time had been a part of Edwards, was es-

tablished by an act of the territorial legislature, the county seat was fixed at Hill's Fort until a commission appointed for that purpose, could choose a permanent location.

On April 15, 1817, this committee reported that they had selected a site on the west bank of the Hurricane, which on account of its natural advantages, the commission considered a desirable location for the seat of justice. Accordingly the new county seat was platted and named Perryville. Three years later, however, the formation of new counties out of the then pretentious Bond, left Perryville in Fayette county, and unfortunate for the youthful city, with its court house and jail, remote from the geographical center.

The undoing of Perryville, however, redounded to the good of Greenville, and Bond county in 1821, reduced to nearly her present dimensions, turned her eyes to the center of her domain and there beheld, sitting loftily on the bluffs of Shoal Creek, the town laid out in 1819 by George Davidson.

The selection of Greenville as a permanent seat of justice for Bond county came about by legislative enactment and the same legislature that placed Perryville in Fayette county, also appointed James B. Moore, Samuel Whitesides, Abraham Eyeman, Joshua Ogelsby and John Howard commissioners to locate the county seat in Bond, provided the proprietor of the land selected would donate to the county for the purpose specified, at least twenty acres of land. This commission was also detailed to fix the damages sustained by the proprie-

JOEL ELAM, *Deceased.*
One of the early business men, who learned the blacksmith trade from his brother, Edward Elam, who was Greenville's first blacksmith.

ELDER PETER LONG, *Deceased.*
Pastor of Mt. Nebo Church, and one of the best known pioneer preachers in the west. Came to Greenville in 1816, and was in the ministry 59 years.

KENDALL P. MORSE, *Deceased.*
Who came to Greenville in 1834; member of the firm of Morse and Brothers. Died here in 1867.

tors of Perryville, in consequence of the removal of the county seat from that place. After due deliberation, the commissioners fixed upon a tract of twenty acres of land in the northeast corner of the original town of Greenville, then belonging to George Davidson. The act provided for the land to be selected in a body. William Russell, Robt. McCord and Jno. Kirkpatrick, then county judges, held a session of the county court on April 18, 1821, and having under consideration the said location, made a demand on Mr. Davidson for the twenty acres immediately around and contiguous to a stake driven by the commissioners. Mr. Davidson, by his attorney, Benjamin Mills, executed a bond to the county commissioners with Peter Hubbard and John Kirkpatrick as securities, agreeing to transfer the land for the purposes selected, excepting therefrom a small tract previously sold to Samuel Whitcomb, and for which Whitcomb held Davidson's bond for a deed. The court declined to act at this time, but at a session held June 5, 1821, Mr. Davidson was permitted to withdraw and cancel the bond previously executed by him to the court, and substitute a new bond for the same purpose with Samuel G. Blanchard, Robert G. White, Samuel Whitcomb, Daniel Ferguson, Milo Wood and Samuel Houston as securities. The court accepted this bond and Greenville was henceforth acknowledged to be, in fact and in law, the permanent seat of justice of Bond county.

The first county court held at the new county seat of Greenville was on June 4 and 5, 1821, William Russell, Robert McCord and John Kirkpatrick being the judges. The first circuit court was held at Greenville on July 12, 1821, with Hon. Joseph Phillips, judge; Samuel Houston, sheriff; and James M. Johnson, clerk. The petit jury was composed of John D. Alexander, John White, George Denny, James Wafer, Andrew Finley, Alexander Robinson, James McCord, Richard Worley, John Prickett, William Gracey, Silas Lee Wait, Abel Sparks, Charles Gillham, Jr., Wm. M. Stewart, Philip Moore, James B. Rutherford, Milo Wood, Wm. Black, Samuel Whitcomb, Harrison Kirkpatrick, James Kirkpatrick, Jr., Absolom Watkins, John Loughlan and Wyatt Stubblefield.

By order of the county court part of the land donated by Davidson was laid off into town lots, and on the first Monday in July, 1821, thirty lots were exposed for sale, the town having been surveyed by John Russell the June previous. The proceeds from the sale of these lots was used for the erection of a court house.

Mr. Davidson, in many ways one of Greenville's greatest benefactors, and his wife Jennet, remained in the town until 1827, when they moved to Galena, Jo Daviess county, realizing but little for their property.

In 1821, when the sale of public lots was held, the present public square was covered with a dense growth of cottonwood and sycamore trees. This was all cleared off by Asahel Enloe and his sons, who

planted the land in corn. At a session of the county court in September, 1821, it was ordered that a court house for Bond county be let to the lowest bidder and when the bids were opened, it was found that Robert G. White's bid of $2,135 was the lowest. This bid was accepted September 19, 1821, and he gave bond for the faithful performance of his duties. The sale of the town lots brought $1,338 and the judges of the county court entered into bond for the remainder. The court house was made of a poor quality of brick and was badly damaged by storms before it was completed, which was not until 1822. The court room was heated by an old-fashioned fire place. No stoves were in use in Greenville at that time, nor for a long time afterward.

There was little respect for the temple of justice and its custodians were sorely beset for means for its preservation. It was the delight of the small boy, hiding behind tree or bush, to hurl stones through the eight by ten window panes, just to hear the glass fall crashing before their aim. Nevertheless the building of this court house was the first real impetus given the town, outside the start given it by Davidson himself. The population of the county at this time was 2,931 and the village of Greenville contained but a few houses, a hotel and a store or two.

Origin of Greenville's Name.

AUTHORITIES differ as to the origin of the name given Greenville. There is a story to the effect

MR AND MRS. WILLIAM S. WAIT, *Deceased,*

William S. Wait, who came to Greenville in 1818. An early writer and journalist; chairman of the National Industrial Convention at New York City in 1845; in 1848 he was nominated for Vice President on the National Reform ticket but declined. He was the prime mover in the projection of the Vandalia Railroad and was one of the leaders who drafted much of the Illinois Constitution of 1845. He died in 1865.

that Mr. Thomas White, the oldest man present when the town was first surveyed in 1821, was asked to name the town and thereupon, casting his eyes over the green woods, readily answered:

"Everything looks so green and nice, we will call it Greenville." Others say that Mr. White named it for Greenville in North Carolina. Another legend is to the effect that Greenville took the name of Green

P. Rice, the Cumberland Presbyterian minister, who resided here at an early date, and was the first Greenville merchant. Allen Comer, who came here in 1817, is authority for the last story, but Mr. White is commonly given credit for having named the town. At any rate it was well named and to this day, as in the beginning, Greenville is noted far and wide, for the many beautiful trees that surround and interlace it—a city in a veritable green forest.

Taxes and Slavery in 1818.

OLD records show that the assessment of tax for the year 1817 was $161.50, which was charged to the sheriff for collection. It is also recorded that one Samuel Hill paid a tax of one dollar on one negro. Of the $161.50 tax, $106 was used to pay for the killing of fifty-three wolves.

The tax of 1818 was $279.50. The first county order ever issued was

WM. S. WAIT, JR., *Deceased,*
For many years a prominent resident of the county.

RESIDENCE OF MRS. ADELE WAIT, South Third Street.

REV. ROBERT STEWART, *Deceased.*
Who came to Greenville in 1840 and was pastor of the Congregational church. His home was a refuge for escaping slaves during the Civil War days.

to Moses Shipman, for a wolf scalp and the amount was $2.00. In 1818 the following tax was assessed on property owned in the county: "For each bond servant or slave, 16 years old, 100 cents; for each young man, 21 years old and upwards, 100 cents; for each Horse creature, three year old, 50 cents."

In 1817 there were seven slaves in Bond county, under the age of 15 years, registered, as provided by law, in the office of the county clerk. They were owned by Martin Jones, William Vollentine, Hardy Vollentine, one each, and H. Kirkpatrick, four. In 1824 a vote on the question of slavery was taken in Illinois and Bond county voted 63 for and 240 against.

Some Early Industries.

A SHORT time after George Davidson came here, Paul Beck arrived and located near the present site of the old cemetery. He was one of the first to follow Davidson here and was Greenville's first manufacturer. He built the first mill in Bond county in 1817, near the old cemetery. It is described as a "little band horse mill" and every customer had to hitch his own horse to the mill and grind his own corn. The bolt for the flour was turned by hand. Some people carried their grain in a sack on horseback, a distance of ten miles, to Beck's mill and were compelled, in many cases, to wait for three days before their turn at the grind. Near the mill was a fine spring, which was named "Beck's Spring."

In 1818 Asahel Enloe settled on the highest point of the present old cemetery, but a short time afterward he and his sons Ezekiel and James moved to a point about eighty rods southeast of the present Vandalia railroad depot, living near each other in separate houses. Samuel Davidson, a son of the founder of Greenville, married Miss Violet Enloe, a daughter of Asahel Enloe.

Wyatt Stubblefield was another early settler. He entered the land adjoining old Greenville on the east and operated a cotton gin and a horse mill.

In those early days Samuel and Thomas White came to Greenville. Thomas White taught one of the first schools, in 1819, in a little log cabin near the tanyard, which his brother, Samuel White put in operation. This was the first tannery in the county and was located in the western part of Greenville. Soon after he and Moses Hinton put in operation a spinning machine in Greenville, but it was soon demonstrated that cotton could not be raised with any success here and the mill was closed down.

In 1822 James Rutherford commenced the manufacture of hats in Greenville, and carried on the business for several years. Edward Elam was Greenville's first blacksmith. He opened a shop in 1819, and was assisted by his younger brother, Joel.

Among the other early residents of Greenville and vicinity although they were not engaged in industrial work, were George Donnell, who came here in 1819 from North Carolina and was the leader of the first Sunday school ever taught in the county; Samuel G. Morse, who was the first sheriff; Daniel Converse, the first county clerk; Francis Trav-

MRS. L. K. KING,
A resident of Greenville since 1837.

is, the first county treasurer; James Wafer, Daniel Ferguson, Robert Gillespie, Williamson Plant, William Robinson, William S. Wait and others.

Greenville in the Twenties.

THE ground already covered takes up to the 20's and marks the first epoch in the history of Greenville. With the location of the county seat in Greenville in 1821 a spark of new life was infused into the settlement and more people were attracted to the place, because of the fact it had arisen to the dignity of a county seat town.

The earliest records on file in the county clerk's office bear date of

RESIDENCE OF MRS. LOUISA RAVOLD.

COL. RICHARD BENTLEY,
Who came to Bond county in 1829 and moved to Greenville in 1847; deputy sheriff in 1848 and sheriff a few years later; one of the first presidents of the village board in the early fifties; representative in the state legislature with Lincoln and died in 1873.

May 7, 1821, and read as follows:

"Agreeable to an act of the general assembly to remove the seat of justice from Perryville to Greenville, Bond County, the court of probate met at the clerk's office on Monday, the seventh of May, 1821, with Thomas Kirkpatrick as judge."

The records show that the probate court held its sessions, or at least some of them, at the dwelling of Seth Blanchard in 1822. Judge Benjamin Mills presided at this time. In 1823 John Gillmore was judge.

The earliest records on file in the office of the circuit clerk bear date of July 18, 1817, three years before Greenville was the county seat. This record shows that Simon Lindley, of Madison county, transferred 160 acres of land for $100 to John Lindley. The land is described as the northwest quarter of section 32, township 5, range 3, west of the third principal meridian. There were no more transfers until September 2, 1817, when Robert Gillespie sold 320 acres to Jonathan Crowley, of Virginia, for $960.

The census of 1820 gives Bond county a population of 2,931. Greenville was still confined to the extreme western part of the present city, now known as Davidson's Addition, which includes the greater part of Greenville west of Fourth Street, between North and Summer. Present Main Avenue and Sixth Street was the business center then and for many years afterwards. During the period of the twenties Seth Blanchard, Cyrus and Ansel Birge, Thomas Long, Samuel White and William Durley operated stores; most of them in the old brick building on the southwest corner of Main and Sixth, which stood south of the John Baumberger, Sr., homestead until a few years ago, when it was torn down. Dr. J. B. Drake was a physician and merchant of this period.

In 1827 Bond county gave but 250 votes, but in the following year immigration from Tennessee and Kentucky increased the population to a considerable extent.

In the twenties Greenville was a typical frontier town, composed of a cluster of log cabins, a tumbledown brick court house and a frame building or two. All east of the present square was "out in the country," and was merely a dense growth of hazel brush.

During the twenties Samuel White sold his tannery to J. Harvey Black and opened a store in 1829, on the northeast corner of Sixth and Main. Thomas Long bought out Mr. Blanchard's stock of goods and for a while his brother, Rev. Peter Long, clerked for him. Mr. Long soon sold out to Dr. J. B. Drake and William Durley, who continued the business where the present Drake House now stands. Dr. Drake, in a few years, bought the entire stock and continued in business for twenty five years.

Cyrus Birge kept a store on lot No. 8, Davidson's Addition from 1819 to 1824, when he sold out to his brother, Ansel, who continued in business for at least eight years.

In 1822, by order of the court, a "stray pen" was built in Greenville. It was 40 feet square and six feet

MRS. RICHARD BENTLEY,
Born in Virginia in 1799; died here in 1876.

high and was built for the purpose of confining stray stock. On court days and other public occasions the people who had lost stock, would go to the stray pen and endeavor to identify their property.

An abstract of the poll books of an election held in Greenville August 2, 1824, for county officers shows that for Sheriff, Hosea Camp had 151 votes, William White 97, Henry Williams, 47; for County Commissioners, Ransom Geer had 224, Robert McCord, 209; Asahel Enloe, 171; George Donnell, 107 and George Davidson 101. For Coroner, Robert W. Denny had 122,

J. P. GARLAND,
Who came here in 1839 and who lived here continuously until his death in 1903.

MRS. J. P. GARLAND,
Who came here in 1830 and is still a resident; married in 1848 to J. P. Garland.

WM. WATKINS, *Deceased*,
A resident in 1860. Former sheriff and ex-member of the legislature, as he looked 41 years ago.

Edwin A. Mars, 8 and James Durley, 6. The returns were attested by Asahel Enloe, J. P. and Leonard Goss, J. P.

Greenville from 1830 to 1840.

THE census of 1830 shows but a small gain in ten years in Bond county, nevertheless the county seat had made some advancement both in point of business and population. The town was now beginning to reach out timidly toward the east. A new frame court house succeeded the crumbling brick structure and was completed in 1832 on the present square. A new jail had also been built.

MRS. MARTHA G. WATKINS, *Dec'd*,
Whose father once owned much of the land where Greenville stands.

Greenville in the thirties is best described by Joseph T. Fouke, who came here in 1830, and who is still a resident of Greenville.

Mr. Fouke says that his earliest recollection of Greenville in 1830 was the digging of a public well at the corner of Main and Sixth streets, by "Black" Jim Davis, Royer and Hicks. The men quarreled over a dog fight and finally fought and Miss Hicks came out of the house and threatened to whip all the men and the dogs thrown in. The following is Mr. Fouke's description of Greenville in 1830:

"In 1830 Seth Blanchard kept a

ALEXANDER KELSOE, *Deceased*,
Circuit Clerk 1848 to 1860; a prominent character in Greenville for many years.

hotel across the street south of the old Drake House. The south half of the building was log and the north half frame. It was two stories and a porch extended along the west side of the building. Mr. Blanchard had his log stables on the ground where Sheriff Floyd now resides. South of Blanchard's tavern was a square room where Dr. J. B. Drake ran a store. This square room is still standing with additions built to it, on the same ground, and in my opinion is the oldest house in

THE OLD MILL AT THE FOOT OF MILL HILL.

W. A. KELSOE,
A Greenville boy of the sixties, many years a prominent St. Louis newspaper man, manager of the local press bureau of the Louisiana Purchase Exposition. Now a resident of St. Louis.

CHARLES HOILES,

Who came to Greenville in 1840, and who, with his son, C. D. Hoiles, established the State Bank of Hoiles and Son in 1869. A member of the Illinois Legislature at the time of the Lincoln-Douglas contest; delegate from Illinois to the Charleston convention. Died at Union Station, St. Louis, May 14, 1884, and is buried at Montrose cemetery.

town. Across the street, west of the tavern, Samuel White's brick residence stood. This building was also used as a store in the early days and was torn down only a few years ago. South of Mr. White lived John T. Walker in a log cabin, near the present residence of Leitle McCracken. Still farther south lived Mr. Benson in a log cabin and opposite the present residence of W. A. McLain lived John Maddux in a log cabin. There was a cabin in the middle of the street in front of the residence of Fritz Streiff, and Mr. Perigen lived in a cabin near the old cemetery. Back of the present residence of Mrs. Agnes J. Mulford was a log cabin, where the school was taught. It was the first school of which I have recollection. Q. C. Alexander was the teacher. Where H. H. Staub lives was the cabin of Harvey Black. This was probably the first cabin ever built in Greenville, the one built by George Davidson in 1815, although this fact is not definitely established. Mr. Davidson, however, built his cabin on this spot and Black's cabin is sup-

posed to have been the same one. Straight west, at the bottom of the hill, Mr. Black had his tanyard.

"Where the present residence of Mrs. John H. Jett stands was Berry's tavern, where circuit court was sometimes held. On the site of the present Baumberger homestead, Ansel Birge had his store. The Drake house was not then built. East of the site of the present Drake house lived John Ackeridge, a famous hunter, who scarcely ever went out for a tramp without bringing home a deer. Near the present residence of Peter Hentz, Major Davis kept a tavern and lived across the street east, where Emil Brice now resides. There were no other houses until the west side of the present square is reached and there, in about the center of the block, James B. Rutherford lived in a frame house and to the north had a log house in which he made hats. This hat manufacturing establishment stood on the site of the present post office building. There was a log cabin near the present residence of Mrs. K. M. Bennett and Daniel Ferguson had a cabin at the north end of Fifth Street, as it is today. That constituted the village of Greenville in 1830. Near the present residence of E. E. Cox was the suburban home of Samuel Whitcomb, a frame building, and one of the aristocratic residences of

THE STATE BANK OF HOILES AND SONS.

What is now the State Bank of Hoiles and Sons was established in August, 1869, by Charles Hoiles and Charles D. Hoiles, under the firm name of Hoiles and Son. Stephen M. Hoiles was admitted to the firm in 1872 and the firm name was changed to Hoiles and Sons. Charles Hoiles retired from business in 1881 and died May 14, 1884. C. D. and S. M. Hoiles continued the business under the old firm name and in December, 1895, incorporated as the State Bank of Hoiles and Sons with a capital of $25,000. The capital stock was increased in September, 1903, to $50,000, and there is now about $9,000 surplus fund, undivided profits. The present officers are C. D. Hoiles, President; C. E. Hoiles, Vice President; G. B. Hoiles, Cashier

C. D. HOILES,

A native of Greenville, ex-member of the Illinois Legislature. Mayor of Greenville from 1879 to 1887, President of the State Bank of Hoiles and Sons. Delegate to National Democratic conventions of 1872, 1884 and 1892. Member of State Democratic Central Committee for eight years.

the village. This Whitcomb house was in later years moved to the lot south of the residence of Judge A. G. Henry, where it stood until a a few years ago, when it was torn down. The court house stood where the present one stands, but it practically marked the eastern confines of the town. To the east and south, there was nothing but underbrush and a few forest trees. One of the two main roads into town came in on the south, up present Fifth street to present College Avenue and up through the present lawn of Dr. B. F. Coop to Oak street, thence through the middle of what is now Moss Addition and through the south part of S. S. Trindle's eighty striking the main road at the present suburban home of C. E. Cook. Another road came in from the direction of the present farm of Mrs. L. K. King, down Blanchard's hill, past the public school building and on the north side of the old elm that stands near the residence of George O. Morris and up to the business center and down the hill back of the barn of Samuel White and thence to the spring at the tanyard, past Wash Lake, to the Shoal Creek ford and westward. There were no hollows and ravines in the west end of town then, as now.

"Religious services were held in the court house in those days and there were no churches in Greenville until later. Dr. J. B. Drake built the Drake House about 1833, and it was considered the finest house in town by far. In this Dr. Drake lived and kept store for many years. At that time the whole county voted at Greenville and most of the elections were held in the east end of the Berry House. The voting was done by voice and the name of the voter and the party for whom he voted were recorded. Seth Blanchard sold out his tavern and store to Thomas Keyes and William S. Smith, who came here in 1832 from Virginia. Mrs. Keyes kept tavern, while her husband farmed and Mr. Smith remained in the mercantile business in this location for 18 years. Thomas Smith ran a store on the southwest corner of the public square, and conducted it as a branch of the old store until 1845 when the old store was closed and the two brothers joined venture on the square.

"Long rows of wagons could be seen in the thirties unloading at the old store, after returning from St. Louis, laden with goods. Keyes and Smith sold the hotel to Thomas Dakin who kept it many years and it afterward was kept a year or two by Enrico Gaskins, who later moved to the north side of the square into the house built by John T. Morgan.

"Later on in the thirties other buildings were erected, among them the Franklin House and in 1842 Charles Hoiles erected the frame building now standing on the south side of the square and used as a barber shop."

Stephen Morse taught school in the court house in the thirties, Miss Prime taught in a log house in the village and Almira Morse for whom Almira College was named, taught in a frame school house two miles south of Greenville. A little frame school house was built in 1832 on the road to Vandalia, and John Buchanan, father of John T. Buchanan, helped build it. It was used minus doors and windows that summer, and snakes and lizards often

RESIDENCE OF C. D. HOILES.

JUDGE S. A. PHELPS,

Who came to Greenville in 1843, and who has resided here ever since. Ex-County Judge and nestor of the Bond county bar.

RESIDENCE OF JUDGE S. A. PHELPS.

whisked in close proximity to the bare feet of the children. The old court house, which had been used as a school house, fell down that summer. The next year the little frame school house was moved upon land owned by Daniel Ferguson and the doors and windows put in. Daniel Ferguson's land was on the site of the residence of Dr. W. T. Easley.

During the thirties the leading merchants in addition to those already named were Willard Twiss, L. D. Plant, Morse and Brothers, J. M. Davis and Albert Allen.

The well alluded to by J. T. Fouke was the only well in Greenville in 1830. It was public property and was very deep and was also frequently out of repair. The wells and water system of Greenville are treated in a separate chapter, of this history.

During the thirties the stage route was in operation. It was a common expression of warning in those days to say "Look out for the stage," for the stage would look out for no one. The route came into Greenville along the Old National road and, passing along the north side of the square and down the

west side, turned west on Main to the Berry tavern. Frank Berry, son of mine host, was one of the stage drivers. After a rest and change of horses, the lumbering old coach would go clattering out of town on the St. Louis road. There was one stage each way every day, with relays every ten miles. The driver whipped along at a gallop and the ten or a dozen passengers were rocked from side to side with a recklessness born of the early stage drivers.

In 1838, R. F. White cut the trees off the ground where the State Bank of Hoiles and Sons now stands and established a blacksmith shop on the ground. He was a cousin of Prof. J. B. White and a brother-in-law of John S. Hall.

Parker, Keyes and Lansing had a

JOSEPH T. FOUKE,

Who came to Greenville in 1830, and who still lives here.

HOTEL EUREKA,

Better known as the Franklin House. Lincoln stopped at this hotel when he visited Greenville in 1858, during the Lincoln and Douglas campaign.

NATHANIEL DRESSOR,

Who came to Bond County overland from Maine in October, 1837, and has been a resident of the county ever since. He settled on two and one-half acres of cheap land in a log cabin, and is now one of the largest property owners of the county. Director First National Bank. State Senator 1897-8-9. Now in his eightieth year.

R. K. DEWEY,

Came to Greenville in April, 1854. One of the two oldest continuous residents of the city, Judge Henry being the other. Justice of the Peace four years, city clerk several terms, bookkeeper and assistant cashier First National Bank for ten years, Notary Public since 1867, Grand Patriarch of the Grand Encampment I. O. O. F. in 1872, Secretary Bond County Old Settlers' Association.

"still house" in 1838 in the hollow northwest of the old graveyard. They piped water from the spring in wooden pipes to the distillery. They made a great deal of whiskey and shipped it away to St. Louis.

C. H. Stephens, an old settler, read his reminiscenses of Greenville as he remembered it in 1834, before the Old Settlers' Association in 1890. He stated that on the west side of the St. Louis road Edward Elam and his father lived. The house stood where the present residence of W. A. McLain now is. They carried on the only blacksmith shop in Greenville and Joel Elam was learning the trade of his brother Edward. Mr. Stephens says that in 1834 provisions were low in Greenville. Hogs sold for $1.50 per hundred, corn for 25 cents per bushel, wheat 37 1-2 cents per bushel " and as for potatoes" he says, "we could not get them for love nor money. I was on the grand jury in the fall of 1835 and the jurors received fifty cents per day and boarded themselves." Mr. Stephens, in his reminiscenses, says there were no buggies in 1834 and very few two-horse wagons. For the most part people traveled on foot or on horseback, and if a young man wanted to take his best girl to church, he would

take her up on his horse behind him and trot off four or five miles and think nothing of it.

Greenville in the Forties.

IN the forties the business center was transferred from the west end to the public square where it has since remained. The population of the county had jumped to 5,000 but Greenville was still under 300 inhabitants. The slow settlement of the country and the location of railroads on each side of the town held Greenville back. In 1846 the subject of railroads was agitated. A charter was proposed in the General Assembly for a road from Terre Haute to St. Louis, but the policy of the state, at that time, was to give Alton the benefit of being the terminus of all railroads that terminated on the eastern bank of the Mississippi river near St. Louis, in order to overshadow the latter city. And so it was that the Greenville railroad project was knocked in the head by the mistaken idea of up-building Alton to the detriment of St. Louis.

By Judge S. A. Phelps.

"In the fall of 1843, I first came to Illinois and first formed the idea of becoming a settler of Bond coun-

ty. I came from Mississippi, but was a sort of a York yankee. When I reached St. Louis, I got in a stage coach and was ferried across the river. Where East St. Louis now stands the ferry boat butted itself against the bank. There was no platform and nothing to receive the stage except dirt. The stage went up the bank of the Mississippi and on the road to Edwardsville, we did not see a fence, nor a field of corn or wheat in all that trip. The next day I hired a horse and came to Greenville, putting up at the old stage house, on the northwest corner of the square, where the store of Weise and Bradford now stands. It was the best house in town, two stories high, with a double porch on the front, and withal a fine building for those days.

"East of this hotel on the north side of the square, was a small frame house in which Enrico Gaskins afterwards lived. On the spot where Joy and Co's store now stands, was a blacksmith shop run by Isaac Smith, a brother of Wm. S. Smith On the corner immediately south was a small store kept by S. B. Bulkley, and afterwards by Alexander Buie. A little way below that was a one story frame building afterwards used as a hotel. On the

SAMUEL COLCORD, *Deceased,*

Who came overland from Maine to Greenville in 1840. A prominent resident for 50 years.

MRS. SAMUEL COLCORD, *Deceased.*

REV. SAMUEL COLCORD,

A former resident; now a resident of New York City.

OTIS B. COLCORD, *Deceased,*

Who came from Maine to Greenville in 1838 and who lived here more than 60 years.

WM. S. COLCORD,

Who came here from Maine in 1840. Former postmaster of Greenville, and a prominent resident for many years. Now deceased.

operated by a man by the name of White. Next to the alley on the south side of the square was the frame building, which is still standing and is now known as the Miller building. In this building lived Charles Hoiles, father of C. D. Hoiles, President of the State Bank, and of S. M. Hoiles, now deceased. In the corner room of this building Mr. Hoiles had started a store. Later on he moved to the site of the present Thomas House. There were no buildings from the alley west to the corner. On the corner was a small, one story building which was conspicuously labeled "Allen" but was vacant. On the corner where Hussong's store stood prior to the fire of Oct. 27, 1904, was the store of Morse and Brothers, a one story

corner where Masonic Temple now stands was an old two story frame house. It was the headquarters for every unlicensed saloon that was started. These unlicensed saloons always ran until the grand jury met. In a hollow where Dixon's store now stands, there was a small frame house in which D. P. Hagee lived, and had a tailor shop. A blacksmith shop stood on the ground where the State Bank of Hoiles and Sons is now. It was

brick and frame, and a little farther to the north was a story and a half hewed log building used as a furniture store. Still a little farther north was the one story law office of M. G. Dale. On the present Post Office corner was another log house. Dr. J. W. Fitch had his office where Mulford and Monroe's drug store now stands and his house where the Bennett residence now is.

"The people were moral and upright. Very little use was there for constables, marshals, juries or courts. They had no marshal and no mayor in Greenville in those days, only a constable and a justice of the peace. Of course there were occasional offenses against the law but as a whole the people compared favorably in morality, honesty and intelligence with the people of today.

"When I came to Greenville, I found that the county was a temperance county and there was not a licensed saloon in it. It so continued for thirty, if not forty years. People could vote any where in the county for the judges took it for granted that we would vote but once. That was before the days of "repeaters."

"There were plenty of good springs here and that was the reason Greenville was located here. When I came to Greenville there was a spring, a kind of reservoir at the bottom of the hill and we used

Mrs. N. W. McLain,

Aged 87 years, probably the oldest native born resident in the county.

to ride down and water our horses. The spring, however, was rather inconvenient and so a public spirited man sunk a well on the south west corner of the square. It was 70 feet deep but was not much of a success on account of quicksand, and the bucket invariably came up only half full. They had just commenced the fad of making cisterns when I came to Greenville.

"The schools scattered throughout the country gave evidence of the intelligence of the country. They had commenced the church building

which was torn down in 1903. Subscription papers were circulated for this church, with a school under the basement, and, when I came to Greenville, the church was completed and in use, but they had not completed the school part and there were those who did not relish this action. So in 1842, Deacon Saunders made his trip to the east on foot to raise money to complete the building. He was successful and the basement was finished. The school in 1845 was held in a little brick building that was torn down a few years ago at the west end of Main Street. When the church with the school building under it was completed, the event was properly celebrated with dedicatory exercises. Among others I received an invitation and all the best men and women of Greenville were there. I was called upon to make a few remarks and did so apparently to the satisfaction of those assembled. The school was commenced that fall and was continued in the basement of that church for a good many years. That was not the only case of the public spirit of the people of Greenville. When Wm. S. Wait laid out his land into lots he laid out a large lot as Academy Square. This Academy Square is the site of our present magnificent school building. The same spirit was shown by others.

"Greenville has progressed and is an entirely new town. Greenville of 1844 has passed away; a new town has come.

"Greenville was, however, quite a thriving business place in '44, having four good stores and no saloons. There were no factories, except the blacksmith shops, where they made plows and now and then a wagon. Now we have factories and the volume of business has increased ten-fold or more. In '44 we had an every other day stage. It went east one day and the next day west. It carried all the passengers and the driver had the mail sack under his feet. When he drew near the post office, he heralded his coming with a tin horn. This was our best means of transportation.

"Compare this with the great Vandalia railroad, running its long trains of palace coaches through the city many times a day and you have a proper comparison of the business between the dates of 1844 and 1905. A little stage coach represents 1844 and the Vandalia Railroad represents 1905. This is the kind of progress we have been making and I want you to look forward with me to the future with the same degree of hope and the same degree of confidence. I can see no reason why we cannot look forward to this same continued prosperity; why the coming years may not hold achieve-

N. W. McLain,

Who came here in 1831, and has lived here and at Elm Point ever since.

ments as great or greater than those of the century of 1800, right here in Greenville."

Cholera Epidemic of 1849.

IN 1849, Greenville was visited by a terrible epidemic of cholera and many deaths resulted. The only account of this scourge, the worst that has ever visited Greenville, is preserved by Mr. Jacob Koonce, in the Western Fountain, which paper copied the following from the issue of the Greenville Journal of July 20, 1849.

Samuel H. Crocker, *Deceased,*

Three times elected Sheriff, and was Ex-Postmaster.

Joseph M. Donnell, *Deceased,*

Who lived in and near Greenville from 1819 to 1894.

JAMES BRADFORD,

Founder of the banking house of Bradford and Son, who came to Greenville in 1824 and served in the Black Hawk war. He was circuit clerk and recorder, county clerk, master in chancery, county commissioner, member of the Illinois Legislature, and county judge. He was the first mayor of Greenville, elected in 1872. He died January 29, 1889.

"The Cholera, this mighty agent of death, has spread destruction in our village since our last issue. Our lively and business like town has put on the habiliments of mourning and sadness.

"The first case of cholera, in our town, was the stage driver to whom we referred last week. He is recovering. The next, we also alluded to last week—a young woman named Sarah Woosley, living with the family of Charles Hoiles Esq. She was taken on Friday morning last and died on Saturday morning about two o'clock. This was the first death from cholera.

"Early the same morning a child of Dr. Sprague's, two or three years old was taken and died in five or six hours. The same day Charles Horton Esq., an infant child of C. Hoiles, Esq., a daughter of Mrs. Kellam's aged 11 or 12 years, and I. N. Reed were all taken. The infant died in the afternoon some time; Mr. Horton died about 11 o'clock and Isadora Kellam about 12 o'clock the same night. Mr. Reed died about four o'clock Sunday afternoon.

"There have been other cases of cholera but these are all the deaths, and these all occurred in less than 48 hours."

In the issue of the Journal of July 27, 1849 the editor says:

"Since our last issue there have been two more deaths from cholera, Mrs. Park and Mr. Hopton, but no cases have come to our knowledge since Monday last."

There were 13 cases of cholera and eight deaths. The Journal says: "Some of our citizens have, perhaps, become unnecessarily alarmed and a number have left with their families. It is due to our physicians to state that they have attended the sick during the present crisis, with an industry and self-denial worthy of all praise. Some of our citizens have also distinguished themselves for their unyielding and disinterested care for the sick and if from this worthy number we were requested to designate, we might speak the names of Rev. Robert Stewart and Elam Rust, Esq."

To these names we may also add the names of J. P. Garland, Wyatt Causey, Isaac Enloe and others.

Greenville had splendid physicians in the forties and fifties, Dr. Drake, Dr. Fitch, Dr. Brooks and Dr. Brown. Dr. Brooks met death by suffocation in 1874 at his home in the brick building that stood across the alley east of the old Baptist church.

Greenville in the Fifties.

INCREASED business on every hand marks the period from 1850 to 1860. In 1850 the first govern-

BRADFORD AND SON'S BANK

The bank of Bradford & Son was founded by James Bradford and son Samuel in 1867, in the frame building one door south of the present location, but moved into the present location soon after the business was established. At the death of James Bradford on January 29, 1889, Samuel Bradford became the head of the institution and so remained until his death September 14, 1891. John S. Bradford, who was admitted to the firm in 1890, then became the head of the banking house and so remains at the present time.

RESIDENCE OF JOHN S. BRADFORD, East College Avenue.

ment census was taken in Greenville, the population being 378. The census of 1860 shows a population of 1000 which tells the story of the growth of this period.

W. S. and T. W. Smith, Morse and Brother, Charles Hoiles and G. W. Hill were still in business and E. A. Floyd, Elliott and Kershner, A. W. Hynes, Barr and Elliott and many others come upon the scene. The hotels had by this time centered at or near the public square. The St. Charles Hotel was kept by E. R. McCord and the Franklin House by Franklin G. Morse, from whom it took its name. From this time on business increased to such an extent that it would be practically an impossibility to note all the changes in detail.

All south of the brick building now used as Plant's Livery stables on Third street was timber and brush in 1857. A few years later R. L. Mu'd built a home near the present residence of George O. Morris, and everybody told him he was building so far out in the timber that none of his friends could find him. Some of the big trees that formed the forest of the fifties are still standing on this property. The eastern limits of the town then were about the present site of the Methodist parsonage, and east of that was the farm of Samuel White.

The Drake house was one of the finest, even then, and the present Wirz building on the south side of the square was the largest business house, except the Sprague block, which was built by Dr. Anson Sprague in 1857. The Sprague block was so large that no one had the courage to occupy it, until Charles Hoiles bought it and opened a store therein.

Robert G. Ingersoll came to Greenville with his father in 1851,

remaining here a year. His father, the Reverend John Ingersoll, was pastor of the Congregational church. The old gentleman was quite eccentric. One son Clark, was a clerk in G. W. Hill's store and was afterward elected to Congress.

Ingersoll and his father boarded for a time with the family of Wm. S. Colcord. They also boarded with the Reverend W. D. H. Johnson. "Bob" was then seventeen years of age and was extraordinarily bright for one of his age. For six months he was seatmate of E. J. C. Alexander, who now lives on his farm north of Greenville. They attended school in the basement of the old Congregational church. Socrates Smith being the teacher. "Bob" was very devout in those days. He lived in Greenville for about two years and it was while here that he

commenced writing poetry, some of which was printed in the Greenville Journal, at the time.

Some of Greenville's citizens were not deaf to the wants of the refugee slaves, who were on their way from the sunny south to Canada. It has been handed down by tradition that the Reverend Robert Stewart gave many a slave shelter and food and helped him on his way. Such assistance in those days was called the "Underground Railroad."

Several times an effort has been made to mark with marble the spot where Lincoln and Douglas delivered their memorable addresses in Greenville. The visits of these intellectual giants were coveted by many towns but were secured by but few. Greenville, however, was one of the favored ones and Lincoln and Douglas spoke at different times in Greenville in 1858, near the residence property of Miss Sallie Colcord.

In the course of his speech Lincoln said that although Bond county was called the "Widow Bond" and was in the way of territory one of the most insignificant in Illinois, she towered way above many larger ones in the intellectuality of her people. He said he had practiced law all around Bond county but had little occasion to practice in it, for there seemed so little contention among the people, that litigation was scarcely known.

Douglas had ridden twenty miles through the heat and dust and after pushing his way through a throng, such as Greenville never had harbored before, he sought opportunity to refresh and re-clothe himself in his room at the old McCord House, on the east side of the square. But the cries of the multitude were so great and so persistent, that it was

RESIDENCE OF MRS. SAMUEL BRADFORD, East College Avenue.

J. M. MILLER, Attorney-at-Law and Capitalist.

Who came to Greenville in 1856, and who has been prominently identified with the city ever since; joined the Federal Army in 1862; was hospital stewart 130th Ill. Infty.; First Lieut. 93rd U. S. C. I.; Vice President First National Bank; Mayor of Greenville 1891 to 1893.

deemed best that he should say a few words to them at once. He stepped out on the upper floor of the two story veranda, which adorned the front of the hotel and talked probably five minutes. He was in his stocking feet, bareheaded and in his shirtsleeves. The sight of him

and the words he spoke brought forth the most enthusiastic applause and so reassured the surging throng that they were content to disperse until after dinner, when the speaking was held. While here he was the guest of his warm personal friend, Charles Hoiles.

Greenville in the Sixties.

THE period of Greenville's history from 1860 to 1870 stands out prominently because of two things, the participation of its citizenship in the Civil War and the great industrial impetus given the city by the building of the Vandalia Line. Both of these subjects are fully treated in separate chapters, in this history.

The early sixties were troublous times in Greenville as elsewhere in this country. The people lived on excitement and news from the front was eagerly sought.

News from the battle field usually came by mail from St. Louis, reaching Greenville with the stagecoach from Carlyle in the afternoon. Victories were celebrated at night with bonfires in the court yard and the ringing of church bells by the youngsters, until most of the grown people, patriotic as they were, wished there had been no battle and no victory to celebrate.

One day in 1863 the mail brought the news of a great victory for the Union arms and the patriots were celebrating in the southeast section

View of Main Avenue, looking east from the southwest corner of the public square in 1892.

J. H. LIVINGSTON,
A prominent business man and a
large land and property owner.

WILLIAM H. DAWDY,
Who came to Greenville in August 1868 and has practiced law here ever
since. Was City Attorney from 1872 to 1874; State's Attorney 1872-
80; Master-in-Chancery for six years; Assistant United States Attorney,
1887-9; Member Illinois Legislature 1890-92; Judge Illinois Court of
Claims 1892-6; Candidate for Democratic Presidential elector 1896.

of the court yard, when a premature
explosion of the cannon killed a
Mr. Zimmerman, one of the gunners
and badly injured a man named
Bates.

Every night the streets were pa-
trolled and many were the nights of
vigil in the homes of Greenville's
citizens. One hundred guns and
ammunition were procured and at
one time, in December 1864, a military post was established in Greenville, in charge of Lieutenant R. H.
Moses, with quarters in the court
house. Even in 1861 a company
was formed, primarily for the purpose of combating Clingman's Band.
Clingman was a noted guerilla and

horsethief and operated in Bond,
Montgomery and Fayette counties.
His real name was said to be Eras-
mus Wood.

On August 4, 1861, a band of
Greenville and Bond county men
formed a party to attack Clingman,
who was thought to be encamped
near Van Burensburg from fifty to
one thousand strong. The attacking
party numbered six hundred, including those from Montgomery
county. Some fifteen or twenty
men, said to have been under the
leadership of John H. Jett, were
scouring the county near its north
boundary line, when a squad of
some thirty five men, under command of Lieutenant Joel B. Paisley,
a veteran soldier, were discovered at
a halt, watering their horses. Each
party mistook the other for Clingman's Band. Paisley, at once, made
a strategetic movement upon Jett's
party for the purpose of hemming
them in the lane and forcing a
surrender. It did not take long for
Jett's force which was the smaller
and was composed entirely of citizens, to decide upon a retreat. Accordingly they put whip and spur to
their horses in order to pass out at
the mouth of the lane before the
others could reach it. They barely
escaped and the race continued for
seven miles, with the swiftest speed
of which the horses were capable.
T. S. Hubbard, one of Jett's men
was overtaken and asked to surrender and failing to do so was
shot twice. Paisley's men, at first,
did not recognize Hubbard, and
Hubbard, on the other hand, did not
recognize his captors. Finally, how-

ever, the recognition was mutual
and further hostilities were averted.

The Greenville company, under
the able leadership of Sheriff Plant
made a brilliant campaign but
Clingman was never encountered
and he finally left the country, but
not until he had done considerable
damage.

One of the tragedies of this period
in Greenville was the murder of
Captain Samuel G. McAdams.
Among others Captain McAdams
was summoned by Provost Marshal
Murdock to assist in the arrest of
one Jacob Sanner, who lived near

WILLIAM MORRIS,
A pioneer real estate man, now deceased.

ROBERT C. MORRIS,
A former real estate man, now living
at Toledo, Ohio.

D. H. KINGSBURY,

A prominent lawyer from 1856 until his death in 1893.

Bethel. They went to Sanner's house at nine o'clock the night of December 8, 1864, with the expectation of finding some deserters, as it was said that Sanner harboured such persons. The marshal first approached the door and made his business known, and being refused admittance, the Captain stepped up, and, taking hold of the door knob, said to Sanner that he had better not offer any resistance but comply with the law and he would be treated like a man. Sanner refused and at the same time made some threat. Captain McAdams replied that he was not afraid but that he insisted on what he had a lawful right to do. At that Sanner fired a musket through the door shutter, the entire load taking effect in the Captain's abdomen, making eight holes in his person, there being one ball and seven buck shot in the gun.

The Captain fell, but soon arose and helped himself off the porch and then fell again.

Five or six men were seen to pass from the house at the time, two more than were with the Provost Marshal. Several shots were fired by the marshal and his men but to no effect. Captain McAdams was conveyed to the home of D. B. Harned, where he lived nineteen hours. There was probably not another man so universally loved in the county as was Captain McAdams.

Sanner was arrested four miles southeast of Salem, Ill., January 7, 1862. He started to run but was wounded and halted. He was brought to Greenville where he was an object of much curiosity. He was later taken to Springfield and his trial was postponed and he was finally acquitted on a technicality. In May 1865 a stranger rode up to

Sanner's house and asked for lodging and without further conversation, drew a pistol and shot Sanner through the head. Three other balls were then fired into his body and the stranger deliberately rode away. It was never known who killed Sanner, although there were various rumors as to the identity of the party.

The bodies of Captain William Colby and Lieutenant Ives, who were killed in battle, arrived in town June 29, 1863. There was a great sorrow because of the death of these two beloved men. The funeral was held at the court house, addresses being made by the Reverend G. W. Goodale and Prof. J. B. White. There were thirty-four pall bearers, and the bodies were laid away with military honors.

Feeling was high in war times and such feeling culminated in the killing of Terrell Reavis by Lawyer J. P. Shields on August 12, 1861. Reavis, who was said to be a southern sympathizer and Shields, who espoused the cause of the Union, met near Wm. S. Smith's store, and after some harsh words, Shields drew a poinard from his cane and stabbed Reavis near the heart. Reavis died in a few hours.

Turning now to the industrial side of this period of the sixties, it may be stated without fear of successful contradiction that from the time the first passenger train was run from Greenville to St. Louis, on the morning of December 8, 1868, the improvement in Greenville was more marked than ever before. The population nearly doubled and the effect of the railroad was very perceptible, as these figures show. The advent of this road gave Greenville an impetus such as it had never

DR. DAVID WILKINS, *Deceased*,

Who came to Greenville in 1854 and practiced medicine until a few years prior to his death July 22, 1905.

before known. As soon as the farmers found here a market for their products, they came here to trade, and merchants soon discovered that a new order of things had been inaugurated. Business increased, brick blocks replaced frame buildings in the business center and an uncertain and transient trade became augmented and permanent.

The railroad awakened a spirit of enterprise that had been lying dormant for want of opportunity or development. Old stage coach lines offered no chance for an expansion of business of any kind. But with the railroad came progress and expansion.

SUBURBAN RESIDENCE OF JAMES F. CARROLL.

JAMES H. MOSS.

A resident since 1835. Trustee and one of the founders of Greenville College. Owner of large property interests.

During the year 1869 no less than 75 buildings were erected in Greenville—more than all the improvements of the previous decade. Among the new blocks and buildings were the Morse block, (destroyed by fire October 27, 1904) the J. B. Reid block, A. Buie's addition to his store, Hoiles and Sons' brick bank building, the brick with the mansard roof by Wm. S. Smith & Co., known later as the National Bank building, and many other business houses, besides residences, as well as two new flouring mills, one by McLain and Wafer and the other by C. P. Staub, and J. M. McDowell's elevator.

In these days of the sixties Greenville boasted a county fair, which thrived for several years but finally succumbed. It was held where "Buzzard Roost" now stands.

Among the most important industries in the sixties were Stahl's woolen mill, Lansing and Ostrom's flour mill, Elam's carriage factory, the sorghum molasses mill of Samuel Colcord on the site of the present post office, and a turning lathe operated by a Mr. Alexander, called Buffalo, and his boys.

Greenville in the Seventies.

THE spirit of public improvement continued through the seventies, although at the beginning of the decade there was at first a lull, and then a decline, in the city's growth and prosperity. But Greenville weathered the panic of 1873, and though she stood still, she did not retrograde. In the fall of 1873 there was a pressing demand for houses and the town began to go forward again.

In the year 1874 there were so many burglaries that the business men met at the First National Bank and arranged for a night watchman and Greenville has not been without such an official since. In 1876, the centennial year, the Greenville Advocate paid special attention to the early history of the city and county, and through the efforts of the Reverend Thomas W. Hynes, George M. Tatham, R. O. White and others, much of this early history was collated and some of it was published. Toward the end of the decade, in 1877, to be exact, many new residences spoke of increased population. Greenville then had three banks, the First National, Bradford's and Hoiles'.

Greenville in the Eighties.

WE are now coming rapidly to days well remembered by many people who now live in Greenville and as we approach the present there is less to be said, without going into an exhaustive resume of the times.

The eighties opened up in Greenville with a cyclone, the most severe windstorm in the city's history. At eight o'clock Sunday evening April 17, 1880, a terrific wind storm broke over Greenville and great was the damage resulting. The steeple of the Methodist church was blown off, as was also the roof of the National Bank building and many business houses and residences were damaged; in fact but few escaped. The damage was estimated at $20,000. The storm was the third tornado to visit the city within the year, the others being of lesser importance. Fortunately no one was severely injured in the storm but there was great excite-

RESIDENCE OF E. V. GASKINS.

DR. W. A. ALLEN, *Deceased*,

Who came to Greenville in 1855, and formed a partnership with Dr. T. S. Brooks. At the time of his death, March, 1891, he was Mayor of Greenville, President of the Board of Education, and Chairman of the Board of Trustees of the Congregational Church.

ment and services at the church were dismissed, while people rushed frantically about searching for their loved ones, and finding all safe, although some were bruised. Several years later when Mt. Vernon was visited by a cyclone Greenville sent $257.30 to the sufferers of that city.

This was a good year for wheat, for the local papers tell us that in one week the last of July 1880, two Greenville banks paid out $84,245 for wheat and this did not include the business of the mills and small buyers.

Greenville in the Nineties.

THE opening of this decade marks a new era in the history of Greenville. It is chiefly the industrial spirit that predominates in the nineties, and, in fact, up to the present time. It was in the period of the nineties that nearly all of Greenville's present thriving industries were launched.

As early as March, 1890, the business men organized and subscribed money for the purpose of advertising Greenville in the eastern papers. Up to this time the growth had been slow but steady. After the Vandalia Line had been safely launched, the people sank back on their

laurels and the usual course of business was allowed to run smoothly and without interruption. And there was really no especially marked advancement until the industrial period of a few years ago swept over the city and the era of factories dawned in Greenville. Since then the advancement has been by rapid strides and the city is eagerly seeking the rolling lands to the northeast, east, southeast, and south, where modern homes are almost daily being built.

In 1890 the Postal Telegraph came, and the same fall, when dingy street lamps cost the city $250 a year, the agitation for electric lights commenced, nor did it cease until June 1, 1895, when the first electric lights were turned on in the streets of Greenville.

The telephone exchange came in 1894. The factory of DeMoulin and Brother was established in 1896 and the Helvetia Milk Condensing Company came in 1898. The Greenville Milk Condensing Company commenced operations in 1902, but all these have enlarged and are still enlarging and their history in detail is given elsewhere in this volume.

The growth of Greenville has not been of the mushroom character, nor has it been by fits and starts but

rather its evolution from the log cabin in 1815 to the growing city of today, has been the result of carefully laid plans and persistent execution of those plans.

Greenville of Today.

AND now we come to the Greenville of 1905, with its population of at least 3,000, and with its prosperous business houses and hundreds of happy homes. In the institutions of this city and in the many channels of business are each day seen evidences of increasing opportunities for intellectual, moral, financial and spiritual gain and growth.

We all know what Greenville of the present day is and we will use no space in telling present day history, for, as has been truthfully said, the history of any community, is the history of its men and women, and in the pages which follow there is portrayed by pen and picture what Greenville is today.

The Civic History of Greenville.

GREENVILLE was one of the first towns in the state to take advantage of the laws to incorporate under special charter. Just fifty years ago, to be exact February 15, 1855, Greenville was incorporated by special act of the Illinois Legislature. The special act incorporating the village clearly indicated that the town of Greenville was already in existence, as a municipality, incorporated under the general laws in force at that time. Section 2, of the act of 1855, provided that "the boundaries of said incorporation shall be those as established

DR. T. S. BROOKS, *Deceased.*

A Greenville practitioner for 40 years; a Yale graduate.

MRS. DORCAS DENNY, *Deceased,*
Wife of J. S. Denny, Deceased.

by the first ordinances passed by the present board of trustees of said town, which said ordinances are hereby legalized for that purpose."

Section 5, of the same act, provided that "the corporate powers and duties of said town shall be vested in five persons, who shall form a board for the transaction of business, and the persons who may be in office as trustees of said town under the general incorporation act of this state shall, after the passage of this act, be deemed to hold their offices by virtue of this act until the first Monday in May, 1855, and until their successors in office are elected and qualified, and to discharge their duties in conformity to this act."

There are no records of the doings and acts of the board prior to the act of 1855, and the first three years records of the new board, from 1855 to 1858, have been lost and diligent research has failed to reveal who were the first officers under the special act of 1855, but from old newspaper files the names of the officers from 1856 to 1858 have been obtained and the city records, complete from 1858 to date supply the necessary information from that time to date.

As early as 1856, the first year of the new village government, the question of license or no license was raised and it has been the chief issue at all municipal elections ever since. The first board of trustees passed an ordinance declaring "the sale of ardent spirits a nuisance when sold as a beverage." At the election in 1856, according to the American Courier, 149 votes were cast and the anti-

license ticket had a majority of 37.

The following is a complete record of the elective officers of Greenville from 1856 to date.

Boards of Trustees.

1856—J. Burchsted, J. K. McLean, M. P. Ormsby, L. P. Littlefield, J. W. Elliott.

1857—President, Col. R. Bentley, J. T. Barr, Wm. S. Smith, A. G. Henry, J. B. Reid.

1858—President, Alexander Buie; Clerk, Joseph H. Birge; Treasurer, J. B. Reid; J. T. Barr, A. G. Henry, Samuel White.

1859—President, J. K. McLean; Clerk, Joseph H. Birge; Treasurer, J. B. Reid; James Bradford, W. S. Colcord, George Gibson.

1860—President, J. K. McLean; Clerk, James Bradford; Treasurer, J. B. Reid; W. S. Colcord, Alexander Buie.

1861—President, J. Burchsted; Clerk and Attorney, L. C. Hawley; Treasurer, J. S. Denny; W. S. Colcord, Wm. M. Colby, S. R. Perry.

1862—President, Alexander Buie; Clerk, L. C. Hawley and M. V. Denny; Treasurer, J. B. Reid; H. B. Alexander, Wm. M. Colby, Joel Elam, S. R. Perry.

1863—President, J. S. Denny; Clerk, M. V. Denny; Treasurer, Alexander Buie; H. B. Alexander, Lemuel Adams, D. H. Kingsbury, W. H. Williams.

1864—President, J. S. Denny; Clerk, M. V. Denny; Treasurer, James Bradford; Alexander Buie, M. Ives, J. P. Shields, S. R. Perry, J. T. Laws.

1865—President, Seth Fuller; Clerk, M. V. Denny; Treasurer, James Bradford; Othniel Buchanan, M. B. Chittenden, W. S. Colcord, J. W. Elliott.

J. S. DENNY, *Deceased,*
Village President in 1863; Mayor in 1873.

1866—President, O. Buchanan; Clerk, M. V. Denny; Treasurer, James Bradford; M. B. Chittenden, D. H. Kingsbury, J. W. Elliott, E. B. White.

1867—President, Rev. Thomas W. Hynes; Clerk, Edward Bigelow; Treasurer, J. B. Reid; R. C. Sprague, E. B. White.

1868—President, Wm. S. Smith, Sr.; Clerk, M. V. Denny; Treasurer, Lemuel Adams; J. E. Walls, John Wenting; Police Magistrate, James Bradford.

1869—President, S. A. Phelps; Clerk, M. V. Denny and R. K. Dewey; Treasurer, Wm. S. Smith, Jr.; P. Boll, C. A. Darlington.

1870—President, R. C. Sprague; Clerk and Attorney, W. H. Dawdy;

The old jail on Third Street, built in 1859, and now used as a tenement house.

Burning of the court house at Greenville, Saturday, March 24, 1883.
Photograph loaned by J. H. Hawley.

1872—(Special Election) Mayor, James Bradford; Clerk, R. K. Dewey; Treasurer, C. D. Hoiles; Attorney, W. H. Dawdy; Aldermen, P. C. Henry and P. C. Reed, first ward; Joseph W. Dewald and C. D. Harris, second ward; W. A. Allen and G. W. Miller, third ward. License 119; Anti-license, 85.

1873—(Regular Election) Mayor, J. S. Denny; Clerk, R. K. Dewey; Treasurer, M. V. Denny; Attorney, W. H. Dawdy; Aldermen, C. D. Harris and John T. Barr, Sr.; Wm. Koch and R. L. Mudd; G. W. Miller and P. C. Reed.

1874—Clerk, George Berry; Treasurer, M. V. Denny; Attorney, W. H. Dawdy; Aldermen, C. D. Harris, J. T. Barr, Jr., R. C. Sprague.

1875—Mayor, James Bradford; Clerk, D. B. Evans; Treasurer, M. V. Denny; Attorney, J. H. Dawdy; Aldermen, Lemuel Adams, R. L. Mudd, Stephen Wait.

1876—Attorney, D. H. Kingsbury; Police Magistrate, M. B. Chittenden; Aldermen, Ed Birge, Wm. Koch, R. C. Sprague.

1877—Mayor G. W. Miller; Clerk, D. B. Evans; Treasurer, M. V. Denny; Attorney, D. H. Kingsbury; Aldermen, J. L. Wood, R. L. Mudd, J. H. Davis.

1878—Aldermen, J. R. Whittaker, M. W. Van Valkenburg, R. C. Sprague.

1879—Mayor, C. D. Hoiles; Clerk, D. B. Evans; Treasurer, J. H. Davis; Attorney, George S. Phelps; Aldermen, W. H. Williams, J. G. Taylor, W. E. Robinson.

1880—Aldermen, F. Parent, M. W. VanValkenburg, W. A. Allen; Police Magistrate, M. B. Chittenden.

1881—Mayor, C. D. Hoiles; Clerk, J. T. Fonke; Treasurer, Joseph Dewall; Attorney, L. H. Craig;

Treasurer, Samuel Bradford; S. E. Black, J. N. Pogue, Wm. S. Smith, Jr.

1871—President, W. S. Thomas; Clerk and Attorney, W. H. Dawdy; Treasurer, George M. Tatham; J. C. Gericks, J. Perryman, E. B. White.

1872—President, John T. Barr; Clerk and Attorney, W. H. Dawdy; Treasurer, C. D. Hoiles; A. G. Henry, J. B. Reid, Stephen Wait.

Incorporated As a City.

At a special election held August 13, 1872, Greenville was incorporated as a city under the state law, the vote being 140 for the proposition to 5 against. The first election under this law was held September 17, 1872. The following paragraphs give the names of all elective officers at regular municipal elections from that time to date. In each case the first named alderman represented the first ward; the second named, the second ward; and the third named, the third ward.

Bond County Jail, built in 1897.

E. B. WISE, *Deceased*,

A prominent merchant for many years. Former Alderman and Member Board of Education.

Aldermen, W. H. Williams, John Schlup, G. W. Miller. (Wm. S. Smith was elected to fill the unexpired term of G. W. Miller, who died.)

1882—Treasurer, Wm. Koch, (to fill vacancy) Aldermen, S. Hutchinson, John A. Elam, W. A. Allen.

1883—Mayor, C. D. Hoiles; Clerk, Ward Reid; Treasurer, D. B. Evans; Attorney, L. H. Craig; Police Magistrate, Henry Howard; Aldermen, W. H. Williams, M. W. VanValkenburg, E. B. Wise.

1884—Aldermen, C. D. Harris, John Baumberger Sr., W. A. Allen.

1885—Mayor, C. D. Hoiles; Clerk, Ward Reid; Treasurer, F. Thraner; Attorney, S. A. Phelps; Aldermen, W. H. Williams, T. L. Vest, W. H. H. Beeson.

1886—Aldermen, J. Seaman, E. D. Wallace, W. A. Allen. For Saloon license, 137; against, 38.

1887—Mayor, U. B. Harris; Clerk, Ward Reid; Treasurer, W. O. Holdzkom; Attorney, S. A. Phelps; Aldermen, F. P. Joy, James Vollentine, E. P. Justice. Majority for anti-license 83.

1888—Aldermen, J. Seaman, Clayton Travis, A. Maynard; Police Magistrate, Henry Howard.

1889—Mayor, Dr. W. A. Allen; Clerk, Ward Reid; Treasurer, J. Seaman; Attorney, Solon A. Enloe; Aldermen, J. C. Sanderson, J. P. Thompson, M. S. Oudyn.

1890—Aldermen, J. A. Harris, Ed Baumberger, J. F. Watts. In 1890 Mayor Allen died in office and M. S. Oudyn was Mayor pro tem for one month.

1891—Mayor, J. M. Miller; Clerk, Ward Reid; Treasurer, W. A. McLain; Attorney, C. E. Cook; Aldermen, Emil Broeker, Clayton Travis, A. W. Mahle.

1892—Police Magistrate, J. J. Sutton; Superintendent of Streets, S. W. Robinson; City Marshal, Fay Z. Dibble; Aldermen, John L. Rogier, L. L. Tice, (to fill vacancy) George W. Hickman, Ed DeMoulin. For electric lights, 166; against, 137. On July 6, 1892, at a special election W. V. Weise and J. A. Harris were elected aldermen to fill vacancies.

1893—Mayor, J. Seaman; Clerk, Frank T. Reid; Treasurer, W. E. Robinson; Attorney, C. E. Cook; Aldermen, L. L. Tice, W. O. Holdzkom, H. A. Hubbard.

1894—City Marshal, W. E. Davis, Superintendent of Streets, Cleve McVey; Aldermen, H. C. Birge, John Dagen, E. B. Wise.

1895—Mayor, J. Seaman; Clerk, John L. Bunch; Treasurer, H. W. Park; Attorney, C. E. Cook; Aldermen, L. L. Tice, N. H. Jackson, H. A. Hubbard.

1896—Aldermen, Horace McNeill, E. M. Gullick, Alfred Blizzard; Police Magistrate, J. J. Sutton.

1897—Mayor, Ed DeMoulin; Clerk, John L. Bunch; Treasurer, S. D. Hoiles; Attorney, C. E. Cook; Aldermen, W. H. Williams, P. Boll, Charles Ingles.

1898—Aldermen, F. P. Joy, S. VanDeusen, E. B. Wise; Treasurer, C. D. Hoiles, (to fill vacancy.)

1899—Mayor, Ed DeMoulin; Clerk, L. A. Holdener; Attorney, C. E. Cook; Treasurer, Guy B. Hoiles; Aldermen, W. H. Williams, James T. Kirkham, H. W. Blizzard, A. C. Culp, (to fill vacancy).

1900—Aldermen, Frank N. Blanchard, Daniel Lutz, E. E. Wise; Superintendent of Streets, Ben Hull; City Marshal, E. D. Wallace; Police Magistrate, J. J. Sutton. The seat of F. N. Blanchard, alderman of the first ward was contested by N. B. Jernigan, who was finally seated.

1901—Mayor, F. P. Joy; Clerk, S. M. Harnetiaux; Attorney, W. A. Orr; Treasurer, Abe McNeill, Jr.; Aldermen, W. H. Williams, Sam Mueller, Ell Armstrong.

1902—Aldermen, J. A. Warren, Daniel Lutz, Fred Durr; City Marshal, C. C. Smith.

1903—Mayor, Ed DeMoulin; Clerk, Frank N. Blanchard; Treasurer, R. W. Wilson; Attorney, C. E. Cook; Aldermen, G. W. Bass; S. Van Deusen, J. E. Wafer. For Mayor Ed DeMoulin and J. H. Livingston each received 316 votes. The two men cast lots, DeMoulin winning.

1904—Aldermen, W. D. Donnell, F. O. Leidel, John S. Bradford; City Attorney, J. H. Allio; Police Magistrate, W. H. Taylor.

1905—Mayor, W. A. Orr; Clerk, J. Finis Johnston; Treasurer, Abe McNeill Jr.; Attorney, J. H. Allio; Aldermen, G. W. Bass, Horace McNeill, (to fill vacancy) Charles White, James E. Wafer.

1905—Special Election to fill vacancy, caused by the resignation of Mayor Orr and his removal to Springfield, held September 12, 1905, resulted in the election of Edmond DeMoulin as Mayor to fill the unexpired term.

Greenville's Geographical Growth.

The original plat of Greenville was made by John Russell, in June, 1821. The exact date is not known, but it must have been before June 6th, of that year, for on that day a sale of thirty of the lots was ordered, "for the benefit of the county." The land platted by John Russell belonged to George Davidson, the founder of Greenville. In this plat was embraced what is now Davidson's Addition, and was bounded on the north by College Avenue, on the east by Fourth Street, on the south by Summer Street and on the west by the west city limits. It is related that Davidson became dissatisfied with this plat and thrust it in the fireplace.

Then the original town of 71 lots was laid out and stands today bounded on the north by Oak Street, on the east by Mulberry Alley, on the south by the first tier of lots south of South Street and on the west by Fourth Street.

The area of Greenville is a mile square, 640 acres, and includes the south half of the northeast quarter of Section 10, the south half of the northwest quarter of Section 11, the southeast quarter of section 10, the southwest quarter of section 11, north half of the northwest quarter of section 14 and the north half of the northeast quarter of section 15. The additions to the city, or original town have been as follows:

Davidson's Addition of 61 lots was made October 7, 1831, by Vance L. Davidson agent for George Davidson, who had moved to JoDaviess county. This was the first addition made to the original town, now city of Greenville.

On May 29, 1839, "a plat of the town of Greenville, laid out in a re-survey by Asahel Enloe, county surveyor," was recorded. Then came the additions in order as follows:

East Addition by Timothy P. Eldrege, Ariel Eldrege and Edward Cotton, April 25, 1839; Asahel Enloe, surveyor; 28 lots.

Greenwood's Addition by John Greenwood, proprietor, September 28, 1841, Seth Fuller, surveyor; 40 lots.

Dallam's Addition, by Aquilla P. Dallam, by Richard B. Dallam, his attorney, September 11, 1848; Seth Fuller, surveyor; 29 lots.

South Addition by William S. Wait, April 29, 1854; John Hughs, surveyor; 121 lots.

White's First Addition, by Samuel White, February 14, 1855; Seth Fuller, deputy surveyor; 68 lots.

College Addition by John B. White, Stephen Morse, Seth Fuller, W. D. H. Johnson and William T. Hull, trustees of Almira College, July 29, 1857; Seth Fuller, surveyor. An addition of the lots across the street south of the college was made in a subsequent survey by A. Buie, president of the Board of Trustees; 72 lots.

Smith's Central Addition by William S. Smith and Willam S. Smith Jr., March 12, 1866; R. K. Dewey, surveyor; 18 lots.

Stewart's Addition by Robert Stewart, J. F. Alexander and Edward Bigelow April 6, 1869; Ira Kingsbury, surveyor; 14 lots.

White's Second Addition by Samuel White July 21, 1869; R. K. Dewey, surveyor; 32 lots.

Railroad Addition by William A. Allen, and Belle E. Holcomb, August 7, 1869; R. K. Dewey, surveyor; 65 lots.

Hutchinson's Addition, by Sylvanus Hutchinson, September 18, 1869, R. K. Dewey, surveyor; 32 lots.

Montrose Cemetery was surveyed by R. K. Dewey April 29, 1877 and was given to the city by the Montrose Cemetery Association.

Evans Addition by Mary A. Evans and Margaret J. Hubbard October 4, 1881; R. K. Dewey, surveyor. Evans addition was vacated January 9, 1886, and is now McLain's Addition.

Justice's Addition by E. P. Justice, W. S. Robinson, G. S. Haven, J. F. Dann, W. H. Dawdy and Caroline Childers, October 4, 1881; John Kingsbury, surveyor; 16 lots.

Koch's Addition by William Koch, April 19, 1883; John Kingsbury, surveyor; 12 lots.

Vest's Addition by T. L. Vest, March 29, 1884; John Kingsbury, surveyor; 40 lots.

McCasland's Addition by John McCasland October 3, 1884; R. K. Dewey, surveyor; 17 lots.

Douglas Place by C. D. Hoiles and Ward Reid, April 15, 1887; R. K. Dewey, surveyor; 75 lots.

Moss's First Addition by James H. Moss, October 13, 1892; R. K. Dewey, surveyor; 35 lots.

Moss's Second Addition by James H. Moss, April 21, 1894; R. K. Dewey, surveyor; 58 lots.

Moss's Third Addition by James H. Moss, June 2, 1898; R. K. Dewey, surveyor; 20 lots.

Colcord's Addition by Hattie J. Colcord and Otis T. Colcord, September 5, 1898; R. K. Dewey, surveyor; 29 lots.

"Baumberger's Out Lots," by John Baumberger Sr., August 31, 1899; R. K. Dewey, surv.; 16 lots.

Rutschmann's Addition by Chas. Rutschmann October 8, 1900; R. K. Dewey, surveyor; 11 lots.

McLain's Addition by Thomas R. McLain by N. W. McLain, agent, May 2, 1902; John Kingsbury, surveyor; 32 lots.

Sherman's Addition by Washington Sherman, June 6, 1902; R. K. Dewey, surveyor; 40 lots.

Hockett's Addition by Oliver Hockett December 8, 1902; R. K. Dewey, surveyor; 20 lots.

College Second Addition by the Board of Trustees of Greenville College June 8, 1903; R. K. Dewey, surveyor; 12 lots.

Moss's Fourth Addition by James H. Moss August 18, 1903; R. K. Dewey, surveyor; 38 lots.

Ashcraft's Addition by Franklin H. Ashcraft, March 17, 1905; R. K. Dewey, surveyor; 92 lots.

DeMoulin's Addition by Ed DeMoulin, March 22, 1905; R. K. Dewey, surveyor; 34 lots.

Dixon's Addition, by Cyrus C. Dixon and H. Harrison Dixon, April 3, 1905; R. K. Dewey, surv.; 41 lots.

Woodlawn Addition by Dr. B. F. Coop, George V. Weise, Ernest E. Wise, E. W. Miller and Cicero J. Lindly, April 6, 1905, John Kingsbury, surveyor; 123 lots.

Armstrong's Addition by Joseph H. Armstrong, Elizabeth J. Armstrong and Ward Reid, April 20, 1905; Jno. Kingsbury, surv.; 20 lots.

Bradford's Addition by Franklin H. Ashcraft, Rose B. Dixon, Cyrus C. Dixon and Otto Schafer, May 4, 1905; R. K. Dewey, surv.; 68 lots.

Kimbro's Addition by Daniel Kimbro, May 16, 1905; R. K. Dewey, surveyor; 10 lots.

College Avenue Addition by F. H. Ashcraft, June 24, 1905; R. K. Dewey, surveyor; 254 lots.

The city of Greenville is composed of three wards, the boundary lines of which have been changed several times. The present first ward is all that part of Greenville east of First Street, the line turning east from First Street down the center of College Avenue, thence east on College to Spruce, thence north on Spruce one block, thence east on Oak to the city limits. The second ward is all south of Main Avenue and west of First Street. The third ward from the west city limits is all north of Main until the intersection of Main and First is reached from which point the line runs north on First to College Avenue and so on through as detailed in the first ward boundaries.

Greenville Census Report.

United States government census reports show that the first census taken in Bond county was in 1820, when the county had a population of 2931, but no government census of Greenville village was taken until 1850. The government census reports here given bear out the statement made in the history of the Vandalia Railroad, that the greatest increase in population was during the building of the road.

1850	378	1880	1886
1860	1000	1890	1988
1870	1989	1900	2504

Since the federal census of 1900, there has been material increase in the population of Greenville and today the city shelters, at a conservative estimate, at least 3,000 souls, although the figure is placed much higher by many. The rapid increase in population is due to the fact that many families are moving here to take advantage of the city's superior educational advantages, while, at the same time the city supplies employment to many, through its flourishing and ever enlarging industries.

Greenville's Military History

By Col. J. B. Reid.

CAPTAIN PAUL BECK, Greenville's first miller, was also Greenville's first military captain. He was commissioned captain May 12, 1817, and mustered a company in the prairie near Greenville.

Samuel Davidson, a son of the founder of Greenville, was made an ensign at the same time. On June 14, 1817, John Laughlin was elected captain, John Hopton, lieutenant, and John Whitley, Jr., ensign.

These military companies were organized for the purpose of keeping alive the spirit of patriotism, engendered by the Revolutionary War and the War of 1812, both of which were only a few years in the past, at this time, and also for the purpose of combating the Indians, if necessary. In this way the military spirit was cultivated until the Black Hawk war of 1831-2, when Greenville sent some of her sons to the front, among whom were James Bradford, William Black, J. Perryman, Thomas Stout and others.

MEXICAN WAR.

When the United States engaged in war with Mexico, Greenville was again in the front. The Protestant Monitor states that on June 4, 1846, citizens of the county assembled in Greenville to respond to a call from the Governor for three regiments of volunteers to go to the front. Although the day was unfavorable the meeting was large and eighty-five citizens, chiefly young men, enrolled and elected Wilson W. Willey captain; James M. Hubbard, first lieutenant; Benjamin E. Sellers, second lieutenant; Matthew Harvey, John A. Washburn, James I. Adams and Josiah F. Sugg, sergeants; Richard Roberts, Lemuel Washburn, Larkin Jackson and Allen Harris, corporals. The privates who volunteered were:

Samuel G. McAdams, John M. Smith, R. B. Alexander, John C. Mackey, R. O. White, Samuel J. Ewing, Stephen White, Thomas A. Ewing, N. D. Higinbotham, Robert Patterson, George P. Etzler, John Patterson, William Alderman, Henry D. Rhea, William Wood, Nelson H. Elam, Joseph A. Jay, Sowel Smith, Joel H. Sherrob, Robert Booth, Henry C. Thacker, James Blankenship, Thomas L. Smith, Henry H. Hill, George A. Reed, John C. Gaston, Nathan McCracken, Daniel Royer, John P. McCracken, Elias Coleman, Samuel Roberts, Thomas Weldon, James Hignight, Peter S. Lyttaker, James Kuykendall, Theophilus Short, James W. Alderman, Charles Hilliard, David Phipps, John Alexander, John Little, William

Ray, Isaac Redfearn, Nathan B. Willis, Alexander McCollum, Isaac N. Reed, William Madray, John Holland, John A. Laws, Thomas J. Jett, Felix Gower, William M. Hunter, Robert Arnold, Andrew Gilbert, Henry B. Alexander, Hardin Elmore, Henry Cruthis, William Lucas, Samuel Gray, Robert Willeford, Milton F. Neatherly, Francis Webster, William Allen, Calvin Brown, John H. Gilmore, Andrew J. Steel, Calvin Denson, James C. Cruthis, Hampton Cruthis, Enoch M. Noland, H. W. Jarvis, George Allen, Michael Tucker, John Spratt, and Joseph W. Grigg.

The above list is taken from the Protestant Monitor of June 19, 1846.

These volunteers departed from Greenville June 19, 1846 for Alton. Before departing they were adressed in the court house by Rev. Mr. Stafford. The company was given a dinner at the home of John West, four miles west of Greenville and after the meal speeches were made by Mr. West, J. M. Davis and Judge M. G. Dale. The Protestant Monitor says: "The amateur musicians, Messrs Garland, Lane, and Humes, with martial music, and the Greenville band, in their spacious band carriage, drawn by four bays, kindly furnished by our enterprising citizen Mr. F. Berry, accompanied the volunteers to Alton."

The ladies of Greenville aided in equipping this company and the volunteers passed resolutions thanking the ladies for their generous assistance and kindly feeling. The company left Alton July 22 for New Orleans.

When the war was over and the veterans returned in 1848 from con-

COL. JOHN B. REID,
Who has had a prominent part in Greenville's Civil and Military life.

Group of old veterans taken on the occasion of the 15th annual reunion of the Bond County Soldiers' and Sailors'
   Association held at Greenville October 19 and 20, 1904.   Photo by McLeod.

quering the Montezumas on the plains of Mexico, they were given an ovation in a grove about a mile and a half southwest of Greenville.

William M. Hunter, who lives on his farm about four miles west of Greenville, was one of the veterans of the Mexican war. The others of the company named above have all passed away.

Greenville's Civil War History.

In the history of Greenville, there should be no chapter of more general interest than that which tells of the "brave boys in blue" who went out in '61 to '65 to fight for the perpetuity of the American Republic.

This history is familiar to the most of us, and that very fact proves its value. It is presumable that no enlightened parent, no true hearted American citizen will wish to have his sons and daughters grow up without becoming more or less familiar with the heroism of these gallant men.

It is impossible to enter into detail and give a complete history of

each soldier who enlisted from "Little Bond," but the writer has endeavored to give a brief sketch of each company and the officers of each.

This civil war in a land so peculiarly blessed, between a people so enlightened and refined, this fratricidal war, as we now review it, having seen its commencement, its continuance and its close, seems only a dream of the past; yet it was to many hundreds of thousands a fatal dream.

Bond county was in the front in furnishing her full quota of brave and patriotic soldiers to defend and uphold the flag and honor of our whole country. They went promptly at every call for volunteers, carrying with them the prayers of sympathizing friends and relatives, many of whom never returned, some returning with lost or shattered limbs or a diseased body as can be attested by a large pension roll in our county.

There is no official history of the men who went from Bond county except that furnished by the state, through the Adjutant General's office. The history of the civil war

soldiers who went from Greenville cannot be separated from those who went from the county and though this history in general is confined principally to Greenville, it will be impossible for me to make the distinction in this article as Greenville was the central point in the county, where soldiers from various parts of its confines came to enlist.

Companies D and E served in the 22nd. infantry. Company D was mustered in May 11, 1861 and the following served as officers: Captains, J. A. Hubbard, John H. Phillips; First Lieutenants, E. J. C. Alexander, Lemuel Adams, John H. Phillips, and E. J. File; Second Lieutenants, Lemuel Adams, Edward Stearns, J. H. Phillips, C. M. Galloway, E. F. File and Joel B. Paisley. Company E was organized June 17, 1861 and the following served as officers: Captains, Samuel G. McAdams, George Gibson; First Lieutenants, James M. Hamilton, George Gibson and J. M. McAdams; Second Lieutenants, George Gibson and J. M. McAdams. Capt. P. E. Holcomb was elected captain of Co. E in Greenville by the company but failed to qualify as a member of the

OFFICERS AND MEMBERS OF COLBY POST NO. 301, G. A. R.

First Row:—(Reading from left to right), John H Hawley, R. K. Dewey, J. T. Buchanan, Officer of the Day; Ransom Pope Junior Vice Commander; Miss Helen Reid, Daughter of the Post; J. H. Ladd, Commander; W. W. Lowis, Adjutant; H. H. Staub; Oliver Hockett, Chaplain.

Second Row:—W. A. McLain, George F. Harlan, J. L. Koonce, A. C. Jett, S. G. Enloe, Colonel J. B. Reid, Thomas J. Long, J. C. Sanderson, Wm. D. Matney.

Third Row:—Samuel Spratt, Frank Parent, G. B. Keesecker, Jacob Dowell, O. T. Lee, M. F. Book, C. I. Young, J. W. Anthony, Joseph L. Turner, George Sherer, F. B. Sells.

Fourth Row:—Joseph Armstrong, Joseph F. Watts, A. A. Thompson, Noah Vaughn, John W. Miles, H. C. Burton, Dr. David Wilkins, Surgeon; Philip Leidner, Archie Ewing.

Fifth Row:—J. M. Alexander, George W. Grigg, H. W. Wait, Nelson Adams, E. S. Valentine, T. R. Loggins, James Ewing, William Ingles, H. E. Sapp.

Sixth Row:—Wm. Green, Francis Kinney, Wm. M. Goad, Fred Dommert, L. T. Ellingsworth, B. F. Schweitzer, Rufus Cox, George Johnson, John A. Finney.

regiment at the muster in, having received an appointment in the regular army.

The 22nd. regiment was mustered into the United States service for three years June 25, 1861 and was mustered out July 7, 1864. The veterans were transferred to the 42d Ill. and were mustered out and discharged Jan. 12, 1866. The 22d. and 42nd. served their country well at Belmont, Charleston, New Madrid, Island No. 10, Farmington, siege of Corinth and Stone River. December 31, 1862 and January 1-2, 1863, the regiment was in the battle of Chickamauga. Here they lost 135 officers and men out of 300 engaged. In storming the heights of Mission Ridge, they lost 10 men out of their reduced ranks; were engaged at Resacca and lost 20 men killed and wounded. On June 10, they were ordered to Springfield, Ill., and were mustered out. The county may be proud of the record made by this grand regiment. The 22nd. Ill., was one of the regiments mentioned in "Fox's History of the Rebellion," that lost the greatest number of men during the three years of service.

July 7, 1861 a squad of 18 men of Co. E of the 1st. Ill. Cavalry were from Bond county. They were captured at Lexington, Mo., which was the principal engagement of the 1st Cavalry, after a siege of 52 hours of hard fighting; 2500 Union men under General Mulligan to 10,000 of the enemy. They were mustered out of the service July '62 and joined other commands. Among the contingent from Bond county were the Dennys, Gordons, Potters, Rankins, and Knights and others just as worthy and brave, who did their whole duty at Lexington, Mo.

August 20, 1861, Co. D., 3rd. Ill. Cavalry was organized in Greenville under command of Capt. Thomas

CHARLES W. WATSON,

A leading druggist from 1881 to 1902, member of Colby Post, and connected with many lodges and organizations in Greenville.

DR. J. B. CARY,

Born and raised in Bond County. Member of Colby Post. For many years a practicing physician in Bond County.

CHARLES TAYLOR, *Deceased*,

A member of Colby Post, G. A. R., who was on his death-bed when the picture of Colby Post was taken.

M. Davis and was assigned to the 3rd. Ill. Cavalry under Col. Eugene Carr of the regular army. All those who at different times served as officers of Co. D. were: Captains, Thomas M. Davis, and James K. McLain: First Lieutenants, J. K. McLain and Jonathan Keshner; Second Lieutenants, Moses Lytaker, Jonathan Keshner and Solomon M. Tabor. The regimental organization took place at Camp Butler in August, 1861 and after an eventful career of fighting, raiding and scouting, were mustered out of service October 18, 1865, having borne an honorable part in the battles of Pea Ridge to Vicksburg and from Vicksburg to Memphis, Tenn., where they took part in driving Forrest from that city the night of August 21, and did many other good things not to be mentioned in history; but with all that was accomplished by this grand organization, by both officers and men, it may be said in all candor that as a patriotic body of men, soldiers and citizens, they deserve well of the state and nation. We met them at Port Gibson, Champion Hills, Black River Bridge and Jackson, Miss. Co. D was always ready when the bugle sounded "Boots and Saddles."

Company C was mustered in August 31, 1861 and assigned to the 26th. Ill. Infantry at Camp Butler, Ill. The various officers of the company were Captains, G. M. Keener, James A. Dugger, Owen W. Walls, and Isaac N. Enloe: First Lieutenants, T. L. Vest, J. A. Dugger, O. W. Walls, James Means, and John McAlister: Second Lieutenants, J. A.

Dugger and E. B. Wise. The 26th. regiment, of which Company C was a part, went from Hannibal, Mo., to New Madrid, Mo., March 3, and were engaged at Farmington, where they lost 5 killed, 30 wounded. From Missouri to Tennessee and Mississippi they went and were in the siege of Jackson, Miss., which was disastrous to Co. C. They lost Capt. Dugger, killed, and also a number of men were killed and wounded at the same time. The regiment of which Co. C was a part marched 6,931 miles, fought 28 battles, among them New Madrid, Farmington, Island No. 10, Corinth, Holly Springs, Iuka, Jackson, Miss., Vicksburg, Mission Ridge, Resacca, Kenesaw and many others. Their service was hard and honorable.

On August 28, 1861, part of Co. I, 45 men, were recruited in Bond county and were mustered into the 30th. Ill. Volunteers, by Col. Phillip B. Fouke. Wm. C. Kershner, of Bond county was commissioned Captain, November 29, 1861. They were in the battle of Belmont, Mo., at the taking of Fort Henry and at the siege of Fort Donnellson, February 13, 14, 15, 1862; were with Grant on the Vicksburg campaign, were engaged at Raymond, Jackson, Champion Hills and Black River Bridge, arriving at Vicksburg, May 19, 1863; moved to Jackson, July 25, marched with Sherman through the Carolinas to Richmond, Va., and took part in the grand review at Washington. They were discharged at Camp Butler July 27, 1865. The men from Bond county in the 30th. did their whole duty and under

Bond county officers, Capt. Kershner and Lieutenants Taylor and Fouke made an honorable record.

July 3, 1861 a squad of 25 men was recruited and assigned to the 35th. Ill. under Capain Han, of Vandalia. The 35th. was mustered out of the service September 27, 1864, after serving their country well for three years and three months. The total distance marched by this regiment was 3,056 miles, and they saw hard service in their country's defense from secession and ruin. Some of the boys from Bond county in the 35th. Ill. were A. A. Thompson, J. M. Brown, G. W. Woodling, and many others.

In 1862, April 3, I find a squad of 14 men went from Bond county and were assigned to the 65th. Ill. Infantry, under Col. Cameron, of Chicago and were mustered out July 26, 1865. The 65th. was known as the "Scotch" regiment under Daniel Cameron, Jr., and did grand service for the country. The squad from Bond county had such men as Comrade J. T. Buchanan, our Past Post Commander, the Sprague brothers, Tate, Frampton, Prouty, Sanders, Tom K. White and others just as true and brave, who did their whole duty and honored the county from which they went. They were in battle at Knoxville, Lost Mountain, Rough and Ready Station, Jonesboro, Columbia, Franklin, Nashville, and Smithtown Creek, and the part taken by the Bond county boys is an honor to our state and county.

Company E was organized August 12, 1862. The men were from Millersburg, Beaver Creek, Pocahontas, and Old Ripley. The different officers of Co. E, were Captains, U. B. Harris and W. C. Harned; First Lieutenants, Wm. Harlan, W. C. Harned, and C. W. Johnson; Second Lieutenants, W. C. Harned and C. W. Johnson.

Company F was organized in Greenville, August 7, 1862 by John B. Reid and was assigned to the 130th. Ill., then being recruited in camp at Belleville, by Col. Nathaniel Niles of that city. The various officers of Co. F were Captains, John B. Reid, W. M. Colby, John D. Donnell and F. W. Phillips; First Lieutenants, W. M. Colby, J. D. Donnell, Charles Ives and F. D. Phillips; Second Lieutenants, Chas. Ives, F. D. Phillips, and John Murdock; Rev. W. D. H. Johnson of Greenville was Chaplain of the 130th, and Dr. David Wilkins was one of the surgeons.

Both companies E and F were assigned to the 130th. Ill., under Col. Niles. The regiment was mustered into the United States service October 25, 1862 and left Camp Butler, Nov. 11 for Memphis, Tenn., where they remained on duty the winter of '62-'63, doing provost and garrison duty at Memphis and Fort Pickering. The regiment left Memphis for Milliken's Bend and was assigned to the 13th. Army Corps, commanded by Gen. J. A. McClernand, and, with a grand army under Grant, swept on to Vicksburg, met the enemy at Port Gibson, Champion Hills, Raymond, Baker's Creek, Black River Bridge and invested the city on May 18, 1863 and during the siege and until the surrender, July 4, was on the firing line or in the trenches. On July 5, the regiment marched to Jackson, Miss., and was at its surrender after a ten day's siege and vigorous defense. The Confederates burned and sacked the town before they left. The regiment returned to Vicksburg and from there was transferred to the Department of the Gulf and shipped from New Orleans to Texas, where they spent the winter of '63-'64 on the Rio Grande, returning to Louisiana in '64 and entering on the Red River expedition, which resulted disastrously for the regiment. In '65 they were at Spanish Fort and Blakeley and the capture of Mobile. They returned to Illinois August 29th, 1869, and were mustered out and paid at Camp Butler August 31, having served their country well. For faithful service a number of the officers were promoted, among them Lieutenant Col. Reid to Colonel, Captain Wilkins to Major, and Adjutant Dewey to Captain. They were engaged at Port Gibson, Champion Hills, Raymond, Black River Bridge, capture of Vicksburg and Jackson, Miss., Mansfield, La., Cane River, Atchafalaya, Spanish Fort and Blakeley, Ala., and at the surrender of Mobile. The companies from Bond in the 130th. did their whole duty to their country and their flag. Modesty will not permit me to say more, as I was identified with it from August '62 to August '65.

June 6, 1864 Co. F of the 135th. Ill. was recruited in Bond county for three months service and was under Capt. S. G. McAdams, formerly of the 22d. Ill. The other officers were James A. Hubbard, first lieutenant; Edward Stearns, second lieutenant and C. W. Holden, adjutant. The command of which Co. F was a part was on out-post duty in Missouri on the Iron Mountain railroad and other parts of Missouri and was mustered out of the service at Camp Butler, September 28, 1864. Of the service performed by these 100 day troops, Governor Yates, in his last message paid a high compliment to the men of the 135th., and all others who responded to his call for men to garrison the posts and forts and relieve the veterans for field service.

February 14, 1865 a squad of ten Bond county men was recruited for Co. F, 150th. regiment, for one year and was discharged Jan. 16, 1866, at Atlanta, Ga., and arrived at Springfield, Ill., having served 11 months in the state of Georgia, on guard duty most of the time. Their service was disastrous to both officers and men. I find the names of Cole, Keshner, Lytle, Pierson, Norman, Barcroft and Howard among the Bond county boys.

February 25, 1865, Co. D was organized in Bond county by Captain Henry A. White and was assigned to the 154th regiment. Wm. H. Ellis was 1st Lieutenant and John E. Sawrey, 2nd Lieutenant. This was a one year regiment and served in Tennessee most of the winter and summer and suffered a great deal by sickness and was mustered out at Nashville, Tenn., September 18, 1865. A majority of the men was recruited from Bond county.

I find a squad from Bond county, Co. K, in the 54th. of which our late comrade George P. Stahl was a lieutenant and the President of the Monument Association, Dr. W. D. Matney, was also a member of the 54th., as were also Humphrey Jett, S. P. Laws and L. J Myers.

I also find in the 29th. Colored, Co. H, three brothers, George, Archie and James Ewing, who were recruited at McCord, now Reno, January 28, 1864, and were mustered out November 6, 1865, who like their brothers in the south, knew the issue was the freedom of their race.

During the summer and fall of 1863 General Thomas visited General Grant at Vicksburg and recommended the organization of a colored regiment with white men to be detailed as officers. Dr. D. Wilkins of the 130th. was made surgeon of the 50th. Colored Infantry. James M. Miller, hospital steward of the 130th., became first lieutenant and Edward Bigelow, Fred Jones and W. P. Wattles of Co. F 130th. became first and second lieutenants of the 50th. Colored.

Greenville had the distinction of furnishing the first brass band for the state. The offer was made by the Greenville Mechanics band in May 1861, and was promptly accepted by Governor Yates. Among the musicians in this band were Wyatt Causey, Cary Darlington and Thomas R. Phillips. The band was assigned to the 20th. Infantry. A band from Jamestown went with the 26th. Ill. Volunteers.

Bond county was required to furnish 1,161 men during President Lincoln's calls from '61 to '65 inclusive, and according to the Adjutant General's report, December 31, 1865, the county had furnished 1,148, leaving a deficit of 13 men. But this is more than made up by men in this county credited to other counties: to-wit, Co. I, of Montgomery, 18 men, all credited to that county. Others from Bond were credited to Clinton and Madison, when to Bond really belonged the honor.

The history of the men who went from Bond county is not as complete, as I would like to have it, for the names of many good men and true, whose names I cannot find are of necessity omitted, a fact that I greatly regret.

The people of Bond county have honored themselves by erecting a monument of granite that will be as enduring as the everlasting hills, in memory of the men who never returned to home and friends.

The Hilliard Rifles.

A company of state militia was organized in Greenville, December 30, 1878 and for want of a better name called themselves the "Greenville Blues," until it was later voted to name the company the Hilliard Rifles, in honor of Adjutant General Hilliard. Major P. E. Holcomb was captain, S. M. Inglis, first lieutenant and Dr. C. H. Beatty, second lieutenant.

The company later became Company F. It had headquarters in Armory Hall, the present opera house. The company was called out at the time of the East St. Louis railroad strike.

The company was disbanded July 6, 1896 by Captain John F. Harris, upon orders of the Adjutant General. At the time the company was disbanded J. F. Harris was captain, F. T. Denny was first lieutenant and

Will J. Bruner was second lieutenant.

Spanish American War.

When war with Spain commenced in 1898, E. Trautman organized a company of volunteers but there was no call for them and hence they did not go to the front. Greenville, however, had many representatives in the thick of the fray.

Lyman Fuller, a grandson of Seth Fuller, Greenville's early surveyor, and a son of Lyman Fuller, a Civil War veteran, was with Admiral Dewey, on his flagship at the battle of Manila on the memorable first of May, 1898. Lyman Fuller was a gunner and was at his post during the fight, when the Spanish squadron was sunk and the city of Manila was captured.

Arthur Rogier was a seaman on the "Iowa" and participated in the naval engagements around Santiago.

John Heston, grandson of a Mexican War veteran of the same name, was in the navy and was an eye witness of the Maine disaster in the harbor at Havana, Cuba.

Harry Williams, now of California, was on board the "Yale" during the war with Spain and saw some service.

Among the boys in the land forces were Lieutenants L. E. Bennett and A. O. Seaman, now U. S. A. officers, Sergeant Major W. H. Boughman, Harry and Berl Murdock, Charles Dixon, Orlay Larrabee, Will Foster, Will Bruner, Charles Rowdybush, Charles Stearns, Edward A. Stearns, George N. Koonce, Charles Kingsbury and many others.

The four last named died of disease while in the service.

COUNTY BUILDINGS.

GREENVILLE has had four court houses, all located within the present public square. For a year or two after Greenville became the county seat there was no court house and court was held in the dwellings in the west end of town, and there, also, the county officers were located.

In 1821 when the sale of lots was held, the present public square was covered with a dense growth of sycamore trees. At a court held the September of that year, it was duly ordered that a court house for Bond county be let to the lowest bidder and on September 19, when the bids were opened, Robert G. White's bid of $2,135 was found to be the lowest, and he at once entered into bond for the fulfillment of the contract, and was paid in notes of purchasers of the thirty town lots. These lots sold at an average of $44.60 each.

The court house was made of a poor quality of brick and was badly damaged by storms before it was completed. The building stood on a natural mound where the present one now stands and was practically completed in 1823. The eight by ten window panes proved too great a temptation for the small boy of that time, and hidden from view behind tree or bush, he would watch with delight the accuracy of his aim as the stones from his sling shot crashed through the glass and sent it flying in every direction. There was little respect for the temple of justice and its custodians were sorely beset for means for its preservation. In a few years this brick court house was so shaky that

it was necessary to build a new one.

The same foundation was used for the second court house, which was a frame building. The brick from the old building was used for flooring. Eben Twiss was given the contract of putting up the frame building, on October 9, 1832. It was completed in September 1833 and was used as a court house for twenty years. J. T. Fouke, who came here in 1830, says this frame court house had a large chimney and fireplace on the north side and a brick floor, except on the south, where there was a plank floor, surrounding the judge's seat. On the second floor were four rooms with low ceilings. The circuit clerk and the county clerk had the two rooms in the north part and on the south were two jury rooms.

This frame court house was too small for the county's needs and was so badly out of repair that on April 14, 1853 the contract for a new one was let. The frame building was sold by the county at public auction July 20, 1853, and was purchased by E. B. White for $193. Mr. White moved it to the lot east of Williams' blacksmith shop, where it was still used by the county until the new court house was completed. Afterwards it was used as the home of the Greenville Journal, a store, a carpenter shop, livery stable and marble shop. It was the first investment in Greenville real estate made by J. M. Miller, now one of the city's largest property owners. The cyclone of 1880 unroofed it and it was later torn down.

Daniel W. Norris, of Carlyle, was the contractor who built the third

court house and James Bradford, Rufus Dressor and M. G. Dale were the county commissioners, who let the contract. The building was of brick on a sandstone foundation, 40 by 60 feet, two stories high. The contract price was $9750 but subsequent improvements ran the amount up to $12,000. It was turned over to the county commissioners as completed September 1, 1854. In 1869 a new roof was put on the building and a large, shapely dome took the place of a little hen coop observatory on the building. In 1880 the offices on the ground floor were remodeled and vaults for the county records were made. The hallway running east and west through the building was closed up and the space thus gained was utilized for the vaults.

This building was becoming too small for the county's needs when it was destroyed by fire on Saturday, March 24, 1883. A defective flue probably caused the fire, which started in the southwest corner of the attic about 9:15 a. m., and was first discovered by Ernest Bigard, who was in an upper room on the south side of the square. He gave the alarm and soon the entire populace was out trying to cope with the flames. The fire had burned some time before it was discovered. There were no water works and a bucket brigade with State's Attorney W. A. Northcott, County Treasurer A. J. Utiger and Robert Donnell in the attic pouring on water, fought the flames, but the dense smoke strangled them and the fight had to be abandoned. All the records were saved by the systematic management of Circuit Clerk T. P. Morey within fifteen minutes and then the crowd watched the court house burn. All day long it burned, but the walls remained standing. The loss was covered by $8,000 insurance, of which $6,981.80 was paid by the insurance company. The county officers had their offices scattered around in various places until the new court house was completed.

Soon after the burning of the court house some of the people of Smithboro started an agitation to move the county seat to that place, but it did not materialize. The matter went so far, however, that petitions were drawn up, and a paper, advocating the change, was started at Smithboro. One hundred eighty-four of the signers of the petition, however, withdrew their names by power of attorney to C. D. Hoiles and the court decided the petition was insufficient to warrant the ordering of an election on the question.

At the election on November 6, 1883, the proposition to appropriate $20,000 for the building of a new court house carried by a vote of

Laying of the cornerstone of the present court house by A. F. and A. M., June 4, 1884.   Photograph
Loaned by J. H. Hawley.

1365 to 768. The county commissioners on January 5, 1884, accepted the plans of W. R. Parsons and son, of Quincy, Ill., for the present court house, 91 by 82 feet. From the ground to the cornice the distance is 42 feet and from the ground to the flag staff the distance is 89 feet. The contract for building this temple of justice was on March 20, 1884, awarded to M. T. Lewman, of Greencastle, Ind., for $20,000. The corner stone was laid on June 4, 1884 by Greenville Lodge No. 245 A. F. and A. M.

John Buchanan, father of J. T. Buchanan, helped build two court houses and two jails in Greenville.

Jail Buildings.

At least three jails had been built in Greenville before the one now in use. The first jail was built by Andrew Moody and Thomas Stout near the location of the old Sargeant House on College Avenue. It was built of square logs at a cost of $244.50, in state paper, and the contract was dated July 4, 1829.

The second jail was built by Richard Tatom on the southeast corner of the public square for $321.74 in 1835.

The third jail was a brick building and was built in 1859 on Third street and is still standing and used for a tenement house. It was built at a cost of $5000 and R. H. Phillips & Co., of St. Louis, was the contractor.

The present jail is an up-to-date and commodious structure in the

northwest part of town and was occupied for the first time June 16, 1897, by Jailer J. E. Wright and family and five prisoners. It required two elections to secure this jail. The first time the proposition was voted on it was defeated by a vote of 1087 to 659. This was in

November 1894. In November 1896 the proposition to issue $5000 jail bonds carried by a vote of 895 to 767. The bonds were taken by Hoiles and Sons. The jail is located on the brow of Mill Hill on a two acre tract purchased by the county of E. M. Gullick for $290.

The present Bond county court house, built in 1884. In front are the present county officers and members of the Board of Review.

✒ The Greenville Shoools ✒

the place made vacant by Mr. Clark, whose wife, Mrs. Phoebe F. Clark, took charge until the vacancy could

THE first school in this city and county was probably taught in the old brick house that stood for many years in the west end of town. This was probably in 1819, the school being taught by Thomas White.

At this time the school was necessarily small, but as years passed, and the town grew the interest in education increased and, although school was taught in several log cabins at different places about the town, the school trustees finally combined interest with the members of the Congregational church and erected the building on West Main Ave., that stood for more than sixty years, and was recently dismantled to make room for the new Carnegie Library. The upper portion of the Congregational church was used for a house of worship and the basement was used for a school house and was, for a time, called the Greenville Academy. Considerable difficulty was experienced in raising the necessary amount of money to carry out this project and it was only after Captain A. L. Saunders had been dispatched to Boston, on foot, to raise funds that it was a success. For a time the school flourished under the management of Socrates Smith, John Marston and others.

When the common school law was passed by the legislature the trustees concluded to take the advantages it offered, so they deeded their part of the building to the church, but the academy proper was used as a school room for many years after, and was used as a primary room until the present new school building was erected in 1894.

The oldest schedule in possession of Mr. C. F. Thraner, school treasurer, of this district, who a few years ago classified all his records and filed them away in proper shape, is signed by William Cunningham as principal and is dated in 1855. Mr. Cunningham taught for seven years at a salary of $50 a month. H. B. Taylor followed him as principal, and was employed for two years, the last year receiving a salary of $60 a month. He was a Methodist minister and divided his time between teaching and preaching. While gathering apples he met with an accident and was forced to give up his duties and return to New England.

Charles Clark, for many years a resident of Greenville, next took the school, but resigned after three months and opened a book store. The school board had some difficulty in securing a suitable person to take

OLD PUBLIC SCHOOL BUILDING.

OLD HIGH SCHOOL BUILDING,
Built in 1859, dismantled in 1894.

OLD PUBLIC SCHOOL BUILDING.

be filled. Rev. Thomas W. Hynes, who recently died here and who was so well known to all, was induced to take the position. Mr. Hynes had been professor of mathematics at Hanover, Ind., and was well qualified for the place. He taught but a few months, however, and in order that he might preach the Gospel, resigned in favor of R. L. Mudd. Mr. Mudd taught for a year at a salary of $75 a month and resigned to accept the office of county clerk.

The next principal was an inovation in the matter of sex. Miss Florence Holden accepting the principalship at a salary of $40 a month. Miss Holden finished the school year and then accepted a position in St. Mary's Institute in St. Louis where she remained for eight years, becoming the principal of the institution. Miss Holden married a gentleman named Houghton, who was connected with the Alton schools. Mr. Houghton died soon after and Mrs. Houghton, in connection with James P. Slade, purchased Almira College. Marrying a Mr. Addis she sold her interest in Almira College to Mr. Slade and moved to Emporia, Kansas, where she died.

James A. Dean was the next principal at a salary of $80 a month. He was succeeded by Prof. S. M. Inglis, who held the principalship for fifteen years, and to his untiring zeal and ability as a teacher is due, in a large measure, the high standard which the school has attained and which has given it a reputation for excellence all over Illinois. Mr. Inglis introduced the graded sys-

tem and added the high school. During his term of service he organized the Alpha Society, members of the high school, and, in about 1873, the Alumni. Mr. Inglis received $133 a month. He resigned to accept the chair of mathematics at Carbondale, which position he held until elected state superintendent of public instruction.

A. K. Carmichael came next and was followed by J. B. Burns, who added Latin to the course. He cultivated a taste for horticulture among the pupils and as a result the school grounds were beautified with flowers and growing trees. D. W. Lindsay, a graduate of Carbondale, was next employed upon the recommendation of Prof. Inglis. Prof. Lindsay made a special feature of music, and remained in Greenville for six years going from here to California. He received a salary of $100 a month while here.

Prof. J. T. Ellis of Carbondale was next employed. He introduced several new features, increasing the high school course to four years. He received $125 a month.

M. G. Clark succeeded Prof. Ellis, who resigned to accept the chair of history in the Southern Illinois Normal at Carbondale. Prof. Clark, who was formerly principal of the business department at the college was principal for two years and was succee'ed by Prof. W. Duff Piercy, fresh from McKendree College at Lebanon. Prof. Piercy remained for two years and went to Harvard to take a special course in English and was succeeded by Prof. E. B.

PROF. SAMUEL M. INGLIS,

Who came to Greenville in 1868 and took charge of the Greenville schools, remaining for 15 years, and graded the schools; State Superintendent of Public Instruction in 1894, serving until his death in June 1898.

Brooks, who after two years was succeeded by Prof. C. N. Peak.

In 1859 the brick school building was built on the site of the present school building and its erection was quite a local event. Many at that time opposed the erection of that building as a wasteful expenditure. The present modern school building

THE GREENVILLE PUBLIC SCHOOL BUILDING, Built in 1894.

was erected in 1894. The building was proposed by the Board of Education that was elected in the spring of 1893. The proposition was submitted to a vote of the legal voters of the district with the result that the proposition to issue the necessary bonds carried by thirty majority. The members of the Board of Education at that time were Col. J. B. Reid, president; W. E. Robinson, C. E. Cook, T. P. Morey, J. Seaman, E. B. Wise and Dr. W. T. Easley. In the following spring Col Reid and T. P. Morey retired and Dr. E. P. Poindexter was elected president and H. B. Henninger a member instead of T. P. Morey.

The initiatory steps to secure the new building were taken by the circulation of a petition by Ward Reid and R. C. Morris, asking for a special election. The election was

PROF. C. N. PEAK,
Superintendent of the Greenville public schools, 1905, succeeding E. B. Brooks, who resigned.

held on February 23, 1894. The vote stood 315 for and 285 against. The building cost $19,600, the bonds being taken by Hoiles and Sons at their face value. The contract was awarded to W. B. Bradsby and Chas. Stewart, of Greenville. The corner stone was laid by the Masonic fraternity Friday, August 10, 1894. The building was ready for occupancy about the first of the year 1895.

For the school year 1905-6 the following teachers were employed: Superintendent, C. N. Peak; Principal, Miss Mame Graff; Assistant Principal, J. C. Hemphill; Latin, Miss Louise McCord; Grade teachers, Misses Emma Streuber, Pearl Sanderson, Lillie Apple, Mary Lewis, Mrs. Ida Travis, Misses Neva Young, Mary Mulford, Anna Leppard, Anna Mulford and Esther Chapman.

FACULTY OF THE GREENVILLE PUBLIC SCHOOLS. 1904-5.

Reading from left to right, top row—Miss Pearl Sanderson, J. C. Hemphill, Miss Mary Lewis, Miss Esther Chapman, Prof. E. B. Brooks, Miss Mame Graff, Miss Louise McCord.
Second Row—Miss Lillie Apple, Miss Neva Young, Miss Mary Mulford, Miss Emma Streuber, Miss Anna Mulford, Miss Anna Leppard, Mrs. Ida Travis.

PROF. JOHN B. WHITE, *Deceased*,
President of Almira College 23 years
and one of its largest supporters.

ALMIRA BLANCHARD MORSE, *Dec'd*.
Who gave $6,000 to Almira College
and for whom it was named.

STEPHEN MORSE, *Deceased*,
A successful merchant and large benefactor of Greenville College.

Almira College

THE conception of the work of
building up this institution for
the higher education of women had
its origin in the minds of two young
New Hampshire lads, Stephen Morse

and John B. White, between whom
a strong and life-long friendship
began while preparing for college
at New Hampton, N. H.

They were each the eldest son of
a large family with sisters whose
educational advantages were in
their day very limited. It must be

remembered that while colleges and
universities opened their doors un-
wittingly to young men, they were
closed against young women. Girls
must be content with an education
which only prepared their brothers
for college. This injustice these
young men keenly felt and deter-

GREENVILLE COLLEGE,
Built as Almira College in 1855, now owned by the Central Illinois conference of the Free Methodist Church.

mined to accomplish something toward elevating the educational standard for women.

They entered Brown University in the fall of 1828, where they were room-mates and class-mates for four years, graduating in 1832 under Dr. Francis Wayland. Both at that time began to pursue a course of law, and in 1836 Mr. White came west, and practiced law, first in Alton, Ill., and later in Greenville, where he became probate judge. In 1838 he married Miss Mary P. Merriam and went south, having accepted the presidency of a flourish-

cessful teacher, but in 1840 came west to Greenville and turned his attention to mercantile pursuits, under the conviction that in this way he could do more for the cause of education and make himself more permanently useful. As a business man he was very successful. The mercantile firm known as Morse and Brothers was for many years the leading firm of Bond County and at one time was estimated to be worth $100,000.

Mr. Morse was a man of high intellectual ability and of rare repose and courtesy of manner. He was

the work and Greenville, on the high table land, between the Wabash and Mississippi rivers, was selected as the location, because its elevation and natural drainage afforded healthy surroundings and lovely landscape views.

Mrs. White died in the spring of 1855, and Prof. White came in the summer of that year with his children, four daughters and two sons, and entered upon the work, it being understood that Mr. Morse was to be relied upon for the financial arrangements and Prof. White for the development of the character of

REV. W. T. HOGUE,
First President of Greenville College, 1892 to 1904. Now General Superintendent of the Free Methodist church.

MRS. W. T. HOGUE,
For several years prominently connected with Greenville College, as a teacher.

ing college for young men at Wake Forest, N. C., which had been tendered him, and remained at the head of that institution for fifteen years. He became a Christian in early life and united with the Baptist church, and while at Wake Forest consecrated himself to the gospel ministry, not with the intention of taking charge of churches, but to better equip himself to the wants, intellectual and spiritual, of the young men and women under his influence.

Mr. Morse, raised by an unusually intelligent Christian mother, was from childhood very conscientious and grew up with an earnest desire to be useful. He was a good scholar and for some years a suc-

married in 1843 to Miss Almira Blanchard, a Christian lady of thorough and accomplished education, who was fully in sympathy with her husband in all efforts for good.

In 1854, at the request of his old class-mate, Prof. White visited Greenville. Enthusiasm for their long cherished scheme was re-kindled and the initiatory steps taken to establish a school for young women. The citizens of Greenville entered heartily into the project and gave liberally toward it, but Mrs. Almira Morse, who had that year come into a legacy of $6,000, from an uncle's estate, gladly donated it all, as a free-will offering to the new project so dear to her heart. This gift made it possible to start

the school. He devoted four years almost exclusively to travel in order to awaken an interest in the institution and secure pupils and funds for its up-building.

It is difficult to go back a half century and give a clear idea of what Southern Illinois was, as an educational field, at that time. To raise the necessary funds for a building in those days was no easy matter. The country was sparsely settled, few of the people were wealthy, farm lands, now valued at $50 or $60 per acre, were then worth $10 or $15. But there was need of the work, for a field more destitute in advantages for higher education than this section could not be found elsewhere in the state.

Rev. A. L. Whitcomb,
President of Greenville College.

Prof. E. G. Burritt,
Vice President of Greenville College.

But these early promoters worked with determination, the citizens of Greenville and friends in the east generously responding with financial aid and the school was founded in 1855 and chartered in 1857, under the name of Almira College, in honor of her whose large donation at the beginning of the work made the institution possible, Mrs. Almira Blanchard Morse.

In this year Miss Elizabeth R. Wright, a native of Vermont, but for twelve years a teacher in Springfield, Ill., came to Greenville as the second wife of Prof. White. She quietly and wisely assumed the care of his family and enthusiastically entered into and made it her especial work to create an atmosphere of home for the girls, who leaving their own homes, came year after year to obtain an education. On account of the motherly interest which she took in each one, and especially in those with limited financial resources, who were obtaining an education by their own efforts, she holds today an exalted place to which few could attain, in the hearts of hundreds of women scattered over many states.

When she had made the new building comfortable within, she turned her attention to the campus, which was literally a brick and lumber yard, without even trees, for every brick (and there were more than 1,000,000 used in the walls and partitions) was made on the ground. Elms, maples and evergreen trees, choice shrubs, vines and flowers Prof. and Mrs. White planted with their own hands and in a few years the place was transformed into a garden of beauty. Her enthusiastic love for flowers and her great success in their cultivation

strongly inspired, in the girls, a love for horticulture.

Ten years elapsed before the building was completed, during which time it was crowded to its utmost capacity to accommodate those who applied for entrance, and during the twenty-three years Prof. White was closely identified with the school, there was always a good attendance and the interest and patronage was always very flattering to his administration, especially as a depression was felt in all enterprises consequent upon the Civil War.

The corps of teachers was selected with care, usually being brought from the east because of the superior advantages there for education, culture and refinement. The course of study was made as extended as possible under existing conditions. There were few high schools outside of the large cities and the district schools were a lower grade than those of the towns, consequently the majority of the pupils were obliged to spend two years in the preparatory department before entering upon the college course, which required four years longer,

and yet the records show, out of an attendance of 2,000 students, an average of 4.2 graduated for each year, although there were none the first two years.

Rev. F. H. Ashcraft,
Financial Agent of Greenville College.

WM. E. MILLIKEN,
Of the Class of 1905, Greenville College.

EZRA WHITTEN,
Of the Class of 1905, Greenville College.

H. K. McGEARY,
Now Secretary to Congressman Martin, Deadwood, S. D.

The college also made its impress on the social life of the town. This was made possible by the custom of monthly receptions at which time the parlors and halls were thronged with old and young, promenading and music being favorite amusements.

Rules and penalties were, of course, necessary to secure the best results where so many types of character composed the family. Some girls lacking promptness in heeding the rising and breakfast bells, were required to commit lines of "Paradise Lost" to memory, while others became far more familiar with verses of Scripture than they otherwise would have been, save for some remissness in duty.

Prof. White won, in a remarkable degree, the confidence, esteem and love of his pupils. He was thorough and clear in his manner of instruction, original, kind but firm in discipline, and invariably made his pupils his friends for life. He was away for two years while serving in the army as chaplain of the 117th. Illinois Infantry, during which time Rev. D. P. French had charge of the school.

Heavy reverses of fortune came to Mr. Morse in 1870, and he moved with his family to Paola, Kansas. Although the attendance continued to be large and the school flourishing, yet the debt which they had carried since the building was completed still embarassed them. Prof. White was no longer a young man, and broken in health as a result of army life, withdrew from active management, and the property was sold to Prof. James P. Slade and Mrs. Flor-

ence K. Houghton, who conducted it until 1892, when it passed into the hands of the Free Methodist Conference.

Greenville College

BY PRESIDENT A. L. WHITCOMB.

THE Institution known and legally incorporated as Greenville College is located at Greenville, the county seat of Bond Co., Ill. The city is on the St. Louis and Terre Haute Railroad line, fifty miles east of St. Louis, Mo., twenty miles west of Vandalia, Ill., and in close proximity to other important railroad centers, thus making it easy of access from nearly all parts of the Union. Greenville is an attractive city of 3000 inhabitants, situated on the highest table lands between the Wabash and Mississippi Rivers, and is the center of a thriving agricultural district.

The College is situated in the eastern part of the city and commands a fine view of the surrounding country. The grounds comprise several acres, consisting of a beautiful shaded campus in front of the building, and lands in the rear for domestic purposes. The main building is a fine brick structure erected especially for educational purposes. Its entire length is 144 feet, and it has an average width of 44 feet. It is a four-story building and contains seventy-two rooms. Within this building are the recitation rooms, chapel, reading room, and library of 6000 volumes, business rooms,

physical and chemical laboratories, music and art rooms, and also a fully developed boarding department; a veritable beehive of industry during the school season.

The College was established in 1855 as a school for young ladies only and in 1857 was legally incorporated as Almira College, by which name it was known until its transfer to the present owners. In 1892 the property was purchased for $12,200 by the Central Illinois Conference of the Free Methodist church with a view to establishing a college for the higher education of both young men and young women, "which should be conducted on strictly christian principles."

Greenville College is held in trust by a Board of fifteen trustees and its affairs are directed by an executive committee consisting of five members. The members of the original board of trustees were as follows: Rev. R. W. Sanderson, Rev. F. H. Ashcraft, Rev. T. H. Marsh, Rev. W. B. M. Colt, Isaac Kesler, Rev. C. A. Fleming, Milton Rowdybush, James H. Moss, Wm. Neece, W. T. Branson, J. M. Gilmore, W. S. Dann, Francis Schneeberger, Shell D. Young, J. D. Springer, Rev. W. T. Hogue, Ex Officio.

On the purchase of this property in 1892, the Rev. W. T. Hogue of Buffalo, New York, a prominent clergyman in the Genesee Conference of the Free Methodist church, was elected President of Greenville College. On the nomination of President Hogue, the following persons were elected and constituted the faculty for the year 1892-3, the first year in the history of the in-

WM. E. WHITE,

Now Superintendent of Coal City, Ill., Schools.

R. W. UPTON,

Graduate of Greenville College, Superintendent of Stronghurst, Ill., schools.

stitution: A. H. Stillwell, Prof. of Latin and Philosophy; E. G. Burritt, Prof. of Greek; Melvin G. Clark, Prof. of Business Science and Mathematics; Charles W. Hogg, Assistant in Greek and Latin; Miss Helen O. Shay, Preceptress and Instructor in English; Miss Emma Adine Phillips, Mathematics and Natural Science; Miss Jessie Augusta Duff, Director of Music; Miss Catherine H. Duff, Assistant in Instrumental Music; Miss Anna Brodhead, Instructor in Art; Mrs. Emma Luella Hogue, Principal of Primary School; Mrs. Marcia A. Jones, Governess; Mrs. Henrietta B. Maxson, Matron.

School opened in September 1892 with about 80 students, the attendance increasing to 163 for all departments for the school year. Greenville College has had a healthy and possibly slow but steady growth from its origin to the present time. About 200 students have graduated from all departments since 1893.

The prosperity of the school is due not only to its careful management by President Hogue and his assistants, but also to the generous bequests of the friends of the institution. In addition to the splendid gift of $6000 made by Mr. J. T. Grice, of Abingdon, Ill., a gift that made the purchase of the property a possibility, other friends have remembered the school and its needs. Mrs. Ellen Roland, of Cowden, Ill., in August 1896, deeded a farm to the institution, valued at $4000. The late W. S. Dann, of Greenville, gave $1000 toward the purchase of the building and later donated a vocalion organ for which he paid

$765. Mr. James Moss, of Greenville, has also contributed upwards of $2000 and Mr. John A. Augsbury, of Watertown, N. Y., has donated $7000 in all to the College, to assist needy students and enlarge the library. Other friends just as loyal though not as able financially, have given to the institution their thought, their prayers and their gifts.

In 1903 the General Conference of the Free Methodist church elected President Hogue to the office of General Superintendent in said church and hence in Feb. 1904 President Hogue tendered his resig-

nation and Rev. A. L. Whitcomb was elected to fill the vacancy.

The following persons were chosen by the Board of Trustees as members of the College Faculty for 1905-6: Rev. Augustin L. Whitcomb, M. S., President, Ethics; Eldon Grant Burritt, A. M., Vice-President, Philosophy and Greek; Archibald Edmund Layman, A. M., Dean, Latin Language and Literature; Rev. John La Due, A. M., Hebrew and Theology; Luella Helen Eakins, A. M., Greek, English and Pedagogy; Charles August Stoll, Ph. B., Preceptor, German and History; Alfred Clay Millican, A. B., Economics and Mathematics; Emma Baldwin Stoll, Ph. B., Preceptress, French; Clara Wilmot Uglow, Science and Mathematics; Zilpha Mae Barnes, Ph. B., Academic English; William Edward Milliken, B. C. S., Ph. B., Principal of Commercial School, Shorthand and Penmanship; Rumsey Osmen Young, B. C. S., Commercial Branches; Emily Grace Kay, Director of Music, Piano, Organ and Harmony; Alice Leta Hull, Voice Culture; Tutor, Ernest Lesley Bost.

At the June 1904 meeting of the Board of Trustees the Rev. F. H. Ashcraft was appointed financial agent with a view to raising funds for the erection of a new Administration Building for the College, and also a heating plant to heat both the old and the new buildings. On Sabbath, Jan. 29th, 1905, Rev. Ashcraft presented the needs of the school to an audience in the Free Methodist church at Greenville and in response to the appeal made, $8000 was soon pledged by the faculty and students of the College and by members of the Free Methodist church.

R. N. THOMPSON, '05.

GEORGE W. EAKINS, '05.

OCTAVO MERRIMO.

Reading from left to right—Alfred H. Joy, instructor in the Syrian Protestant College, Beirut Syria; John M. Smith, student at Greenville College; Wm. F. Murden, assistant editor of Waterloo Gazette, Waterloo, Nebraska; Walter A. Joy, with F. P. Joy and Co., Greenville, Ill ; Wm. E. White, Superintendent of Public Schools, Coal City, Ill.; Wm. E. Milliken, Ph. B. B. C. S., Principal of Greenville Business College; Herbert K. McGeary, Secretary to Congressman Martin, Deadwood, South Dakota; Robert Neil Thompson, Student at Harvard University; Robert E. Adams, B. A., M. A., Professor of Science, Meridian Male College, Meridian, Miss.

The Octavo Merrimo, composed of nine young men who were associated together in Greenville College, is one of our well known Literary and Social Clubs. It has had a continuous and flourishing existence since eight of the college boys founded the organization in 1898. In spite of peculiar difficulties and wide separation, the Merrimo has grown stronger from year to year, while similar aims and ideals, frequent correspondence and annual reunions have kept the members in closest touch with each other. The Merrimo stands for a perpetuation of the congenial friendship of college days, for mutual helpfulness in all possible ways, and for the highest ambitions and worthiest endeavors in life.

Class of 1905 of Greenville College

A male quartet formed the class of 1905 from Greenville College, and as they are strong and hardy in sex, so are they in robust, mental attainment and achievement.

William Edward Milliken, Greenville, Illinois, class treasurer, took his intermediate work in the preparatory department of the college and has finished the Ph. B. course in the college.

Ezra Whitton, Newmansville, Penn., vice-president, and a village curate, took his preparatory course in the High School at Sheffield, Pa., and has completed the A. B. course in the college.

Robert Neil Thompson, of Dallas, Texas, class secretary, after a preparatory course in Chili Seminary, Chili, N. Y., has finished the A. B. course in the college.

George Woodruff Eakins, after graduating from Wilkesbarre High School, Penn., took one year in the University of Pennsylvania and has completed the Ph. B. course in the college.

The class had a remarkable career while in the college, holding all the posts of honor the student body could bestow, and its members being acknowledged as exceptionally profi-

ROBERT E. ADAMS.

Class of 1903, Greenville College. Member of the faculty of Meridian Male College, Meridian, Miss.

cient in scholastic and literary efforts; the Ph. B's. for special science work, and the A. B's. for extraordinary rhetorical accomplishments.

Class Song.
By Robert E. Adams.

Our joy and our gladness
    On reaching our goal,
Is mixed with a sadness
    That's filling our soul;
For year after year, as
    We held on our way,
All things became dearer
    With each passing day.

We think of the struggles
    And conflicts we've met,
But the joy of our triumph
    Is tinged with regret;
For the faces of class-mates
    And kind friends so dear,
Will never more greet us
    Our lone hearts to cheer.

To-morrow we leave them
    And bid them farewell,
And turn to the future
    That none can foretell;
To-morrow we leave thee,
    Our dear College Home,
May Heaven protect thee
    In days that shall come!

In far away countries
    And far away climes,
We'll think of the College
    And all the old times.
Where'er we may wander
    And what be life's part,
These bands we'll not sunder
    Nor loose from our hearts.

⚘ History of Greenville Churches ⚘

Methodist Episcopal Church.

By Rev. Theodore Cates.

NO early records of the Greenville M. E. church have been kept and it is therefore impossible to give anything like a complete history of it. It is recorded, however, that the first sermon preached in the county by a minister of any denomination was by Rev. John Powers, a Methodist minister at Jones' Fort in February 1816. The first Methodist meetings were conducted by Rev. John Kirkpatrick. The first Methodist church was built about a mile and a half southwest of Greenville, where camp meetings were held for several years. For more than twenty years after the settlement of the country services were very irregular and it is related that those who attended church stacked their guns outside the door while two sentinels stood watch to give the alarm, at the first approach of Indians.

John H. Benson conducted meetings at the house of Mr. Knapp. Next came Rev. Thomas Brown, who died in 1844, and then for several years there were none to take up the work except transient preachers. Until this time class meetings and other religious services were held at private homes, in Odd Fellows' Hall and in the old court house.

In 1848 the trustees of the church bought two lots in Davidson's Addition of Thomas Kirkpatrick for $3.00 which indicates that he gave the lots to the church. The building was finished the following year.

In May 1848 the trustees of the church bought their first parsonage of Seth Fuller for $425. It was the property on Second street north of the present Garland residence.

Until 1872 this church belonged to the circuit consisting of Dudleyville, Centenary and Greenville and only had preaching regularly twice a month, but at that time the church was able to support itself with preaching every Sabbath. Rev. House was the last minister of the circuit and Rev. Van Treese the first minister of the station. Soon after the old church was sold to the Christian denomination for $600 and the old parsonage was sold to George Hill for $1,000. A lot on Second and Summer streets was purchased for $1,000, and the present brick edifice was built at a cost of $8,000. Rev. Cyrus Gibson was pastor at that time and did much toward pushing the movement. The contract for building the new church was let May 29, 1877, to Jno. H. Perry for $4885. The corner stone was laid by Greenville Lodge, 245, A. F. and A. M., July 10, 1877, Rev. W. H. Scott, of Troy, acting as

REV. THEODORE CATES,
Pastor of the M. E. Church.

Grand Master. The church was dedicated December 17, 1877, by Bishop Bowman.

The church was without a parsonage from 1877 until 1892, when C. D. Hoiles and Ward Reid donated a lot in Douglas Place and a house of eight rooms was built and was occupied by Rev. L. W. Thrall, who was pastor at that time. Later the property was sold and the present parsonage on Main Ave. was purchased.

The following ministers have served the church between the dates mentioned: V. Ridgly, 1852; J. W. Caldwell, 1853; J. S. Estep, 1854; W. G. Moore, 1855-7; C. M. Holliday, 1857; V. D. Lingenfelter, 1858-9; Levi Walker, 1860; F. M. Woolard, 1861; H. B. Taylor, 1862-3; G. W. Waggoner, 1864-6; J. S. Morrison, 1867; M. N. Powers, 1868-9; M. House, 1870-71; F. M. Van Treese, 1872-3; I. A. Smith, 1874; R. H. Massey, 1875; J. Gibson, 1876-7; J. A. Robinson, 1878-9; J. W. Van Cleve, 1880; E. A. Hoyt, 1881; W. F. Davis, 1882; F. L. Thompson, 1883; W. E. Ravenscroft, 1884-6; S. P. Groves, 1887-8; L. W. Thrall, 1889-92; C. W. Bonner, 1893; C. D. Shumard, 1894-98; J. B. Ravenscroft, 1899-1901; J. G. Dee, 1902; C. B. Besse, 1902-3; Theodore Cates, 1904 and the present pastor.

The following are the present officers of the church: Pastor, Rev. Theodore Cates; Board of Trustees, J. Seaman, J. S. Bradford, Dr. Wm. T. Easley, Dr. J. A. Warren, Samuel McGowan, Jesse McAdams, T. R. Robinson, W. W. Hussong and A. L. Bone; Board of Stewards, J. H. Ladd, Dr. Fred C. Jones, R. W.

THE M. E. CHURCH,
Built in 1877. South Second Street.

Rev. Thomas W. Hynes, D. D.,
Who was born in Kentucky in 1815, and who died in Greenville July 26, 1905. Came here in 1851; County Superintendent of schools for 20 years, a minister 60 years.

Wilson, H. W. Blizzard, E. R. Gum, Mrs. N. R. Bradford, Mrs. K. M. Bennett, Mrs. E. A. Gullick, Mrs. Jennie Warren, Mrs. Lena Davis, Mrs. Minnie Easley, Mrs. Alma Davis; Superintendent of the Sunday School, J. Seaman; Assistant Superintendent, Dr. Wm. T. Easley; Treasurer, Dr. Fred C. Jones; Secretary of the church, J. H. Ladd.

Presbyterian Church.

(Embracing the History of the Congregational Church.)

By the Reverend W. B. Minton.

MARCH 10, 1819, a church was formed in Bond county called "Shoal Creek church," embracing all the Presbyterians in the county. The center of this congregation was in what was called the "Ohio Settlement" about six miles north of Greenville. In 1825, Shoal Creek was divided into three, Bethel, Shoal Creek and Greenville churches. In 1832, Greenville and Shoal Creek were united under the name of Greenville. This church enjoyed the labors of Rev. Solomon Hardy, William J. Fraser, A. Ewing, William K. Stewart and James Stafford up to 1838. The house of worship, which was built at the time

Shoal Creek church and Greenville church united, was located about two miles north of the village of Greenville, on the left hand side of the Hillsboro road, near what is now known as Hazel Dell Cemetery. This was known as an old school church. In 1838, under the leadership of Dr. D. C. Lansing and those who sympathized with his views a new school church was organized in Greenville.

They commenced a house of worship in 1839 and dedicated it January 1, 1843. This is the building which stood for sixty years on the site of the present Carnegie Library. In 1846 the congregation worshipping in this house became Congregational in its internal government, though still retaining its exterior Presbyterian connection. In 1870 those members preferring complete Presbyterian polity united with the old school people, who had erected a church in Greenville in 1844-5. The remainder took the entire Congregational order. The ministers who have served, for a year or more, this church, which passed through the different changes in form of government just mentioned, are as follows: Revs. D. C. Lansing, 1838-41; Robert Stewart, 1841-9; John Ingersoll, 1850-1; George C. Woods, 1852-7; F. A. Armstrong, 1857-9; G. W. Goodale, 1862-5; M. M. Longley, 1868-72; M. A. Crawford, 1879-81; Isaac Wolfe, 1882-3; R. Adams,

1883-6; A. L. Grindley, 1887-90; L. E. Jesseph, 1891-3; J. P. Preston, 1893-5.

As has been stated, in 1845 the old school Presbyterian church people erected a building in Greenville. The union of 1871 wiped out all distinctions of new school and old school, and the Presbyterian and Congregational churches of Greenville remained as the outgrowth of all the past fifty years of changes from 1819 to 1871.

In 1840 Rev. James Stafford became pastor the second time of the church worshipping near Hazel Dell, and was pastor when the new church building was erected in town, during the years 1844 and 1845, and continued with this church until 1850. He was followed by these brethren: William Goodner, 1850; William Hamilton, 1851-2; T. W. Hynes, 1852-67; Arthur Rose, 1867; George Fraser, 1869-72; N. S. Dickey, 1873-6; Albert B. Byram, 1877-80; Wm. H. Hillis, 1881-3; O. G. Morton, 1884-7; Joseph Swindt, 1887-1891; George J. E. Richards, 1891-1900; W. B. Minton, 1900 to the present time.

Going back once more to 1870 and 1871, we find the Presbyterian and Congregational churches existing side by side with varying success until October 23, 1897, when the Presbyterian house of worship burned. The Congregational people at once invited the homeless Presbyterians to share with them the Congregational church building and together it was arranged that Rev. George J. E. Richards, then pastor of the Presbyterian church, should become the minister of the two congregations, which were like two rain drops on the window pane, very close together, yet distinct. On the first Sabbath in April, 1898, the two drops got so close together that they coalesced around the communion table and as a united church have since had place and influence in Greenville, under the name and polity of the Presbyterian church. In 1902 and 1903 the united church erected the present commodious and comfortable house of worship at a cost of $9,000. The membership of the church, according to the last report to the General Assembly, is 377.

The present elders are James Hepburn, Dr. N. H. Jackson, H. C. Burton, S. S. Trindle, Frank P. Joy, S. Curtis White, Alfred Maynard, W. D. Donnell, Geo. Colcord, W. T. Carson, Col. J. B. Reid, Robert Fangenroth. Of these James Hepburn has been in continuous service since 1872.

The deacons are W. O. Holdzkom, W. A. McLain, Walter Joy and H. Allendorph. The trustees are W. O. Holdzkom, James Wafer, Horace McNeill, Walter Joy and A. D. Ross.

REV. W. B. MINTON,
Pastor of the Presbyterian Church
since June, 1900.

THE PRESBYTERIAN CHURCH.

The Sunday School officers are, Superintendent, Alfred Maynard; Assistant Superintendent, W. A. McLain; Superintendent of Primary Department, Mrs. W. A. McLain; Assistant Superintendent Primary Department, Miss Eula Carson; Superintendent of Home Department, Mrs. W. T. Carson; Superintendent of Cradle Roll, Miss Ola Coen; Secretary and Treasurer, Miss Lizzie Colcord; Librarian, Bertha Drayton; Organist, Misses Hattie Carson and Mabel Grube.

Including Home Department and Cradle Roll, the school reports 369 members.

The Senior and Junior Christian Endeavor Societies are well attended and doing good service. The Women's Home and Foreign Missionary society is progressive and faithful.

Rev. T. W. Hynes, D. D., who died in July, 1905, in his ninetieth year, had the honor of serving the church for the longest time, 1852 to 1867, fifteen years consecutively, and for short periods since, for a few weeks or months as the church had occasion to look to him for his always acceptable services.

The present minister is Rev. W. B. Minton, who began his ministry with the church in June, 1900. Since his coming the new church has been built and dedicated free of debt. The outlook is full of encouragement.

Baptist Church.

By Mrs Ellen R. Stearns.

THE Baptist church of Greenville was organized September 18, 1836, with six members: Lemuel Blanchard, Charles Norton, Eunice Norton, A. N. Norton, Elizabeth Norton and Sibbel Blanchard. In 1842 the total membership was forty-two. From that time the

THE OLD PRESBYTERIAN CHURCH,
Built in 1845 and destroyed by fire in 1897.

REV. GEORGE J. E. RICHARDS,
Pastor Presbyterian church from December 15, 1891, to April 1, 1900, now a resident of Mt. Carmel, Illinois.

church declined in numerical strength. During these eleven years of its existence, it never had a regular pastor and with one brief exception never had preaching service, oftener than once a month.

In May 1847 it was decided to dissolve the church relationship and enter into a new church organization. July 4, 1847, the church was re-organized by Rev. Ebenezer Rodgers and Rev. I. D. Newell, with fifteen members: K. P. and Elizabeth Morse, Sibbel Blanchard, Elizabeth Foster, C. J. and Almira Wightman, John and Sophia Jett, Benjamin Floyd, Susan Morse, Priscilla Morse, Elizabeth Hoiles, Serena Hull, Wm. T. and Maria Hull. Of these, one, Mrs. Sophia Jett, survives. Six hundred twenty-two names have been enrolled. The present membership is 121.

Prior to 1854 meetings of the church were held in private houses, in the court house, or in the Presbyterian church. From 1847 to April 1854, the meetings were held in the Presbyterian church and for more than three years of that time we occupied that building one half of the time. In April 1854 a building 32x50 feet was completed at a cost of $2500. This building was called at that time, the prettiest church building in southern Illinois. This house was occupied till September 1902, when it was sold. In October, 1902, our present house of worship was completed but was not dedicated till July 12, 1903, at a cost of $5,000. The first pastor of the new organization was Rev. Moses Lemen, who served one year. In February 1851 a call was extended to Rev. W. D. H. Johnson, of Woodburn, Ill., and in December 1851 he moved his family to Greenville, with the condition that a meeting house should be built as soon as possible. He continued as pastor till October 1858. Other pastors were Rev. J. B. White, 1858 to 1861; Rev. D. P. French, 1862 to 1866; Rev. R. G. Hall, 1867 to 1869; Rev. M. D. Bevan, 1870 to 1875; Rev. R. M. Neil, 1876 to 1877; Rev. George Kline, 1877 to 1879. In 1881 Rev. M. D. Bevan was again called to the pastorate, serving until 1884, when Rev. P. Reynolds came, remaining till 1886. Then Rev. H. W. Thiele from 1887 to 1890; Rev. J. W. Titterington, 1890 to 1893; Rev. Stephen Crockett 1893 to 1894; Rev. W. L. Jones, 1895 to 1898; Rev. R. Wiley, 1900 to 1903; Rev. G. E. Milford, 1903 to 1905. Our present pastor, Rev. E. M. Ryan, commenced his labors in October 1905.

As early as February 1838 initial steps were taken towards building an academy but the effort failed at that time. However the desire of

THE OLD CONGREGATIONAL CHURCH,
Built in 1839, and dismantled in 1903, for the site of the Carnegie Library

the church to do something in the line of education, strengthened and matured and in the fall of 1854 developed in plans for the erection of Almira College, now Greenville College. This effort was not made by the church in its church capacity but all of its originators, except one, were members of the church and its members always took a deep interest in the advancement of the school. About one hundred of the pupils of the school were converted and united with the church so that the church and school were closely linked together as long as the school remained in the hands of the Baptist denomination and the history of the church would be incomplete without reference to the College.

The Sunday School was held in connection with the Presbyterians until 1854, when we occupied our own house of worship. A school of forty-three members was then organized with Alexander Buie as Superintendent. In 1860-5 the average attendance was 115. During the Rebellion thirty-eight of those who were or had been members of this school joined the Union army, eight of whom gave their lives for their country. The present officers of the school are: Superintendent, Fred Scheele; Assistant Superintendent, Miss Lizzie Blanchard; Secretary, Della Jett; Treasurer, A. B. Scheele; Organist, Mrs. A. B. Scheele. The present enrollment is ninety.

The young people of the church are organized into a B. Y. P. U. with thirty members. The officers are: President, Miss Lizzie Blanchard; Secretary and Treasurer, Miss Lola Nevinger; Organist, Mrs. A. B. Scheele.

The ladies of the church maintain a mission circle which meets once a month. It has a membership of twenty. The officers are: President, Mrs. E. R. Stearns; Secretary and Treasurer, Mrs. J. B. White.

The present officers of the church are: Trustees, Fred Scheele, G. B. Hoiles, E. Sohn, F. N. Blanchard, J. W. Blanchard, J. W. Wrightsman and Erastus DeMoulin; Deacons, F. Scheele, E. Sohn, John Wenting, Ransom Pope, W. Donnell and G. B.

Keesecker; Clerk, Mrs. E. R.
Stearns; Treasurer, G. B. Hoiles;
Organist, Miss Lizzie Blanchard.

St. Lawrence Congregation.

By The Reverend Wm. Pachlhofer.

THE first mass known to have
been celebrated at Greenville
was said by a Franciscan Father of
Teutopolis, Ill., at the home of
Frank Seewald in the year 1875.
On May 6, 1877 a small congregation was organized under the direction of Rev. L. Quitter, of Vandalia, and services were held at first
in a hall on the third floor of the
First National Bank Building on the
southwest corner of the square,
which is now the property of J. M.
Miller.

Prominent among the first promoters of the new mission were
Lawrence McGinness, Peter Pepin,
Frank Parent, Frank Seewald, Philip Cable, Patrick Clare and Louis
Lehn. Several months after the
opening of the services in the hall
arrangements were made for the
building of a special house of worship. A suitable site was secured
at the corner of present Prairie and
Spring streets and a small brick
church was erected thereon, which
was given the name of St. Lawrence
the Martyr, a compliment to Lawrence McGinness. On completion
of the church the congregation continued to be visited about once a
month as an out-mission of Vandalia, viz., 1877-81 by Rev. L. Quitter; August 14, 1881-85 by Rev.
Charles Geier; in the summer of

THE FIRST BAPTIST CHURCH, built in 1902.

1885 by Rev. John J. Higgins; November 1885-88 by Rev. Hy. Beck-
er, D. D.; October 1888 to December
1893 by Rev. P. M. Bourke; January 1894 to June 1895 by Rev. Ber-
nard Lee.

In June 1895 the congregation received its first resident pastor, in
the person of Rev. John P. Moroney,
who enlisted for his work the good
will and co-operation, not only of
the regular parishioners, but also
of numerous non-Catholic friends.
With their aid, Father Moroney
erected a parsonage in 1895 and
built a front addition to the church
in 1897. He likewise placed in the
church the present main altar which

was donated by the congregation of
Jacksonville, Ill. When Father Moroney was transferred to Vandalia
in June 1898, he was succeeded by
Rev. S. P. Hoffman, who proceeded
to appropriately furnish the parsonage and improve the premises of the
church property. At the same time
he established several church societies, and founded a library for
the use of the congregation. In 1900
a tract of land was purchased on the
southwest limit of the town and
adopted for the purpose of a cemetery.

Moreover during Father Hoffman's term the sanctuary of the
church was artistically frescoed, and
side altars with statues and a new
organ placed in the edifice. When
in October 1901, the zealous pastor

THE OLD BAPTIST CHURCH,
Built in 1847 and used continuously for more than 50 years.

REV. E. M. RYAN,
Pastor First Baptist church.

REV. M. D. BEVAN, D. D., *Deceased,*

Pastor of the Greenville Baptist church from 1870 to 1875 and from 1881 to 1884.

REV. W. D. H. JOHNSON, *Deceased.*

Pastor of the Greenville Baptist Church from December, 1851, to October, 1858.

was compelled by ill-health to resign his charge, he was temporarily replaced by Rev. A. Hochmiller. On October 1, 1902, Rev. William A. Pachlhofer, the present incumbent, was appointed rector of the church. Since his arrival, it has been his endeavor to continue, with the assistance of his flock, the work performed by his predecessors in furthering the spiritual and material progress of the congregation. During the last two years the congregation has secured additional church furniture, renovated the interior of the parsonage, notably reduced the church debt, and added, in September 1904, a commodious sacristy to the church.

Although comparatively small and with the majority of its members living at considerable distance from church, St. Lawrence congregation has, especially during the last ten years, slowly but steadily progressed and, as the Catholic population of the seat of Bond county is increasing, bids fair to contribute even more in the future to the honor of God, the salvation of souls, and the general welfare of the community.

Grace Episcopal Church.

By The Reverend J. G. Wright.

THE Greenville papers of 1877 announced that the Reverend W. M. Steel of Rantoul, a pioneer missionary of the Protestant Episcopal church, held services in this city in the summer of that year. He was, in all probability, the first Episcopal minister to visit our community. On July 20th, 1878, Messrs. W. S. Ogden, C. K. Denny, M. B. Chittenden, Henry Howard and Henry M. Chittenden, (now Archdeacon of Alton) met at Esquire Howard's office and there decided to organize a mission to be known as Grace Church. To the above named gentlemen, seventeen others, who had been baptised in the Episcopal church, and twelve, who were not connected with any religious organization in the city, may be added as constituting a part of the nucleus of the mission.

The Reverend Mr. Van Duzen, of Paris, Edgar county, visited Greenville in August 1878, and held services in the Congregational church. W. S. Ogden attended the Diocesan convention of that year held at Springfield and conferred with Bishop McLaren about the mission. He carried with him the petition for admission, and this being accepted, the mission was canonically established. W. S. Ogden and C. K. Denny were selected as Wardens; M. B. Chittenden, Treasurer and H. A. Stephens, Clerk. At the same time Henry M. Chittenden received a license to act as lay reader. Morse Hall was rented and fitted up for use and Mr. Henry Chittenden conducted for a while, the Sunday services, his sister, Miss Hattie Chittenden, playing the organ. In the same year the Reverend R. E. G. Huntington, of Collinsville took charge and began fortnightly services. He remained in charge until May, 1881.

The first list of communicants of the church is as follows: W. S. Ogden and wife, C. K. Denny, C. R. Jones and wife, M. B. Chittenden, Henry M. Chittenden, Hattie E. Chittenden, Mrs. S. M. Hoiles, and H. F. Stephens. To these were added in the first confirmation Henry Alexander, Mrs. W. H. Williams, and Misses L. E. Daniels, Hattie E. Ogden, May Ellis, Emma Jones and Louisa Jones. At the following visitation of the Bishop, Mmes. W. S. Smith, S. Blanchard, C. K. Denny and the Misses Minnie Blanchard,

MRS. C. J. WIGHTMAN,

One of the first teachers in Almira, and one of the founders of the Ladies' Library Association,

C. J. WIGHTMAN, *Deceased.*

One of the founders of the Greenville Baptist church and a prominent citizen for many years.

ST. LAWRENCE CATHOLIC CHURCH, built in 1877.

REV. WM. PACHLHOFER.
Pastor of St. Lawrence congregation.

Emma Williams, and Carrie Ogden were added. It may be here noted that one hundred and six others have since been confirmed in Greenville by Bishop Seymour.

On Easter Sunday, 1882, the Reverend J. G. Wright was placed in charge of the mission. He was at that time principal of the public schools in Altamont and came over every Sunday to conduct the services. During the administration of his predecessor a lot had been purchased on Third Street, midway between the Vandalia depot and the public square, and soon after Mr. Wright took charge, a movement was made to begin the erection of a church building. "So built we the wall for the people had a mind to work," and on the following Easter Sunday, 1883, the congregation assembled for the first time in their new church, a small but beautiful Gothic structure, well suited to the needs of a small congregation.

In June, 1883, the Reverend J. G. Wright moved from Altamont and took up his residence in Greenville, the first resident clergyman of the mission. He is still in charge, (1905) having completed twenty-two years of service. The church now has a membership of sixty.

To this brief note it may well be added that much support has been given to this struggling mission by the organization of the Ladies' Aid Society. This society purchased the lot on which the church stands, and have from the very first supported every movement made to advance the church's interest. Mainly by their efforts the debt upon the church building was cancelled, thus

REV. J. G. WRIGHT,
Pastor of the Episcopal church for more than 22 years.

GRACE EPISCOPAL CHURCH, built in 1882.

THE CHRISTIAN CHURCH, built in 1891.

enabling the Bishop to consecrate the church. This ceremony took place March 25, 1897. It is also a matter of interest that Henry Chittenden, whose name occurs in the foregoing note as one of the founders of the mission, was ordained deacon in this church, by Bishop Seymour, January 16, 1887, and in the same church and by the same Bishop was advanced to the Priesthood October 15, 1891.

The interior of the church has from time to time been much improved. A handsome carved memorial Altar, the gift of Mr. and Mrs. A. L. Hord, has replaced the more modest altar of the earlier days. The altar cross thereon is a memorial of Lieut. C. C. Ogden of the 13th Infantry, a faithful and devoted son of the church, who died in 1893. A memorial brass altar desk has been presented by Mr. and Mrs. W. W. Lowis, a brass lectern by Mr. and Mrs. Walter von Weise and brass memorial alms basins by Mr. and Mrs. George von Weise. The chancel chairs were the gift of the Ladies' Aid Society and the book of altar services and book for prayer desk were given, as a memorial to his wife and mother, by Charles W. Watson. In addition to these handsome gifts, the church has lately purchased a pipe organ of excellent quality and tone, and the same Ladies' Aid Society which has been so fruitful in good works, is now steadily diminishing the small indebtedness that rests thereon. The choir, as at present constituted, consists of Messrs R. S. Denny, H. C. Diehl, Frank E. Watson and Will C. Wright. Miss Louise Morey is organist.

The Christian Church.

By Mrs. Alice Perryman.

ELDER J. CARROLL STARK, pastor of the Christian church at Augusta, Ill., arrived in Greenville February 7, 1878, and commenced a series of meetings which led up to the organization of the Greenville Christian church on Sunday, February 24, 1878. The meetings were held in the old M. E. church on the southwest corner of College and Fourth Streets. The trustees of the First M. E. church of Greenville deeded this church to M. V. Denny, R. C. Sprague and Wm. Koch, trustees of the Christian church on October 12, 1877, for $600.

Large audiences greeted Elder Stark and the local papers at the time stated that people came six and seven miles through the mud and darkness to hear him.

As above stated the church was organized February 24, 1878, with twenty-six members. Seven more united a few days later and there were many additions every week, during the labors of Elder Stark here. In April of that year a Sunday School was organized with M. V. Denny as superintendent and Miss Cornelia Dry as secretary.

Elder Stark remained with the church as pastor for about two years during which time under his labors and the labors of Elder Trickett, in a protracted meeting held early in the year 1879 there were added to the congregation about 63 persons. In April W. S. Errett came to Greenville as pastor of the church. Others who have served as pastor have been J. M. Tennison, John A. Williams, H. R. Trickett, W. S. Errett, a second time, Dr. Collins, H. H. Peters, E. N. Tucker, J. E. Story and Tallie Defrees, the present pastor. At present E. E. Wise and E. W. Miller are the deacons and E. W. Miller is clerk. The present church on the corner of Main Avenue and Prairie Street was dedicated on Sunday, August 23, 1891, by Elder F. M. Rains of Topeka, Kansas, assisted by the pastor, Elder W. S. Errett. The new church cost, with the furnishings, $3,500.

So-Called Plymouth Brethren.

By One of the Brethren.

THE origin of the Plymouth Brethren, so-called, but which title they do not own, dates from the year 1827 and started in Dublin, Ireland, where four men, who had

RUTSCHLY'S HALL,
In which the Plymouth Brethren, (so-called) worship.

REV. J. H. FLOWER,

Who was pastor of the F. M. church for several years and who built the present church. Now a resident of St. Louis.

been troubled about the state in the established church, left it and met together to study the Scriptures. This resulted in their being gathered unto the name of the Lord alone, and instead of forming another unity, and thus adding to the divisions in Christendom, they simply recognized the unity of the church of Christ, and so were standing on a ground that embraced all Christians.

In the year 1828, Mr. J. N. Darby published his first pamphlet entitled: "The Nature and Unity of the Church of Christ." This tract may be considered as a statement of what these brethren believed and practiced, yet not in the form of a confession.

In the spring of 1830 they commenced breaking bread in their first public meeting room on the first day of the week and the truths which seemed to get most notice were the divinity of the Lord Jesus, the efficacy of redemption, the knowledge of pardon and acceptance, the oneness of the body of Christ, the presence of the Holy Ghost in the assembly, and the Lord's second coming.

The first public meeting room in Plymouth was called "Providence Chapel" and as they refused to give themselves any name, they were known as "Providence People." But when the brothers began to go outside the town and preach the gospel in the villages—then a rare thing—they were spoken of as "Brethren from Plymouth," which naturally resulted in the designation "The Plymouth Brethren." This new title spread rapidly over England and elsewhere but was never accepted by them, as they refuse both the position and name of a sect.

This company has spread all over the civilized world, and the first meeting in Greenville was in 1854, when there were only a few gathered together and the meetings were held in a private house. After a while they rented a hall, when the number increased to about forty or fifty. They do not accept the term or name of member of church but only members of the body of Christ. Hence, there is no such thing among them as members of Plymouth Brethren church as they only recognize one church, composed of all true believers in the Lord Jesus Christ, no matter where they meet.

REV. C. A. FLEMING,

Pastor of the Free Methodist church in 1881 and again in 1904 and 1905.

Free Methodist Church.

By The Reverend C. A. Fleming.

IN the fall of 1880 C. A. Fleming, who was appointed to the Woburn and Walnut Grove circuit, which included Dudleyville and Mulberry Grove, first began preaching in Greenville, in the private house of Mr. Fleeharty, and continued until the following July, at which time a tabernacle meeting was arranged by him. The services of F. H. Haley, T. H. Agnew, Lon E. Myers and Addie Durham were secured to assist in the meeting.

At the close of the tent meeting, W. B. M. Colt, district elder of the Litchfield district, organized a class consisting of seven members, namely W. S. Dann, A. J. Huffman, Lewis Wright, A. L. Alred and Sarah Dann, Hulda Huffman and Clara Wright. The organization took place in the rooms of W. S. Dann, over his store which is now occupied by Joy & Co. This was about July 20, 1881. C. A. Fleming acted as pastor to the end of that conference year, at which time the circuit was divided. Then C. C. Brunner was appointed to the Greenville circuit and served from 1881 to October 1882, at which time C. A. Fleming was re-appointed and served the following year. During this year the first Free Methodist church was built at the corner of Prairie and Vine Streets, at a cost of $1,300. The church was dedicated by B. F. Robert, one of the

THE FREE METHODIST CHURCH, built in 1899.

THE AFRICAN M. E. CHURCH.

General Superintendents of the Free Methodist church.

The membership of the church at this time had increased to about twenty-five, all being in poor circumstances but one. The succeeding pastors were as follows: M. C. Ballew, 1883-5; H. F. Ashcraft, 1885-6; R. Adams, October 1886 to June 1887; M. C. Ballew, June to October 1887; J. W. Kelly, 1887-8; W. C. Kelly, 1888-90; H. G. Ahlemeyer, 1890-92; W. T. Hogue, 1892-3; J. H. Flower, 1893-4; John LaDue, 1894-5; J. N. Eason, 1895-6; B. S. Dewey, 1896-7; J. H. Flower, 1897-1900.

Under the pastorate of J. H. Flower, the present church at the corner of College and Elm Streets was built at a cost of $4,000. This church was dedicated at the close of the annual conference by Superintendent E. P. Hart, September 18, 1899. The membership of the church at this time consisted of 122 full members and 24 probationers, making a total of 146. The succeeding pastors were as follows: S. K. Wheatlake, 1900-2; W. R. Bonham, 1902-3; A. L. Whitcomb, September 1903 to July 1904; W. P. Ferries, July to September 1904; C. A. Fleming, September 1904 to September 1905. The present pastor is Rev. A. L. Whitcomb and the membership is 280. The Board of Trustees are J. H. Moss, J. H. Maxey, W. B. Fink, H. R. McAdams and S. M. Bilyeu; class leaders, Wm. Baker, Wm. Freidlein, Mrs. Minnie Ashcraft and Mrs. G. R. White; Superintendent of Sunday School, J. M. Daniels, with a membership of about 300; Woman's Foreign Missionary Society—President, Mrs. C. A. Fleming; this society raised a total of $336.70 for foreign missions last year. The Junior Missionary Society, Mrs. Emma Haverland, president. This society is raising yearly $15 for the support of one of the Indian orphans.

The African M. E. Church.

THE African M. E. church was organized in 1881 by Rev. Morgan. Meetings were held at the private homes until the Congregational denomination offered the use of their church basement which was used until the present building was erected. In 1882, Henry Nowell, Jacob Bristow and Eli Spriggs bought a lot of Dr. Ravold and donated it in part to the A. M. E. denomination and Rev. D. A. Wilkerson, the pastor in charge, built the present church at a cost of $500.

The Second Baptist Church.

THE Second Baptist church was organized July 19, 1890, at 7 p. m. Rev. J. W. Feat was the moderator and Rev. J. H. Bell secretary. Rev. Metcalf, Rev. Groase, L. D. Blanchard, J. B. Reid, J. H. Jett and C. Anderson sat in the counsel. The church was organized with four members, Archie Ewing, James Ewing, Julia Dukes and Martha Wilson. The present church was erected a few years later.

THE PRESS

The Protestant Monitor.

THE PROTESTANT MONITOR was the first newspaper published in Greenville and the earliest copy of the paper preserved is Volume 1, No. 27, bearing date of December 8, 1845. As the name indicates it was a religious paper and was started in Vandalia the June previous, but was moved soon after to Greenville. The paper was owned and edited by E. M. Lathrap. Incomplete files of the Monitor are preserved in Greenville newspaper offices. The subscription price was $2 per year, if paid in advance; $2.50 at the end of three months, or $3 if payment was delayed to the end of the year. The paper espoused the cause of the Protestant Methodist denomination and paid but little attention to local news. The local news was contained principally in the quaint advertisements and the death of a prominent citizen was disposed of in three lines in a remote part of the paper.

In March 1846 James Shoaff became associated with Mr. Lathrap and in November of that year the name of John Waite appears as assistant. Mr. Waite was a Protestant Methodist minister. He was drowned in Shoal Creek in 1853. He re-

THE SECOND BAPTIST CHURCH.

OTHNIEL BUCHANAN, *Deceased,*
Editor of the American Courier in
1856-7. A resident of Greenville
for 58 years.

tired in August 1847 and J. McPike
became associated with Mr. Lathrap.
The following October Stephen Fisk
was associate editor for a short
time. The Protestant Monitor was
moved to Alton in January 1848
and was published there for several
years.

While in Greenville the Protestant Monitor was published on the
site of the present residence of T.
R. Robinson, in the west end of
town.

The Barn Burner.

Jediah F. Alexander, who came
to Greenville in 1848, at the age of
twenty-one years, started, during
the memorable campaign of that
year, a Free Soil paper, called the
Barn Burner, supporting Martin Van
Buren for President.

The publication was intended only
as a campaign paper, and, having
served its purpose, was discontinued.
Nothing of the Barn Burner is preserved. It was the first journalistic
venture of Mr. Alexander, afterward
promoter and president of the Vandalia Line and founder of the Greenville Advocate.

The Western Fountain.

John Waite was editor of the
Western Fountain, published semi-
monthly and "devoted to Christian-
ity, sacred literature and religious
intelligence." A part of Volume

One is now in possession of Mr.
Jacob Koonce of Greenville. Number 3, bears date of December 6,
1848. It is not definitely known
how long Mr. Waite continued the
publication of this paper but it was
probably not long for he was connected with other journalistic vent-
ures. Mr. Waite published the
Western Fountain in connection
with the Journal.

Rev. Peter Long's Publications.

From 1845 to 1856 Elder Peter
Long published the Western Evan-
gelist a monthly religious paper,
which had a circulation of 2,000 in
this and other states. The paper
was first published from the press
of Lathrop and Waite, in a house
where T. R. Robinson's residence
now stands. It was then moved to
Rockwell, a postoffice on Elder
Long's farm, six miles west of
Greenville. It was afterwards again
printed in Greenville. Elder Long
also published the Primitive Preach-
er, 1850-51, quarterly. It consisted
principally of a reprint of standard
religious works.

From 1860 to 1876 he issued
"The Visitor" occasionally, for
gratuitous distribution. He was also

the author of "The Western
Harp" a book of about two hundred
hymns and sacred poems. Six
editions were printed and about
4000 copies were distributed, many
of which are still in use.

The Greenville Journal.

While Mr. Alexander was running
the Barn Burner, the Journal was
started by John Waite, former assistant editor of the Monitor. After
he had discontinued the publication
of the Barn Burner, J. F. Alexander
became connected with the Journal,
first as a partner of Mr. Waite, and
afterward, in 1850, as sole proprietor. In January 1852 John Waite
again became the editor of the Journal, and the following June the
paper published a poem entitled
"The Wavy West," from the pen of
Robert G. Ingersoll, then a boy in
Greenville.

On September 9, 1853, E. J. C.
Alexander, who is still living on his
farm north of Greenville, together
with his brother, J. H. Alexander became editors and proprietors of the
Journal. In 1856 the old files of
the paper show that D. W. Alexander was publisher and J. F. Alexander was editor. The paper changed

E. J. C. ALEXANDER.
Editor of the Greenville Journal in the fifties and
war time editor of the Advocate.

THE GREENVILLE ADVOCATE OFFICE.
Reading from left to right are J. H. Hawley, Miss Myrtle Loggins, J. H. McHenry, George E. Hines and Will C. Carson.

hands many times and was eventually sold to a Scotchman, who moved it to Staunton, Ill. It was independent in politics until 1856, when it hoisted the Freemont standard.

The American Courier.

Thomas Russell and Othniel Buchanan were the editors and owners of the American Courier, which was launched in the field May 22, 1856, the entire outfit having been purchased new in St. Louis. The paper ardently supported the Native American party and Millard Fillmore, its nominee for the presidency. On March 26, 1857, Mr. Russell retired and Mr. Buchanan subsequently bought the Greenville Journal of J. F. Alexander and then sold both the Journal and Courier to Parson Percy, who moved the two plants to another town.

The Greenville Advocate.

By W. W. Lowis.

On February 11, 1858, the Greenville Advocate made its initial appearance under the editorship and ownership of J. F. Alexander. The paper was born in time to take a stand for the preservation of the Union, which it did. The Advocate witnessed the birth of the Republican party and has come down through the years a staunch supporter of

the principles of this party. At the outbreak of the civil war Mr. Alexander made personal investigation of the situation at Washington, and at the various seats of war, and wrote his impressions for the benefit of his readers. During this time and for years afterward an "Educational Department," was conducted by Rev. Thomas W. Hynes. In all his career as a newspaper writer Mr. Hynes urged with vigor the preservation of the local history of the city and county.

In June 1863 E. J. C. Alexander succeeded his brother as publisher of the Advocate, remaining editor until July 20, 1865, when he sold the paper to S. C. Mace. In April 1865 T. O. Shenick became associated with Mr. Mace as publisher. All this time the paper was published in the second story of a frame building where Masonic Temple now stands. In October 1866 Mace and Shenick moved the plant to the rooms over Denny and Dressor's corner, where J. V. Dixon's store now is. T. O. Shenick left the paper in March 1867, selling his interests to Mr. Mace. In October 1870 Wm. Boll, afterwards one of the editors of the Sun, was made publisher of the Advocate, remaining in that capacity until January 1871, when Mr. Shenick again returned and bought back his old interest. In 1871 the office was moved over Smith's bank where Hawley's jewelry store now is and the proud and happy day dawned when the paper announced that it was "all printed at home."

In August 1871 Mr. Shenick again severed his connection with the paper and the following month the subscription price was reduced from $2 to $1.50 a year and has since remained that price.

In November 1871 Mr. Mace sold the paper to Samuel B. Hynes, under whose proprietorship, his father, Rev. Thomas W. Hynes, was editor. S. B. Hynes himself was the local editor. The paper was in 1872 changed from an eight column folio to a six column quarto, retaining this form two years and then returning to its former dimensions. April 24, 1872, the publication day was

RESIDENCE OF W. W. LOWIS, North Third Street.

W. W. LOWIS,

Publisher of the Greenville Advocate; President
of the Building and Savings Association; Director of the Carnegie Library; Adjutant Colby Post.

changed from Friday to Wednesday.
In July 1872 the office was moved
to Col. Reid's block, up stairs over
McLain and Wafer's store, where F.
E. Watson's store now is.

George M. Tatham purchased the
paper and became editor and publisher October 1, 1873. He straight-

way made a specialty of local news.
The last week in December 1875 he
changed the publication day to
Thursday and increased the size to

seven columns, four pages.

Early in the eighties Mr. Tatham
moved the paper from the south side
to the second floor of the Smith
building, on the west side of the
square, where it remained until
1898.

John H. Hawley is the nestor of
journalism in Greenville. He first
commenced work on the Advocate
November 14, 1860, when J. F.
Alexander was editor and remained
till January 1862, when he enlisted
and went to the front. He went
back on the paper November 11,
1878, and has continued as a member of the force until the present
time with the exception of five
months he was engaged in other
business.

Numerous others have served
their apprenticeship on the Advocate and are now engaged in the
newspaper business in many distant
cities.

In February 1893 Mr. Tatham
slipped on the ice and fell, receiving
injuries which caused his death,
May 21, 1893. During his illness
and for several months after his
death, Mr. Hawley was in charge of
the business and editorial department of the office.

The Advocate was sold at auction
June 26, 1893 to W. W. Lowis, of
Lena, Ill., who moved to Greenville
and took charge of the paper. Mr.
Lowis at once changed the style and
make-up of the paper, making local
news the predominating feature. In
1895 it took its present form. In
July 1898 the office was moved from
the Smith building to the second

WILL C. WRIGHT,
Former Editor of the Sun.

OFFICE OF THE GREENVILLE SUN.

MRS. ALICE ENLOE PERRYMAN.

floor of the Weise building, on the north side of the square, where it remained till July 1901, when the plant was moved to its present location on the ground floor two doors west of the postoffice.

The Greenville Sun.

By Will C. Wright.

The Greenville newspaper now known as The Sun was originally The Bond County Democrat. J. B. Anderson, a practical printer, established the Democrat here in 1876 and the first issue appeared June 2d of that year. The paper

espoused the cause of Democracy. The office was then located on the second floor of the Hoiles building, just over the store now occupied by A. H. Krause, the jeweler. The paper consisted of eight pages, six columns to the page. Local news appeared on only four of these, the remaining four being "patent insides." Mr. Anderson conducted the Democrat until February 2, 1877, when it was purchased by William Boll and Fordyce C. Clark. Both these gentlemen had previously been employed in the composing rooms of the Advocate. The new proprietors promptly changed the name of the paper to The Sun and its policy also was changed so that it became more independent in tone. However, it still retained its democratic proclivities and in 1880 it again became a recognized organ of that party, remaining so up to the present time. Messrs. Boll & Clark retained possession of The Sun for seven years and sold it in 1884 to Vallee Harold, of St. Genevieve, Missouri. Mr. Harold presented the first issue under his management July 4, 1884. He continued the publication of the paper in the same location for about three years and then moved it to the rooms over J. Seaman's hardware store, on the southeast corner of the square.

The next change in The Sun's management took place Nov. 9, 1891, when Chas. E. Davidson, who had been associated with Mr. Harold, became its editor and proprietor. Mr. Davidson retained charge of the paper until Jan. 5, 1901, when ill health compelled him to dispose of it. The Sun then passed into the ownership of Will C. Wright, the present proprietor, who had been

GEORGE PERRYMAN,
Editor of the Item.

doing local work under Mr. Davidson for the four years and a half preceding.

During Mr. Davidson's regime the paper was moved to the second story of the old First National Bank building on the south side and here it remained until the fall of 1898 when a new building was erected for it on the east side of the square and it was, for the first time, located on the ground floor.

Editor's note.—Since the above was written, Mr. Wright has sold The Sun to Charles E. Maynard, who is now the editor and publisher. The sale was made in November, 1905.

The Greenville Item.

By George Perryman.

The Greenville Item entered the journalistic field of Bond county May 28, 1896. It was received by the public with many doubts and misgivings and few believed it would survive longer than three months, as it came in direct competition with two old-established and well-equipped newspaper offices, which seemingly filled every want, but it lived and grew in size from a five-column quarto to its present size, seven-column quarto, the largest paper published in the county, and is now recognized as one of the permanent institutions of the county.

Much of it's success is due to the efforts of the publisher's wife, Mrs. Alice Perryman, who has assisted in every department of the paper. The Item is now in its ninth year and is enjoying a lucrative patronage.

RESIDENCE OF GEORGE PERRYMAN.

MRS. ABRAHAM MCNEILL, *Deceased*.

Who was a resident of Greenville and vicinity for 65 years. A native of Virginia.

The Bench and Bar

BY FORMER LIEUTENANT GOVERNOR W. A. NORTHCOTT.

BOND COUNTY was organized by an act of the territorial legislature passed January 4, 1817, and at that time extended as far north as the Wisconsin line and was one of the fifteen counties comprising the territory of Illinois at the time of its admission as a state.

The first court was held June 30, 1817, at Hill's Station, a fort on Shoal Creek about eight miles southwest of Greenville. Judge Jesse B. Thomas, afterward United States Senator from Illinois, presided. The legal business of the county from this date until about 1837 was conducted by visiting lawyers, and no record can be found or tradition given of any resident attorney. In 1838 Judge M. G. Dale, then a young attorney, located in Greenville and remained until a short time prior to the war, when he removed to Edwardsville, and continued practice until his death in 1896. He was a remarkable man in many respects, and one who retained during his entire life the respect and good will of the people of both Bond and Madison counties. He always dreaded to speak in public and was not strong as an advocate before a jury, but as county judge, at different times in each of these counties, he was a strong judge of law and a most impartial, upright official. He was a very

active man, continuing in practice up to the time of his death.

James M. Davis, the next resident lawyer of the Bond county bar was a man of fiery eloquence and his particular delight was in presenting a case to the jury or in making a political speech in the public forum. In 1849 he went to Vandalia to take a position in connection with United States land office, afterwards removing to Hillsboro, where he was the tutor and benefactor of Congressman Ed Lane, who read law under him and who received his law library as a legacy. Until the beginning of the war Mr. Davis was an active Whig, but at that time became a Democrat and a radical sympathizer with the rebellion. He was a man of considerable talent and great social qualities.

At the beginning of 1850 the following were resident lawyers of Greenville and members of the Bond county bar: Cornelius Lansing, Elam Rust, Tevis Greathouse, Judge S. P. Moore and Samuel Stevenson. Of these Judge Moore continued his residence the longer in Greenville, not removing until during the war or shortly thereafter. Tevis Greathouse was a man of much more than ordinary ability, fond of literature and an omniverous reader. After leaving Greenville, he practiced law until his death, in Vandalia.

Between 1855 and 1860 many new additions were made to the membership of the bar the most notable being the enrollment of Salmon A. Phelps, who can very appropriately be called its nestor. Judge Phelps was admitted to the bar in Mississippi in 1841 and moved to Pocahontas, Bond county, in 1844, living on a farm but practicing law

ABRAHAM MCNEILL, SR.,

One of the stockholders of the Vandalia Railroad, former banker, and a resident of Greenville 40 years.

both before justices of the peace and the courts of record at Greenville until 1855, when he moved to the county seat and was actively engaged in practice up to a few years ago. From the years 1859 to 1879 he and his sons had the bulk of the civil business of the county bar. Judge Phelps never liked the criminal practice and while he was frequently retained in the defense of cases, yet it was always distasteful to him. His honorable conduct, strict integrity, and disposition to discourage litigation has left its impress upon the younger members

RESIDENCE OF ABRAHAM MCNEILL, SR., Fourth Street

MRS. ALICE LINDLY,
Daughter of Mr. and Mrs. Abraham McNeill, one of Greenville's best known literary women.

HON. CICERO J. LINDLY,

Bond County's present member of the House of Representatives; ex-chairman of the Illinois Railroad and Warehouse Commission; ex-county judge of Bond county. A prominent figure in Illinois state campaigns for the past twenty years; was presidential elector in 1884; received the solid Republican vote of the Illinois Legislature in 1890 for United States Senator in the memorable contest against John M. Palmer, which vote was within two votes of election. Judge Lindly is extensively engaged in farming.

CHARLES E. DAVIDSON,

Former editor of the Greenville Sun,
ex-Master in Chancery of Bond
county; stockholder and manager
of the Greenville Lumber Company

RESIDENCE OF CHARLES E. DAVIDSON, South Fourth Street.

of the county bar. He has been a
man of exemplary habits, kind and
courteous and has the honor of living in his old age in the county
where he had resided for sixty-two
years, having the respect and love
of all his neighbors. Two of his
sons were admitted to the bar in
Greenville. One of them, Judge Alfred Phelps, living in Denver, is one
of the leading lawyers of the state
of Colorado, where he has by his
marked ability and high demand as
a lawyer, accumulated a large fortune. Another son, George S.
Phelps, was at one time State's Attorney of Bond county but later
moved to Leadville, Colorado, where
he held the positions of city judge
and district judge. He died at
Leadville about two years ago.

Four sons of Ira Kingsbury were
at different times members of the
county bar. The first to be admitted
was Judge A. N. Kingsbury in 1855.
After practicing a few years in this
county, he moved to Hillsboro,
where he was one of the leading
lawyers until the time of his death.
Dennis H. Kingsbury was admitted
to the bar about 1856 and continued
practice here until his death in
1893. He was a natural born lawyer, with all the instincts for special
pleading and forms of law; besides
he was an aggressive debater and a
hard fighter before a jury. He was
a man of strict integrity and while
of a combative disposition, which
frequently led him into personal en-
counters with his enemies, he was
strong in his friendships as well as
his enmities. He always command-

ed a fair share of the clientage of
the bar. He never allowed politics
or love for place to interfere with
his profession, but was its devotee
to the exclusion of all other masters.
Darius Kingsbury, after admission,
moved to Carlyle where he is still
engaged in the practice of law. John
Kingsbury, after practicing in
Greenville for a number of years,
retired, and lives on a farm south
of Greenville.

J. F. Alexander and A. G. Henry,
who afterwards became two of Bond
county's most distinguished citizens,
were admitted about the same time,
in 1857. Mr. Alexander was at one
time a member of the state senate
and was prominently identified with
the building of the Vandalia railroad and the Louisville and Nashville railroad. He was also at one

THE PRESSED BRICK PLANT OF THE GREENVILLE LUMBER COMPANY.

RESIDENCE OF MR. AND MRS. W. A. NORTHCOTT.

The Greenville residence of Hon. and Mrs. W. A. Northcott for many years. Recently sold by them to J. H. Livingston.

Hon. W. A. Northcott,

Who came to Greenville in 1879 and commenced the practice of law; Supervisor of
the Census in 1880; elected State's Attorney of Bond in 1882, and re-elected for
two terms; elected Head Consul of the Modern Woodmen of America in 1890 and
unanimously re-elected for six terms, finally resigning on account of ill health;
elected Lieutenant Governor of Illinois in 1896, and re-elected in 1900.   Moved to
Springfield, Ill., in June, 1905, to accept the United States district attorneyship.
Member of the law firm of Northcott, Hoff and Orr.

Mrs. W. A. Northcott.

Miss Amy Northcott.

NATHANIEL D. NORTHCOTT, now in business at Huntington, W. Va.

FORMER LAW OFFICE OF W. A. NORTHCOTT.
Now occupied by Ward Reid and Son.

WILLIAMSON PLANT,

First Secretary of the Vandalia Railroad, who held that office for many years with marked success.

SAMUEL B. HYNES, *Deceased.*

Son of the late Rev. Thomas W. Hynes; was first station agent at Greenville and at the time of his death was foreign freight agent for the Burlington system. Died on March 30, 1904.

JEDIAH F. ALEXANDER,

First President of the St. Louis, Vandalia and Terre Haute Railroad; county treasurer in 1853, state senator in 1870.

time grand master of the Odd Fellows of Illinois. He devoted but little attention to the practice of law, but was one of the best parliamentarians in southern Illinois, and had a wide and extensive acquaintance throughout the state. He was a man of elegant manners and strong intellectuality.

Judge A. G. Henry was county judge of Bond county for two terms, and also served two terms in the Illinois legislature. He is a man of strong native ability and uncompromising in his devotion to his political beliefs. Although at an advanced age and confined to his house most of the time by sickness, yet his

mind is clear and his memory good, he being a ready and entertaining conversationalist.

Job A. Cooper was born in Bond county and admitted to practice in 1859, was at one time circuit clerk of the county and was an active member of the bar during the few years he was connected with it.

Burning of the Vandalia Line depot, 7:30 p. m., July 22, 1884. Photograph loaned by Miss Nellie Morris.

D. B. EVANS, *Deceased.*
Circuit Clerk from 1884 to 1892.

E. E. ELLIOTT,
Present agent for the Vandalia Railroad; in service of the company 18 years.

P. BOLL,
Postmaster from 1870 to 1882.

Shortly after the war, he moved to Colorado and rapidly rose in distinction, becoming Governor of the state and one of its wealthiest and most prominent citizens. He died there a few years ago.

William H. Dawdy was admitted to the bar while residing in Vandalia but shortly afterward, in 1868, located in Greenville, where he has practiced law ever since and is still one of the most prominent members

of the bar. Judge Dawdy has been a member of the Court of Claims of the state and also assistant United States district attorney and state's attorney of Bond county. He is a strong advocate before a jury and

VIEW OF THE PENNSYLVANIA RAILROAD STATION.
Reading from left to right are L. S. Matherly, R. I. Clarkson, Agent Elliott and John Clanton.

J. Seaman,

One of Greenville's leading business men. Mayor from 1893 to 1897. President of the Library Board, and former President of the Board of Education. Head of the J. Seaman Hardware Company.

Lieutenant A. Owen Seaman, U. S. A.

Son of Mr. and Mrs. J. Seaman; a veteran of the Spanish-American war and an extensive traveler. Now stationed at Monteray, Cal., with the 15th Infantry.

Ewing Hunter,

Member J. Seaman Hardware Co.

Residence of J. Seaman, East College Avenue.

EMIL BRICE,
Member J. Seaman Hardware Co.

SAMUEL WALLACE,
Member J. Seaman Hardware Co.

MARCEL CALAME,
Member J. Seaman Hardware Co.

during the thirty-five years of practice at this bar has been on one side or the other of nearly every important contest. He is very fond of a story and is of a sociable and courteous disposition. He and Judge Phelps have done much toward giving the county bar its deserved reputation for fairness and honesty, both toward the court, jury and clients.

William A. Northcott, former Lieutenant Governor of Illinois, was admitted to the bar in West Virginia in 1877 but removed to Greenville

in 1879 and has continued in the practice of law ever since. Shortly after coming to Greenville, he formed a partnership with Dennis H. Kingsbury which continued until Mr. Northcott was elected State's Attorney in 1882. He held this office for three successive terms.

Judge Cicero J. Lindly entered upon the practice of law in Greenville in 1882 and held the office of county judge from 1886 to 1892. For a time he lived on his large and profitable farm three miles south of Greenville, but he has been engaged

in many prominent cases. He now resides in Greenville. Judge Lindly is widely known throughout the state of Illinois, having been chairman of the state railroad and warehouse commission and also having received the entire Republican vote for United States Senator in 1890, when Governor John M. Palmer was elected. Judge Lindly is an orator with a state reputation and is well grounded in the principles of law. He has been twice elected representative in the Illinois Legislature from the Forty-seventh Senatorial

WM. H. WILLIAMS, *Deceased*,
Fifty years a resident and business man of Greenville. Alderman from First Ward for 17 years.

J. C. MERRY, *Deceased*,
For many years a prominent farmer near Greenville.

PHINEAS B. CHAPMAN,
Who came to Greenville in 1867, and manufactured brick until his death May 12, 1901.

CLARENCE G. JACKSON,
Member of the firm of Davis and Jackson, Druggists.

district, and is now serving his second consecutive term as such representative.

F. W. Fritz was admitted to the bar in 1889 and immediately formed a partnership with W. A. Northcott which lasted until several years ago. He has been three times elected state's attorney of Bond county and has the past year retired from that office to pursue the practice of law, he having built a commodious law office on the north side of the public square. He is a man of strict integrity, a true friend, and hard

DR. N. H. JACKSON,
For twenty-five years a leading dentist. Former Alderman and former Member Board of Education.

worker in his profession. Mr. Fritz is a public speaker of considerable merit. He is prominently connected with his party, having advocated its principles from the stump since 1888.

C. E. Cook was admitted to the bar in Montgomery county and practiced for a few years at Raymond, locating at Greenville in 1889, where he is still a member of the bar. He

has a good clientage and is an industrious lawyer. He has been city attorney and also attorney for the Greenville Building and Savings Association nearly all the time since coming to Greenville. He is at present holding the office of Master-in-Chancery of Bond county, having been appointed by Judge Burroughs.

H. W. Park was admitted to the bar in Richmond county and located

J. E. WAFER,
Contractor and builder; Alderman from the Third Ward, and Mayor Pro Tem during summer of 1905. A resident of Greenville for many years.

RESIDENCE OF DR. N. H. JACKSON, West College Avenue.

T. P. MOREY,

Circuit clerk from 1876 to 1884; two terms as county superintendent of schools; ex-member Board of Education and member of the 40th General Assembly of the Illinois Legislature. A real estate dealer and prominent citizen

HENRY H. MOREY,

Graduate of the University of Illinois and now a law student there.

James M. Miller, L. H. Craig, H. H. Craig, Thomas Tiffin, Charles E. Davidson, Solon A. Enloe, L. E. Bennett, Joseph Streuber and Alfred Adams were all, for short periods members of the Greenville bar.

Clarence E. Hoiles was admitted to the bar in 1896 and soon became a member of the firm of Northcott, Fritz and Hoiles. He is a grandson of Charles Hoiles, who founded the banking house of Hoiles and Sons and belongs to one of the oldest and most prominent families in Bond Co. Mr. Hoiles was for several years a member of the law firm of Fritz and Hoiles and recently retired from the

in Greenville in 1891 and was connected with the firm of Northcott, Fritz and Hoiles until 1897, when

he opened an office by himself. He later formed a partnership with Judge Joseph Story, which continues to this day. Mr. Park is well learned in the law and was the tutor of Alfred Adams, Joseph Streuber and C. E. Hoiles.

D. R. GRIGG,

Who came to Greenville in 1857; in business 16 years, 13 years in his brick building on the east side of the square.

RESIDENCE OF T. P. MOREY, East Main Avenue.

MRS. E. A. GULLICK,
Wife of the late A. J. Gullick.

A. J. GULLICK, *Deceased*
Sheriff of Bond County from 1872 to
1878, and from 1880 to 1882.
Died in 1894.

commercial department of Greenville College, studied law and was
admitted to the bar in December,
1899. He was elected City Attorney in 1901, serving two years. On
February 1, 1904, he formed a partnership with Lieutenant Governor
Northcott, which still exists.

Editor's Note—Since the history
of the Bench and Bar was written
by Mr. Northcott, he has received
the federal appointment of United
State's District Attorney, and he
and Mr. Orr have moved from
Greenville to Springfield, Ill., where
they are still associated together,
in the practice of law.)

Greenville Postoffice

BY POSTMASTER A. L. HORD.

firm to take the position of Vice
President of the State Bank of
Hoiles and Sons, which he held until
February 1, 1905, when he and Mr.
Fritz again formed partnership.

Joseph H. Story was admitted to
the bar in the summer of 1897 and
was appointed county judge by
Governor Tanner in December of
that year, to fill the vacancy caused
by the resignation of John F. Harris
who was elected in 1894 but who
moved to Montana in 1897.

J. H. Allio was admitted to the
bar in November, 1897, but did not

commence active practice until
April, 1903, when he moved to
Greenville and opened a law office.
He was elected City Attorney of
Greenville without opposition April
19, 1904.

George L. Meyer was admitted to
the bar in June, 1898, and has
practiced in Greenville ever since.
He was elected State's Attorney of
Bond County in November, 1904,
running ahead of the county Republican ticket. He is a native of
Greenville, having been born here
February 7, 1865.

W. A. Orr, while principal of the

Ansel Birge, father of the Misses
Emma and Alice Birge, was the first
postmaster of Greenville. He was
commissioned December 12, 1825,
and his daughters still have the original commission. Tradition has
it that the first postoffice was located in the brick house that stood
across the street south of the John
Baumberger homestead in the west
part of town. For years it was kept
by the various storekeepers as a
"side line" to their mercantile business and it was moved about to different buildings in the west end
until it finally was located on the
public square, where it has since remained.

Lawson Robinson was the second
postmaster, having been commissioned September 28, 1829. The

WM. T. CARSON,
A merchant of Greenville from 1869
to 1873. Now justice of the peace,
real estate and insurance agent.

RESIDENCE OF MRS. E. A. GULLICK, West Main Avenue.

E. M. GULLICK,

A prominent business man; director of the Electric Light Co., and former Alderman.

M. V. DENNY, *Deceased*,

Former Cashier of the First National Bank; Ex-County Superintendent and Ex-County Clerk.

office again reverted to Ansel Birge April 26, 1831.

William S. Wait was the fourth postmaster, commissioned February 14, 1839. Albert Allen, a merchant, was commissioned as the fifth postmaster, February 24, 1841. Charles Hoiles, father of C. D. Hoiles, was the sixth postmaster, commissioned February 21, 1844, and had the office in the building now owned by J. M. Miller, and used as a barber shop on the south side of the square, east of the alley. Parmenas Bond was commissioned as the seventh postmaster April 30, 1849. The eighth postmaster was Franklin G. Morse, commissioned April 21. 1851: the ninth was Dr. T. S. Brooks, May 26, 1853, who had the office where J. V. Dixon's store now is: the tenth Samuel H. Crocker, November 24, 1854. Mr. Crocker had the office in the Denny building on the south side of the square. He was succeeded by J. B. Reid. August 5, 1856. Mr. Reid had the office in the building where Stubblefield's store now is. It was a frame building and afterwards burned. Mr. Reid resigned in 1861 and Wm. S. Colcord was commissioned the twelfth postmaster, February 12. 1861, and had the office on the west side of the square in the E. A. Floyd building.

Pangratz Boll was postmaster from September 17, 1870, until 1882. It was a fourth class office in 1870, but in a year Mr. Boll made it a third class office. He first had the office in his frame building, where the Schott building now stands on Second street. After seven years he moved it to the building where F. E. Watson's drug store now stands and after two or three years moved it to the frame building south of J. M. Hawley's jewelry store. A year later he moved it to the building now used as Joy's cloakroom and kept it there until he resigned and Lemuel Adams was appointed his successor February 5, 1882. Mr. Adams moved the office after several years to the George Hill building, where the H. H. Wirz

RESIDENCE OF E. M. GULLICK, West College Avenue.

S. M. THOMAS,
Proprietor of The Thomas House.

cigar store now does business. Col. Reid was again postmaster from March 15, 1886, until March 1, 1890, when C. K. Denny was commissioned and conducted the office in the Hill building until about six months before the end of his term, when he moved the office to the Sprague block, now occupied by the State Bank of Hoiles and Sons. Mr. Denny was succeeded by Frank T. Reid, June 21, 1894. Mr. Reid kept the office in the Sprague block for several years and then moved it to the Kingsbury building on the east side of the square, where it remained until July 1, 1901.

A. L. Hord, the eighteenth post-master, was commissioned March 31, 1898. He appointed C. F. Thraner assistant postmaster. On July 1, 1901, Mr. Hord moved the office to the new DeMoulin building on the west side of the public square, where it now remains. New fixtures replaced the old ones purchased by Postmaster Adams. The office was raised to second class on July 1, 1900. As the business of the office increased, rural carriers and then city carriers were added, the latter on September 1, 1903. Now the work of the office is done by Postmaster Hord, Assistant Postmaster Thraner, Clerks Harry N. Baumberger and Robert Potter, City Carriers J. L. McCracken and Oscar Wafer; Rural Carriers, H. H. Staub, Marshall Kirkham, J. C. Sanderson, C. T. Myers and Samuel Mueller.

For the year ending March 31, 1905, 5363 money orders were issued for $35,659.14, and 5326 were paid for $43,683.05. The postal receipts for the year amounted to $11,062.00. The amount paid out in salaries and rents was $10,410.-00.

The revenue in the matter of salaries brought into the town through the post office when Mr. Hord became postmaster was $2,220 a year, whereas in the year 1905 it increased to the sum of $10,410.

MRS. S. M. THOMAS,

roads, and in turn the Vandalia Line has been one of the principal makers of Greenville. The early settlers of Greenville had an eye single to the good of the town, for we read, in our early history, that the people of Greenville, in mass convention assembled, passed resolutions condemning the International Improvement System before it began to wreck the state treasury. With judgment equally as good as that which prompted opposition to this reckless expenditure, the people of Greenville took an interest in the old national road from Washington City to St. Louis.

Then came the agitation of the Mississippi and Atlantic railroad, a staunch supporter of which was Hon.

Greenville Railroads

GREENVILLE was the nestor of the Vandalia Line, one of the country's greatest trunk line rail-

MRS. MARY THOMAS, *Deceased.*
Founder of The Thomas House.

THE THOMAS HOUSE,
Established by Mrs. Mary A. Thomas in 1880, and now owned by Mr. and Mrs. S. M. Thomas.

DR. WM. T. EASLEY,

Twenty years a leading physician. Member Board of Health, ex-member and ex-president Board of Education. Surgeon for Vandalia Railroad 18 years.

RESIDENCE OF DR. WM. T. EASLEY, West College Avenue.

William S. Wait, one of Greenville's foremost citizens. This road was projected in 1835 and was agitated until February, 1854, when work was actually commenced, the intention being to connect Terre Haute with St. Louis, through Greenville, but the "Schuyler Fraud," which shocked all railroad enterprises, is assigned by Mr. Wait as the cause of the abandonment of the enterprise.

A charter for the "Highland and St. Louis railroad company" was obtained in 1859. The civil war was one of the causes of the failure of this road.

The Vandalia Line.

On February 10, 1865, a liberal charter was granted for the building of the present "Vandalia Railroad," then known as the "St. Louis, Vandalia and Terre Haute Railroad." Among the persons named as incorporators were the following Greenville men: William S. Smith, Charles Hoiles, William S. Wait, John B. Hunter, Williamson Plant, Andrew G. Henry, Jediah F.

Alexander and Thomas L. Vest.

Greenville and Bond county men led in the enterprise of building the road and were for many years the officers of the road. On Tuesday, January 17, 1867, the vote in Bond county to determine whether or not the county would take stock in the railroad resulted 1,018 for and 143 against taking stock. In the city of Greenville the vote stood 323 for and only 2 against. Bond county subscribed $100,000 and individuals in Greenville subscribed $46,000 more, besides $2,000 for a depot building. The $100,000 subscribed by Bond county was payable in fifteen annual installments, with 10 per cent interest per annum, all of

W. O. HOLDZKOM,

Former Alderman. Proprietor of the Red Front Notion Store, in business in Greenville many years.

RESIDENCE OF PROF. W. E. MILLIKEN,

RESIDENCE OF C. W. SEAWELL.

C. W. SEAWELL,
U. S. Internal Revenue Agent; Member Illinois Legislature in 1887 and again in 1894. A resident of Greenville 32 years.

which was promptly paid. Greenville people paid their first subscription to Williamson Plant at his office in the Hoiles Block.

At a meeting held at Vandalia, April 27, 1865, J. F. Alexander and William S. Wait were appointed commissioners to take stock in Bond county and J. Ravold, H. H. Wait and H. H. Smith were elected members of the Board of Incorporators for Bond county.

R. K. Dewey and S. B. Hynes procured much of the right of way through Bond county, and Mr. Hynes went on through to East St. Louis in this work. In the spring of 1867, the surveyors were at work and by December, 1868, the rails were laid to the depot in Greenville, "thanks to the energy and indomitable perseverance of a few Greenville people." One of the first locomotives on the Vandalia Line was named "Greenville."

Greenville made the first move for the Vandalia Line. Greenville kept the matter agitated and Greenville and Bond county advanced the money required to build the first twenty miles of the road, and that at a time when great doubts were continuously expressed as to the success of the enterprise, by the stockholders themselves.

On Tuesday, December 8, 1868, the first regular passenger train left the Greenville depot at 6:30 a. m. in charge of Mr. Gwynn, for St. Louis. It was a big event but owing to the extreme cold Greenville was not extensively represented,

T. R. ROBINSON,
Manager of the local Postal Telegraph office. Member Board of Education.

RESIDENCE OF J. E. HILLIS, East College Avenue.

JOSEPH F. WATTS,

Sheriff of Bond County from 1886 to 1890; county treasurer from 1894 to 1898, ex-alderman, and resident of Greenville 18 years.

RESIDENCE OF J. F. WATTS, East College Avenue.

nevertheless quite a number boarded the train and made the trip to St. Louis and return. It being the first trip the passengers kept coming and the conductor kept holding the train, waiting for such as were in sight until the train was late.

But at last the bell sounded and the first passenger train in the history of Greenville moved off.

After that, track-laying progressed rapidly to the eastward. The good people of Greenville gave the knights of the pick and shovel frequent suppers and entertainments. At first there were only two trains a day, one each way.

In 1869 the town authorities voted $3,000 for depot improvements. On Wednesday, June 8, 1870, the first through passenger train went through from Indianapolis. Greenville people boarded the train and the trip was made a festive occasion. Soon after the Vandalia Line put on fourteen trains a day.

The first wreck at Greenville was on October 20, 1870, when the express due at 11:15 a. m., collided with an extra freight, killing M. P. Mansheam, the express messenger, and injuring two others.

The first meeting of the Board of Corporators held at Vandalia November 14, 1865, elected nine directors, among whom were William S. Smith, and Williamson Plant of Greenville. J. P. M. Howard, of Effingham, was the first president, and Williamson Plant, of Greenville, was the first secretary of the road.

The railroad received its first severe blow in the death, on July 17, 1865, of Hon. William S. Wait, the father of H. W. Wait, F. F. Wait and Mrs. Louisa Ravold of this city and

J. E. DONNELL,

A former Greenville contractor, now a resident of California.

RESIDENCE OF K. E. GRIGG, West College Avenue.

JOHN L. WATTS,

Deputy county treasurer 1894-7. Now chief clerk
of the U. S. district and circuit courts at Peoria,
Illinois.

EDWARD E. WATTS,

Chief Deputy U. S. Marshal at Danville, Ill., having
held the office from 1889 to 1893, and from 1895
to that date.

W. S. Wait, deceased, whose widow Mrs. Adele Wait, and children, now live in Greenville. Mr. Wait was the earnest leader and judicious friend of the enterprise and his lamented death robbed the promoters of his wise and mature judgment.

At a meeting in January, 1867, a code of laws was adopted and Greenville was designated as the general office of the company. At the annual election in January, 1867, J. P. M. Howard was re-elected president, Williamson Plant, secretary and William S. Smith, treasurer. The following April Mr. Howard gave up the presidency and

J. F. Alexander, of Greenville, was chosen in his place. This gave Greenville all the officers of the company besides three of the nine directors. At the 1868 election five of the nine directors were Greenville men namely, J. F. Alexander, W. S. Smith, A. G. Henry, Wm. S. Wait, Jr., and Francis Dressor. Mr. Alexander continued as president until

WILLIAM BAUMBERGER,

A former resident, now of Peoria, Ill.

RESIDENCE OF FRANK ABRAMS.

W. V. WEISE, *Deceased*,

For many years President of the Weise & Bradford Cor poration. Prominent in business and social life for many years.

WEISE AND BRADFORD'S GREENVILLE STORE.

The Firm of Weise & Bradford.

The firm now known as Weise & Bradford was started by the present management in 1879 when W. V. Weise bought the interest of P. C. Reed, in the firm of Jandt & Reed, the name being changed to Jandt & Weise. This name was continued a number of years when the entire interest of Mr. Jandt was absorbed by W. V. Weise & Geo. D. Bradford, who was then a member of the firm in charge of the parent store at Pocahontas, Ill., the name of the Pocahontas store being changed from H. A. Jandt & Co. to Weise, Bradford & Co., and the Greenville store to Weise & Bradford. This management was continued until 1892 when Mr. Bradford opened the third Star store in Waverly, Ill. At this time Henry Ballman and J. M. Appel were admitted as partners in the Pocahontas store. In 1893 the business was incorporated and Walter White and Henry Hair were admitted as stockholders in the Greenville store. In 1996 Mr. White was transferred to Vandalia, Ill., to manage the fourth Star store and Chas. V. Weise and Geo. V. Weise absorbed the stock held by him. In 1896 the management of the Greenville store was assumed by the two latter named, Mr. W. V. Weise retiring from the active life he had led so long.

In November of 1901 occurred the

GEORGE V. WEISE,

Secretary and treasurer of the Weise and Bradford Corporation, and resident manager of the Greenville branch.

RESIDENCE OF GEORGE V. WEISE.

CHARLES V. WEISE,
Member of the Weise and Bradford Corporation and manager of the Tuscola, Ill., branch.

death of W. V. Weise, senior member and founder of the business. No change occurred in the business until the summer of 1902 when Chas. V. Weise opened the fifth Star store in Tuscola, Ill. Geo. V. Weise assuming full control of the Greenville store. This arrangement still exists.

It has always been the policy of this firm to advance capable employees and three branches of the original firm are now managed by men who were formerly salesmen. They are Joe Murdock, of Bradford and Murdock, Virden, Ill.; W. C. White of Bradford & White, Vandalia, Ill. and E. V. Buchanan of Bradford & Buchanan, Sumner, Ill. The Greenville store which is more closely related to this history has increased its outlet very materially during the last few years and is recognized everywhere as one of the most complete stores of its kind in Southern Illinois. The officers of the concern are Geo. D. Braford, President; Chas. V. Weise, Vice President and Geo. V. Weise, Secretary and Treasurer.

February 15, 1871. William S. Smith was treasurer from January 18, 1867, to April 14, 1869. He was succeeded by Williamson Plant, who was treasurer until February 15, 1871. Mr. Plant was also secretary for many years. C. D. Hoiles was assistant secretary for several years and his son, Guy B. Hoiles, was assistant secretary at the time of the merger of all the lines in December, 1904.

S. B. Hynes, a son of Rev. Thomas W. Hynes, was the first station agent and was afterwards one of the most prominent railroad men of the west,

WARD REID,
Ex-City Clerk; Circuit Clerk from 1892 to 1904; Secretary Building and Savings Association; now in the real estate, loan, abstract and insurance business.

holding high and responsible positions with some of the greatest railroads in the country. He was followed as station agent by J. E. Hunt. M. W. Van Valkenberg was the third station agent serving until 1876, when he was succeeded by W. S. Ogden, who held the place for twenty years and died in 1896, in office. John Geismann was the next agent, serving until August 1, 1903,

when he was succeeded by Edgar E. Elliott, who holds the position at the present time. Mr. Elliott was born August 6, 1866, entered the service of the railroad March 12, 1888, as clerk; was promoted in April, 1893, to the position of cashier at the Brazil, Ind., freight station; in October, 1898, to the position of Agent at Greenup and on August 1, 1903, to the position of

RESIDENCE OF WARD REID, East College Avenue.

FRANK P. JOY,

Head of the firm of F. P. Joy & Co. Mayor of
Greenville from 1901 to 1903. Member of the Library Board.

agent at Greenville.

The name "Pennsylvania Line" is
now used instead of "The Vandalia
Line," the change having been made
recently.

Jacksonville & St. Louis R. R.

President W. S. Hook in September, 1880, wrote to Wm. S. Smith to
confer with the people of Greenville about a road known as the
Jacksonville and St. Louis, then
built as far as Litchfield. On October 1, of that year, Mr. Hook came
to Greenville and twenty-five business men met him at the First National Bank. He wanted a bonus of
$25,000 and the right of way in
consideration of coming to Greenville. After several months parley-
ing Greenville, in 1882, offered
$15,000, the complete right of way
and ample depot grounds, but the
offer was rejected and the road went
to Smithboro.

Chicago, Greenville & Southern.

After the J. & St. L. had passed
Greenville by and had been in oper-
ation for several years, President
Hook, on November 23, 1891, offer-
ed to build a "spur" from Durley to
Greenville, a distance of four miles,
for $25,000 and the right of way.
The solemn promise was made that

the road would be extended south
in a few years to Carlyle. The offer was accepted and the road was
named the Chicago, Greenville and
Southern, but as years passed and it
went no farther south, the name
was facetiously changed to the
"Chicago, Greenville, and Stop."
The first train over this road was
run in August, 1892. In honor of

the completion of the road and because of their liberal subscriptions,
the people of Greenville were given
a free ride to Springfield in October, 1892, and 425 people took advantage of the opportunity to visit
the capital. The road continued in
operation until January 3, 1903,
when it suspended business after
having been sold in pursuance of a
decree of the Federal Court. The
four mile stretch of track was torn
up by the purchaser in April, 1903,
and now nothing remains to show
for the $25,000 invested in it by
Greenville's citizens.

Numerous other railroad projects
have been agitated in Greenville,
among them the St. Louis, Shelby-
ville and Detroit, and the "Black
Diamond Line" as well as some
other north and south railroads.

Greenville can feel proud of the
part it played in the origination and
construction of the Vandalia Line.
From the start this line became one
of the greatest railroads in the
country, having been leased and
operated by the great Pennsylvania
System until 1900, when it became
by purchase a part of the great parent trunk line. It is the connect-
ing link between Indianapolis and
St. Louis and as such carries the
traffic of the great Pennsylvania
System. This traffic now supports
ten passenger trains each way per
day, an aggregate passenger service not equalled by any other line
in the west. There is no nook or
corner in the country where this
popular railroad is not known and
it enjoys a reputation of possessing
the best roadbed, the best passenger
service and the finest as well as the
fastest trains in the country.

RESIDENCE OF F. P. JOY, East College Avenue

RESIDENCE OF W. A. JOY, East Main Avenue.

F. P. Joy & Co.

This firm is one of our largest business houses doing a general merchandise business throughout the city and entire county.

F. P. Joy & Co. in connection with W. S. Dann & Co., whom they succeeded without a change of management, has done a continuous and ever increasing business for thirty-five years. On the ground where now stands the building devoted to their general merchandise stock, in 1870, stood a small one room store, where Mr. W. S. Dann, in that year, opened a stock of general merchandise. Within a few months Mr. F. P. Joy, who now heads the firm, became associated with Mr. Dann and for the last twenty-five years he has had the larger part of the active management of the business.

The store, thus started in the seventy's, soon became widely known throughout the county. In 1880 and again in 1886 additions were made that more than trebled their space. Then in 1899 the necessity for still further room compelled the firm to move their clothing stock into the large and splendidly equipped room on the east side of the square, known as the Kesler building. They now have a complete Clothing Emporium under the management of three of the firm's best salesmen, Mr. Harry E. Maynard, Mr. K. E. Grigg, and Mr. Wm. H. Fink.

In the year just passed extensive improvements have been made in their general store building, including a remodeling of the shoe room, a new office, also a rest and toilet room and a room in the rear of the dry goods room for their stock of ladies' ready made garments.

Mr. W. S. Dann died in 1893, and

F. P. JOY & COMPANY'S STORE.

FIRM MEMBERS AND CLERKS OF F. P. JOY & COMPANY.

Top Row reading from left to right—Miss Lizzie C. Colcord, bookkeeper; George W. Christian, member of firm; Clyde Tate, shoe department; Will Hobbs, grocery department; Clifford Borror, deliveryman; Samuel Spratt, deliveryman.

Second Row—P. H. Tate, underwear, hosiery and notions; W. B. Fink, grocery department; L. Barnes, grocery department; Wm. H. Fink, clothing department, Miss Bertha J. Drayton, saleslady dress goods department; Miss Alice J. Colcord, cashier.

Third Row—Walter A. Joy, dress goods department; K. E. Grigg, clothing department; G. A. Colcord, staple department; A. Maynard, shoe department; S. C. White, carpet department; Harry E. Maynard, clothing department.

F. P. JOY & COMPANY'S ANNEX, Clothing store.

in 1895 the name of the firm was changed to F. P. Joy & Co., the "Company" consisting of several of the firm's oldest salesmen. It might be of interest to insert that Mr. Dann was one of those most interested in the founding of Greenville College. While he only lived to see the opening of the College, he was very deeply interested and gave liberally and was intending to do much larger things for the college when he was called from this earth.

F. P. Joy & Co. in their general store employ fifteen to eighteen clerks, and in their clothing department, three or four more, all of whom are thoroughly interested in making a success of the business. The stock carried comprises all general merchandise, including groceries, shoes, carpets, clothing, fancy and staple dry goods and ladies' ready made goods of all kinds.

MR. AND MRS. C. K. DENNY,
Mr. Denny was Postmaster of Greenville from 1890 to 1894.

SAMUEL McGOWAN,
A resident of Greenville for forty-four years, justice of the Peace for sixteen years.

Greenville's Big Fires

THE first fire of which there is record took place in 1824, when Mr. Kirkpatrick's log house burned. A woman had been picking over cotton, which was raised here then, and while she was absent some of the children set the pile on fire. The nearest water was supplied by a spring, far down the long sand hill to the west and the log house was destroyed before water could be thrown on the flames. It was about this time that fire obliterated the boundary lines of the place.

There were no other big fires until the brick court house burned March 24, 1883. Smoke was first seen issuing out of the southwest corner of the roof. W. A. Northcott, Robert Donnell and others went into the garret to fight the flames, but there was no water system and the bucket brigade was inadequate. The energies of the crowd were directed toward saving the records and this was accomplished. In half an hour the roof was all ablaze and in an hour the dome fell in with a crash, sending embers flying high in the air. These fell on adjacent buildings and they were preserved only by dint of hard fighting. The building cost $9,000. The insurance was $7,000.

The next fire of consequence occurred February 4, 1891, on the west side of the square. The frame building of J. H. Livingston, occupied by Philip Diehl, Charles Wolridge's notion store, the Yarbrough property owned by J. M. Miller and occupied by C. H. Shields, photographer, F. Parent's building, occupied by J. W. Hastings, the McCord hotel, owned by J. M. Miller and D. H. Kingsbury, were destroyed. The loss amounted to sev-

M. S. OUDYN,
Former Mayor Pro Tem. One of the proprietors of Oudyn's Book Store.

RESIDENCE OF MRS. ELIZA JETT, West College Avenue.

A View of Montrose Cemetery.

College Avenue, Looking West from Greenville College.

SOME VIEWS IN AND NEAR GREENVILLE.

A. L. Hord,
Postmaster of Greenville; a prominent business
man and citizen for many years.

The DeMoulin Block,
The Postoffice is located in this building.

Employees of the Greenville Postoffice.
Left to right—J. L. McCracken, city carrier; J. O. Wafer, city carrier; H. N. Baumberger, clerk; Robert Potter,
clerk; C. F. Thraner, assistant postmaster; H. H. Staub, Marshall Kirkham, J. C. Sanderson, Will Hair,
and Samuel Mueller, rural carriers.

W. D. DONNELL,
A leading business man. Ex-Alderman from the First Ward.

RESIDENCE OF W. D. DONNELL, North Third Street.

eral thousand dollars. The fire was caused by a defective flue.

On September 25, 1891, the fine Export Mill and Peter Saile's apple evaporator, both the largest industries of their kind in this section of the state, were totally destroyed by fire, which originated in the evaporator from an unknown cause. The mill was 70x160 feet and was owned by Charles Valier, C. H. Seybt, Charles and Emil Broeker. The loss was $150,000. Mr. Saile's loss was $4,000. This was the most expensive fire in the history of the city.

November 2, 1892, Jernigan's livery stable and some small buildings nearby were destroyed, several horses perishing. John Schlup, Sr., a well known citizen, died during the fire, of heart failure, superinduced by over-exertion and excitement.

Fire of unknown origin started

in the rear of J. M. Miller's shoe store on the southwest corner of the square, July 31, 1893. The third story of the Miller building, known as the old National Bank building, was destroyed, and the Sun office, Wm. Akhurst, grocer, C. W. Watson, druggist, and Hoiles and Sons suffered damage to the extent of $11,000.

Breuchaud's elevator was burned June 10, 1894, with a loss of $18,000. A spark from an engine started the fire.

Blanchard's mill was destroyed by fire of unknown origin October 22, 1897. The loss was $3,500. The following day, October 23, 1897, fire, which started from gasoline in the feed store of Wm. Denham, destroyed the Presbyterian church and the feed store. The loss was $2,600.

The north half of the west side

of the public square was destroyed by fire August 15, 1899. The fire was of unknown origin and destroyed the buildings of Ed DeMoulin, George Grafe, G. D. Chaffee and Hentz's livery barn, beside many stocks of goods. The loss was $10,425 with $2,775 insurance.

The newly completed Greenville Milk Condenser was destroyed by fire on the morning of October 29, 1902. The origin was unknown, the loss was $6,000 with no insurance.

November 18, 1902, fire, which started in a barn on the Kingsbury property, damaged Joy and Co.'s An-

STORE OF W. D. DONNELL & CO. STORE OF WISE, COX AND TITUS.

E. S. TITUS,
Member of the firm of Wise, Cox and Titus. Worshipful Master Greenville Lodge No. 245 A. F. and A. M.

EDMOND DEMOULIN, Mayor of Greenville.

Edmond DeMoulin came to Greenville in October, 1886, and has been a resident here ever since. Mr. DeMoulin served one term as Alderman of the Third Ward and was re-elected Mayor for the fourth time in 1905. He is the founder of the factory of DeMoulin Brothers and Company and is president of the corporation.

MRS. EDMOND DEMOULIN.

RESIDENCE OF MAYOR EDMOND DEMOULIN,
Photographed by himself by moonlight on a snowy night.

ULYSSES S. DeMOULIN.

Born October 3rd, 1871; A citizen of Greenville since February 13th, 1894; Married
Miss Emma Diehl of this city, December 3rd, 1897; Is President and General Manager of the Greenville Electric Light, Heat and Power Company and is Vice President and General Manager of DeMoulin Brothers and Company.

Mrs. Ulysses S. DeMoulin,

Residence of Ulysses S. DeMoulin.

THE MANUFACTURING PLANT OF DEMOULIN BROTHERS AND COMPANY.

This was the first factory ever located in Greenville. The business was started in a small way by Edmond DeMoulin in 1892, and on February 13th, 1894, Edmond and Ulysses S. DeMoulin entered into a partnership in the name of Ed DeMoulin and Brother. The business grew rapidly from the beginning and over one hundred people are now employed in the manufacture of band and society uniforms, lodge supplies, banners, badges, etc.

On December 19, 1905, the firm was incorporated under the laws of the state of Illinois and the following officers were elected: Edmond DeMoulin, President; Ulysses S. DeMoulin, Vice President and General Manager; H. C. Diehl, Secretary and Treasurer; Edmond DeMoulin, Ulysses S. DeMoulin and Erastus DeMoulin, Directors.

The building is four stories, furnishing 27,000 square feet of space and is well equipped with the most up-to-date machinery, is well lighted and ventilated and has good shipping facilities, having its private railroad switch.

GROUP OF EMPLOYES OF THE FACTORY OF DEMOULIN BROTHERS & COMPANY.

RESIDENCE OF PHILIP DIEHL.

PHILIP DIEHL,

Was two years a member of the House of Delegates from the Sixth Ward, St. Louis. In business in Greenville for 19 years; Introduced the method of butchering hogs in the summer time.

nex, J. E. Hillis, The Sun office, F. Parent's bakery and others. The fire was controlled without the loss of buildings. The damage was about $600.

About three o'clock on the morning of October 27, 1904, fire from unknown cause started in the base-

ment of the Seaman Hardware Company's store and by daylight the Morse block, owned by the J. B. White estate, Miss Lucy Smith's building, Mrs. M. V. Allen's building and Mrs. August Pierron's building were in ruins. The Seaman Hardware Co., W. W. Hussong and Co., W. O. Holdzkom, J. A. Johnson, Graff and Eppestine, Dr. W. T. Easley, George O. Morris, the Odd Fellows, the Court of Honor, the Rebekahs, the Maccabees, and the Women's Relief Corps, C. E. Cook and Dr. M. L. Ravold were burned out. It was the most disastrous fire in the city's history, taking into consideration the number of people affected. The total loss was about

$50,000, with about $26,000 insurance. The handsome new business houses known as the Grafe building, the Seaman building, the Hussong Cash Mercantile Company's building and the Miller-Wise building have been erected on the site of the burnt district.

GREENVILLE'S WATER SUPPLY

A BODY of water, in a bed of quicksand underlies the entire city of Greenville, and numerous springs gush from the hills on the north and west of the city.

The first settlers, George Davidson, Paul Beck and Asahel Enloe, located in the west part of town near the springs to obviate any trouble for water. Those later settling farther up in town carried all the water they used from the springs and from Wash Lake.

In 1822 the first attempt was made to sink wells. The first well was dug in the middle of the street where Main and Sixth intersect. The second at the intersection of Third and College and the next was at Second and Main. These wells were dug square and were curbed with wood. An oldfashioned windlass was used for drawing water. Owing to the elevated ground on which Greenville stands it required deep digging to get to water, and the wells were from seventy to ninety feet deep.

Two people met death in these wells. William Gray was in the act

RESIDENCE OF ERASTUS DEMOULIN, Washington Avenue.

LOUIS LATZER,
President of the Helvetia Milk Condensing Company.

HELVETIA MILK CONDENSING CO

JOHN WILDI,
Secretary and Treasurer of the Helvetia Milk Condensing Company.

The Helvetia Milk Con=
⌁ densing Company ⌁

The plant is well located in regard to trackage facilites, drainage and sanitary surroundings. The buildings consist of a power house, the condensing plant proper, canmaking department and a number of warehouses for the storage of metals, box lumber and the finished product. They are all substantial structures, mostly two stories high, and cover over two acres of ground. The machinery in every department is of the latest construction, and several of the apparatus used have been built according to plans original with the Company or persons connected therewith. A striking feature noticed by the visitors is the neatness and cleanliness which prevails throughout the plant. It was established in 1899, and several additions have since been made, so that now it has sufficient capacity for handling about 125,000 pounds of milk daily. The investment in buildings, machinery and materials is about $100,000, and the average monthly expenditures for milk and labor is about $26,000. The product is consumed principally within the United States, but it is also shipped to all parts of the world, including the Islands of the Seas. You cannot travel in any country with exception of some parts of

Europe where you do not find it. The plant has been in charge of its present Manager, Mr. Adolph Meyer, ever since it was established. The main office of the Company is located at Highland, Ill., where the Company was organized in 1885, and where its magnificent home plant is located. It also operates a third plant at Delta, Ohio.

The Company was organized by some of the leading business men in Highland, in 1885. Its first board of directors consisted of Dr. John B. Knoebel, President; John Wildi, Secretary and Treasurer; Louis Latzer, Fritz Kaeser and Geo. Roth, Members, but for many years up to this date the board of directors has been composed as follows: Louis Latzer, President; Fritz Kaeser, Vice President; John Wildi, Secretary and Treasurer; Adolph Meyer and C. W. Buck, Members.

of getting into the bucket to go down to the bottom of the well in the southeast corner of the square, when the rope parted and he was precipitated to the bottom, a distance of 82 feet. When Gray was taken out he was still alive but he died the next day in great agony. A boy by name Cornelius Hildreth fell into the well at the crossing of Sixth and Main and was instantly killed.

In 1849 another well was dug in

ADOLPH MEYER,
Manager of the Greenville Plant of the Helvetia Milk Condensing Company.

the orchard between the J. P. Garland property and the home of Rev. Stafford, on Second street. Seven men formed a company and dug to a depth of 75 feet, when the sand caved in, the cholera epidemic came and the laborers fled the town, leaving Mr. Garland to finish the work himself.

Rear View of a Portion of the Helvetia Milk Condensing Plant.

W. A. McLain,

Member of the firm of McLain and Cable; member board of Education and a prominent citizen for many years

S. M. Harnetiaux,

City Clerk, 1901-2; Proprietor of The Busy Bee Restaurant.

Frank J. Cable.

Member of the firm of McLain and Cable, and a prominent business man for a number of years.

In the fifties these wells gave evidence of caving in and were filled up. Twenty five years after it had been filled up the well on the southeast corner of the square sunk, leaving a hole ten feet deep. A similar depression has been found there several times since.

During the seventies the question of an adequate water supply for the city was agitated and in May 1878 the city employed Richard Strout to make a survey for water works. Prior to this, in October 1877, a petition was circulated by C. D. Hoiles asking the city council to appoint a committee to make profiles, estimates and measurements for water works. On December 10, 1877, C. E. Gray of St. Louis made the estimates and measurements. It was then the plan to tap the springs in the north part of town and the fall from the north end of

Rear View of a Portion of the Helvetia Milk Condensing Company's Plant.

THE PLANT OF THE GREENVILLE MILK CONDENSING COMPANY.

Third street was then estimated at 30,000 gallons a day, sufficient for a city twice the size of Greenville at that time.

It was not until the election of April 17, 1884, that the city voted an appropriation for water works. The vote stood 323 for issuing $18,000 water works bonds to 71 against. At that time it was the understanding that the pumps be located in the north part of town, but later the plans were changed by the city council to the present location in the south part of town, near the Vandalia depot. On April 29, 1885, the first test of the system was made and proved satisfactory. The water works plant is owned by the city but is operated under contract by the Greenville Electric Light, Heat and Power Co.

Cyclone Hose Company No. 1.

By Charles F. Thraner.

Cyclone Hose Company No. 1 was organized May 23, 1885. The following were the organizers of the company: Albert Baumberger, Louis Derleth, Charles G. Derleth, Philip Diehl, Jacob Dowell, William H. Evans, August Faust, Vallee Harold, Ed Heussy, W. O. Holdzkom, Albert W. Holdzkom, N. M. Hurley, William Leidel, Jr., William Leppard, G. L. Loggins, Henry Ostrom, Frank Parent, Sr., Ward Reid, John Schmelzer, Henry Shaw, Charles H. Shields, Thomas A. Stevens, Charles F. Thraner, E. D. Wallace, Samuel Wannamaugher, John Yarbrough, W. Daly Zimmerman—total 27.

The following were the first officers: E. D. Wallace, Foreman; N. M. Hurley, First Assistant; W. O. Holdzkom, Second Assistant; C. F.

Thraner, Secretary and Treasurer; L. Derleth, Philip Diehl, A. W. Holdzkom and S. Wannamaugher, Wheelmen; Ed Heussy, Wm. Leidel, Wm. Leppard, Henry Shaw and W. D. Zimmerman, Branchmen. There were no plugmen until 1892.

Cyclone Hose Company No. 1 was incorporated under the laws of Illinois during the year 1887, and since that time three directors have been added to the lists of officers. The first directors were Ward Reid, Vallee Harold and C. F. Thraner.

The company has responded to seventy-six fire calls since its organization twenty years ago, an average of nearly four per year. There were no fires in 1889 and 1895.

The present officers of the company are: L. Derleth, Foreman; F.

N. Blanchard, First Assistant; L. Senn, Second Assistant; C. F. Thraner, Secretary and Treasurer; F. H. Floyd, George Price, Ab Near, C. Sapp, Wheelmen; C. L. Abbott, Al Chamberlain, E. M. Davis, James Mulford and Al White, Branchmen; J. Dowell and G. L. Loggins, Plugmen; H. N. Baumberger, F. N. Blanchard, E. M. Davis, P. Diehl, Ab Near and L. Senn, Fire Police; J. L. McCracken, Ab Near and J. Dowell, Directors. The Chemical Engine Company is composed of H. N. Baumberger, John Buscher, J. L. McCracken, Lee Loyd, J. A. Scott, J. Schulp and T. D. Stevenson members with F. N. Blanchard, Captain.

The Ladies' Library Association

(NOTE—The following paper, furnished by Mrs. Louisa (Wait) Ravold, one of the first and most active members of the Ladies' Library Association, is, in substance, the same as that placed in the corner stone of the new Carnegie Library.)

FOR nearly half a century the Ladies' Library has been an institution of the city of Greenville which has given great satisfaction to those who appreciate the influence of books and periodicals upon the rising generation.

As the shelves of the Ladies' Library were gradually filled with the choicest of literature, history, poetry, etc. and the books were circulated amongst the community, the benefit which they were doing was soon apparent and there was no one who did not feel a just pride in the good work which had been done.

F. N. BLANCHARD & CO.'S ROLLER MILLS.

View of the west side of the square on the occasion of the J. Seaman Hardware Co. stove drawing, September 3, 1904.

Ruins of the fire of October 27, 1904, when the west side of the square, with the exception of the DeMoulin Block was wiped out. Loss $45,000.

DR. E. P. POINDEXTER,

Former member of the Illinois Legislature and a
practicing physician of Greenville.

PETER SAILE,

Greenville Business man from 1878 to 1891; now
a resident of Batavia, N. Y.

In the year of 1855 some quantities of yellow covered literature having been brought into the town, many of the most intelligent mothers in the city became alarmed for the welfare of the minds and morals of their children, and determined that a more healthy diet should be provided.

Some prominent ladies, among whom were notably Mrs. Almira Morse, Mrs. S. Hutchinson, Mrs. Sarah Wait, Mrs. Robert Stewart and a few others, began immediately proselyting amongst their friends and neighbors with such good effect that it was but a short time before there were quite a number of ladies who were willing and glad to assist in the enterprise of starting a circulating library.

WM. T. HARLAN,

For a number of years a teacher in the schools of Bond county. Elected Co. Superintendent of Schools in November, 1898, which position he still holds.

DR. DON V. POINDEXTER,

A practicing physician of Greenville, in partnership with his father, Dr. E. P. Poindexter. Elected coroner of Bond county in November, 1904.

E. R. GUM,

Deputy Sheriff of Bond county since 1902; was raised on a farm and has resided in the county all his life.

WM. D. MATNEY,
County Clerk of Bond county since 1894; President Board of Education in 1903; Sergeant Co. K 54th Ill. Vols., serving three years and ten months in the Civil War. Resident of Bond since October, 1883.

MRS. WM. D. MATNEY,
Deputy County Clerk.

Ex-Sheriff J. E. Wright,   Bennie Wright.   Mrs. J. E. Wright,
Sheriff from 1898 to 1902; City   (nee Dorris)
Marshal, 1893-4.   Harry Wright.   Lucien Wright, Deceased.

RESIDENCE OF JOHN H. LADD.

JOHN H. LADD,

County Treasurer. Born in Oldham County, Ky. At age of 19 enlisted in Union Army in 1861; Co. B, 6th Ky. Inft. Wounded at the battle of Stone River, and disabled. Was four years supervisor of Lagrange township; elected county treasurer in 1902; Ex-Commander of Colby Post No. 301, G. A. R.

COUNTRY RESIDENCE OF A. J. SHERBURNE.

A. J. SHERBURNE,

Who commenced railroading in 1861 and was one of the first engineers on the Vandalia Line. Was engineer 19 years and passenger conductor 5 years.

JOSEPH H. STORY.

County Judge of Bond County, having been appointed in 1898 and twice elected to that office. Member of law firm of Park and Story and a prominent Republican politician.

H. W. PARK, Lawyer.

Member firm of Park and Story; Ex-City Treasurer of Greenville; For several years attorney for the Sorento Building and Loan Association.

NED C. SHERBURNE,

A former resident, now state deputy for the M. W. A. for Ohio, residing at Newark, O.

E. D. WALLACE,

Well known contractor.

JOHN BREUCHAUD,

Owner of Breuchaud's elevators and lumber yards.

GEORGE L. MEYER,

A resident of Bond for 37 years; taught school 10
years; Graduate of the High School, Almira College and the Illinois Wesleyan University Law
College; Elected State's Attorney of Bond County in the fall of 1904.

DR. S. E. YECK,

Formerly a resident of Greenville, now practicing
medicine in Coffeen.

F. PARENT.

Proprietor of Parent's Bakery.

DANIEL LUTZ,

Alderman from 1900 to 1904, now
a resident of Vandalia.

FRANK HENTZ,

Proprietor of Hentz's livery barn.

MRS. JOHN L. BUNCH.

JOHN L. BUNCH.

Raised on a farm in southern Bond county; Deputy County Clerk several years; two terms city clerk of Greenville; elected circuit clerk and ex-officio Recorder in 1904.

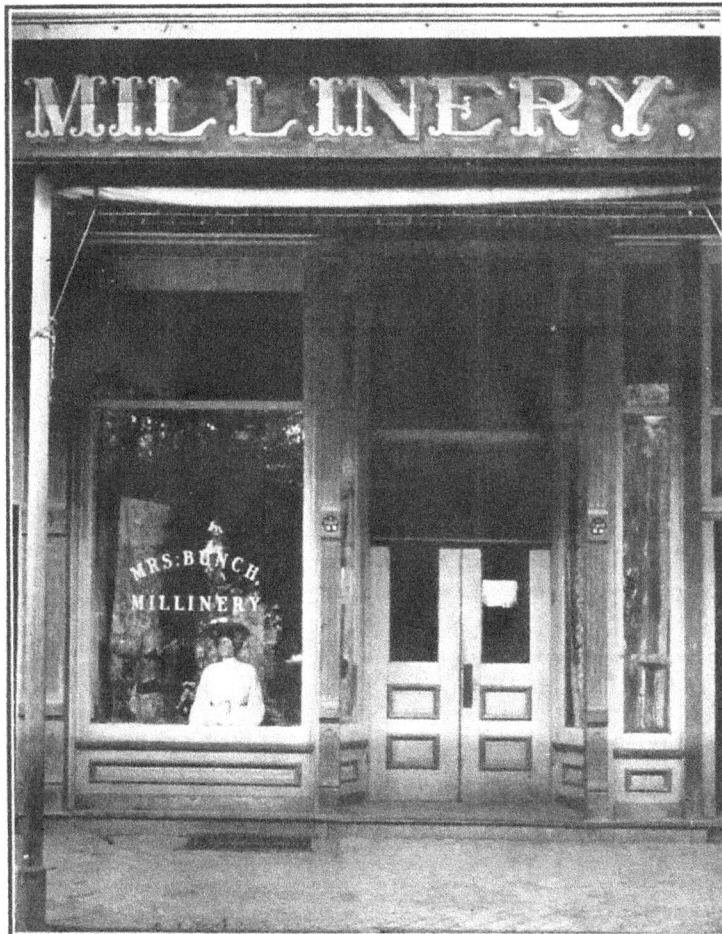

MRS. BUNCH'S MILLINERY STORE.

In a short time "The Ladies' Library Association" was organized with a large number of enthusiastic members. They found that their only way of raising funds for their undertaking would be by getting up entertainments of various kinds. Nothing daunted, they planned a series of suppers, concerts, lectures, etc. Their first supper was given in the old Congregational church, which stood on the site of the present Carnegie Library.

The supper gotten up and prepared by such energetic and accomplished housekeepers and good managers, was a great success and was patronized by a great part of the community. The proceeds amounted to one hundred dollars, and formed the nucleus to which was added the sums accumulated from time to time, which were realized from various entertainments.

With the small beginning of about one hundred dollars worth of books, the number of volumes at present in the library has increased to about four thousand. Added to these is a large number of the best magazines and periodicals, which have been bound annually and placed upon the shelves.

The funds of the society, derived partly from fees paid by the members and patrons, and partly from

Phot graph by McLeod.

Bond County Law Makers.   Members of the Board of Supervisors and Keeper of the County Poor Farm for 1904.

Reading from left to right—(First Row) Emil Harnetiaux, Mills Township; S. Van Deusen, Chairman, Central Township; Ed Mayo, Pleasant Mound Township; William D. Matney, County Clerk.

Second Row, (Left to right) George W. Pigg, Mulberry Grove Township; J. B. Apple, Tamalco; Robert Hurst, Keeper of the County Poor Farm; Simon Brown, Old Ripley Township; A. O. Donnell, Lagrange.

Third Row, (Left to right) Albert G. Schmidt, Burgess; R. H. Pullen, Shoal Creek Township.

endowment, have amounted to $1,-300. This sum has been placed at interest for the purpose of meeting expenses and buying new books. It was slow work but was persevered in by the members often at a sacrifice of time and labor, for the sake of building up an institution, which they knew would benefit the people.

On February 22, 1867, the association was incorporated under the title "The Ladies' Library Association of Greenville, Illinois." The names of the charter members are as follows: Almira A. Morse, Lucy B. Stewart, Sarah Sprague, Elizabeth Smith, Hannah Chittenden, Mary A. Shields, Priscilla W. Alexander, Emily M. Dewey, Sarah H. Walls, Caroline R. Phelps.

There have been many changes in the members of the Association, yet all have been actuated in a remark-able degree by unanimity and a generous desire that the library shall be so managed that it may continue its good influences in time to come.

The Carnegie Library

THE Ladies' Library Association took the initiative in the establishment of the Greenville Carnegie Library or the Greenville Free Public Library, as it is now called. It was their generous offer of money and books that made possible the opening of negotiations with Hon. Andrew Carnegie, the donor of the building.

The matter was discussed by the ladies at their meetings in the year 1902, and finally the association offered to give $1,000 in money and their library of more than 4,000 volumes for the furtherance of the cause, provided the city would levy a two mill tax, as provided by law, for the maintenance of the library. At a meeting of the city council on April 2, 1903, C. D. Hoiles, F. W. Fritz and W. W. Lowis appeared before the council in support of a resolution offered by Alderman W. H. Williams favoring the location of a Carnegie Library in Greenville. This resolution was passed by a unanimous vote. It did not provide for the levy of any tax, but was merely an expression on the part of the city council, paving the way for the opening of negotiations with Mr. Carnegie. At that meeting Mayor Joy appointed Mrs. C. D. Hoiles. President of the Ladies'

SHERIFF W. L. FLOYD,

Born and raised in Bond county;
Constable six years; Deputy Sher-
iff four years and elected Sheriff of
Bond County in 1902.

Library Association, to communicate
with Mr. Carnegie in regard to the
matter. Mrs. Hoiles had already
had correspondence with Mr. Carnegie, having been delegated to
write him by the Ladies' Library
Association. In reply to her first
letter, Mrs. Hoiles received a blank
to be filled out signifying that the
city council was favorable to the establishment of a Carnegie Library.
The resolution passed by the council
was forwarded to Mr. Carnegie as

proof of the good faith of the city
in desiring a Carnegie Library. In
reply to this Mr. Carnegie, through
his private secretary, James Bert-
ram, stated that if the city would,
by resolution of council, agree to
maintain a free public library at a
cost of not less than $1,000 per
year, and provide a suitable site
for the building, he would be pleased
to furnish $10,000 to erect a free
public library for Greenville.

On August 6, 1903, the city council passed a resolution providing for
the establishment of a free Carnegie
Library to cost $10,000, and pledg-
ing the required two mill tax for
the support of the library. In the
same resolution the city accepted
the gift of $1,000 from the Ladies'
Library Association. Mayor Ed De-
Moulin appointed a board of nine
directors as follows: J. Seaman, F.
P. Joy, G. B. Hoiles, W. W. Lowis,
S. Van Deusen and Mesdames C. D.
Hoiles, W. A. Northcott, A. L. Hord,
and K. M. Bennett. The board afterward organized, electing J. Seaman,
president, Mrs. A. L. Hord corresponding secretary and Guy B. Hoiles
recording secretary.

Several sites were under consideration for weeks but the solution
came with the purchase of the
Presbyterian church site, lots 28
and 29 of Davidson's Addition to
Greenville, where the old Congregational church stood for more than
half a century. The purchase price
was $1250, the money being made
up by popular subscription.

On June 17, 1904, the contract
was awarded to J. F. Rees for $8,-
500 and actual work commenced
July 20, 1904. The corner stone
was laid September 9, 1904, by the
Masonic fraternity, Grandmaster
William B. Wright of Effingham
officiating. The chief addresses
were made by Lieutenant Governor
Northcott and Hon. Charles E.
Whelan of Madison, Wis.

On December 14, 1903, the plans
of Paul O. Moratz of Bloomington,
Ill., were adopted, and he was employed as the architect. The building is 50 feet by 50 feet, 22 feet
high, with a large tower on the
northeast 28x28, and 30 feet high.
The building is of pressed brick and
stone, the building is steam heated
and finished in hardwood and has
electric lights, and is equipped with
stacks for 12,000 books. Miss Emma
Colcord is the librarian. The building was completed in the early part
of 1905, and the work of moving the
books was commenced in the month
of May. They were then catalogued
and placed on the shelves.

The library was formally opened
with a public reception and program
on August 4, 1905.

MRS. W. L. FLOYD.

The Greenville Building and Savings Association

By Secretary Ward Reid.

THE history of Greenville would
be lacking in an important particular, if a brief sketch of this corporation were not made a part of
the same, for many of our best citizens are now the owners of beautiful and comfortable homes as a result of the timely acceptance of op-

A. A. JACKSON,
Of Muncie, Ind., a former Greenville
resident.

MRS. A. A. JACKSON,
Of Muncie, Ind., daughter of Sheriff
and Mrs. Floyd.

F. W. FRITZ,
State's Attorney from 1892 to 1904. Member the law firm of Fritz and Hoiles. Prominent in Bond County politics for twenty years.

RESIDENCE OF F. W. FRITZ, East Main Avenue.

portunities offered by this reliable financial institution.

The preliminary paper of "The Greenville Building and Savings Association"—being the license for subscription of Stock—was issued November 9, 1883, by Henry D. Dement, Secretary of State, and gave to Frank Seewald, J. Baumberger, U. B. Bowers, P. H. Grafe, John Schlup, William Boll and L. H. Craig, the right to open books for subscription of Stock of said Association. "F. Seewald, 20 shares" is the first name on the original subscription list and to Mr. Seewald, still one of Greenville's prosperous business men, belongs rightfully the title of "father" of the Association.

The first meeting of Stockholders was held December 17, 1883, and at that time the first Board of Directors was elected, and was composed of the following gentlemen: W. V. Weise, W. H. Watson, William Boll, M. W. Van Valkenburg, J. B. Reid, William Koch, C. D. Hoiles, R. L. Mudd and Frank Seewald. Of these nine original Directors, only two are deceased; four others are still residents of Greenville, and three are residents of other States.

To C. D. Hoiles belongs the distinction of being the only one of the original Board who is now a Director, and he has occupied that position—as well as that of Treasurer, —since the organization of the Association. James P. Slade was chairman and Henry Howard and Ward Reid, secretaries of this first meeting of Stockholders.

At this meeting the Charter and By-laws of the Association were also adopted; M. W. VanValkenburg, being chairman of the Committee to prepare same, and to him should be given credit for the bulk of the work on same, ably assisted by R. L. Mudd, M. V. Denny, L. H. Craig and J. B. Reid, other members of this

LAW OFFICE OF FRITZ AND HOILES, North side public square.

the same positions. To them should be given much credit for able and careful management of the details of the business of the Association.

The first meeting of the Board for loaning money was held February 4th, 1884, and at that meeting was made a loan of $1100 to Dr. W. H. H. Beeson, on his property, at present the location of the handsome residence of W. W. Lowis, on "Piety Hill."

Since organization The Greenville Building and Savings Association has made a total of 885 loans, aggregating many thousands of dollars, and hundreds of homes in Greenville and adjacent towns on which loans have been "matured" show the immense benefit this institution has been to the citizens of the community.

These notes would hardly do justice to the Greenville Building and Savings Association, and would not be complete without especial mention of the name of W. V. Weise, now deceased, who was for many years a Director of the organization. Mr. Weise served for seven years as president and being peculiarly gifted as a financier, he was of great assistance to the officers in the matter of bookkeeping and the distributions. His good judgment was also keenly appreciated and his interest in the welfare of the Association did much to place the organization in the front rank of its class. Other past Presidents who have rendered good service are Frank Seewald, J. Seaman, N. H. Jackson and F. P.

Dr. B. F. Coop,
A leading physician and surgeon. Member of the Board of Education.

Committee.

The Board of Directors held their first meeting December 22, 1883, at which time the following officers were elected: Frank Seewald, President; M. W. Van Valkenburg, Vice President; C. D. Hoiles, Treasurer; Ward Reid, Secretary and L. H.

Craig, Solicitor. Of these officers, only two, viz. C. D. Hoiles, as Treasurer and Ward Reid, Secretary, have served continuously, and now occupy

John H. Adams,
Proprietor of Adams Hotel and Livery.

Residence of Dr. B. F. Coop, West College Avenue.

H. H. WIRZ,
Manufacturer of Wirz's Straight Five Cigars.

BUSINESS HOUSE OF H. H. WIRZ.

Joy, while to W. W. Lowis, elected to fill vacancy caused by the death of W. V. Weise, belongs the distinction of having been elected President for five consecutive years, and Mr. Lowis is now ably filling the position.

As above noted L. H. Craig was the first Solicitor (or Attorney) of the Association, and was again elected for the second year. After him W. A. Northcott gave his able services for four years and at the election for the term beginning 1890 C. E. Cook, was chosen for the place. Since that date Mr. Cook has continuously held the office of Solicitor (or Attorney), of the Association and has rendered careful and conscientious service.

At the last annual meeting of the Stockholders the report of Secretary Reid, showed assets of $119,095.12, and every indication of a prosperous and healthy condition. The report also showed that there has been issued since organization, 10,245 shares and that the total earnings, now distributed to shares, aggregate, $30,683.71. The present Board of Directors is as follows: J. Seaman, F. E. Watson, G. L. Loggins, W. W. Lowis, N. H. Jackson, F. N. Blanchard, C. D. Hoiles, F. P. Joy and Geo. V. Weise. The officers for year of 1906 are W. W. Lowis, President; F. P. Joy, Vice President; Ward

DR. C. C. GORDON,
Ex-Coroner.   Now of Highland, Ill.

RESIDENCE OF CHARLES F. THRANER, East Main Avenue.

S. G. SPARKS,

A former resident, prominent officer of the Modern Woodmen for several years.

tion that the Bond County Soldiers' Association take steps to erect a monument in the city of Greenville, to the memory of the citizens of said county who responded to the call for volunteers in the war of the rebellion; and that a committee be appointed by the commander to take hold of the matter and push the work. This resolution was passed unanimously and the commander later appointed the following committee under the resolution, towit: Wm. D. Matney, Chairman, Greenville; John H. Ladd, Lagrange; John Tischhauser, Burgess; George F. Harlan, Mills; William Meyer, Tamalco; A. D. Cullom, Mulberry Grove; Col. John B. Reid, Greenville; J. W. Daniels, Woburn; Dr. J. A. Black, Pleasant Mound; Anton Phillipsen, Old Ripley; W. W. Lowis, Central; I. H. Denny, Shoal Creek.

The chairman called a meeting of the committee for Saturday, November 11, 1899, and the following named members were present, William Meyer, Dr. J. A. Black, J. W. Daniels, George F. Harlan, Wm. D. Matney, Col. J. B. Reid, W. W. Lowis, John H. Ladd, Anton Phillipsen and I. H. Denny. The committee organized by electing Wm. D. Matney, president, W. W. Lowis, secretary and Charles W. Watson, treasurer.

The chairman told the members present of the desirability of the success of the undertaking and called for suggestions of plans for the pushing of this effort to success, not failing to impress on the committee some of the difficulties we would encounter, but impressing the idea on the comrades that by a "long pull;" a touching of elbows

Reid, Secretary; C. D. Hoiles, Treasurer; and C. E. Cook, Solicitor.

The Greenville Building and Savings Association can truthfully be classed as one of the pioneer institutions of our City, and its officers and members can well be proud of its prosperous and useful career.

Bond County Soldiers' Monument.

By Wm. D. Matney.

AT the eleventh annual meeting of the Bond County Soldiers' Association, held in Greenville, October 18, 1899, the first steps were taken to erect a monument, to the memory of the men who answered to their country's call from 1861 to 1865. The writer hereof started the ball to rolling by introducing a resolu-

RESIDENCE OF J. E. WRIGHT.

RESIDENCE OF FRANK E. WATSON. East College Avenue.

FRANK E. WATSON,

A leading druggist, a resident 13 years; Director B. and S. Association; former member Board of Health; State Inspector Sons of Veterans of Illinois, 1901-3.

as of old, we were bound to succeed. Comrade Lewis advocated the plan of popular subscription as one means and the plan was approved by the committee, as one of the means to be adopted and the sequel shows that the plan succeeded. Col. Reid advanced the idea of interesting the schools in the matter of raising funds among the pupils, offering prizes to the schools raising the largest and the second and third largest amount. Col. Reid was appointed to take charge of this work, to visit the schools and get the citizens of the various school districts, the teachers and pupils to work. The Colonel went to work vigorously and when the contest closed the association had something over $180 to its credit: the first money to be realized, and when this report came in, although the amount was small, the committee felt sure that event-

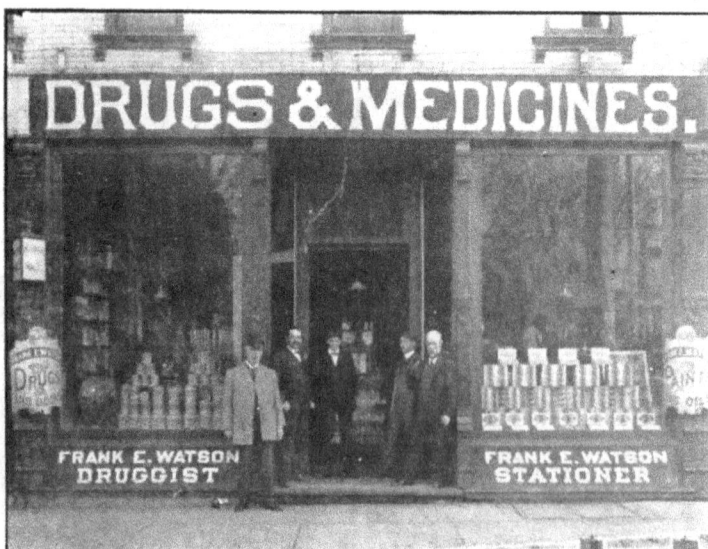

W. H. HUBBARD,

Attorney at Law and Justice of the Peace.

FRANK E. WATSON'S DRUG STORE.

SUBURBAN RESIDENCE OF MRS. CAROLINE IDLER.

JACOB M. APPEL, C. P. A.

Ex-Chief of the Building and Loan department of the state; now chief of the banking department in the State Auditor's
office; Secretary of Republican Senatorial Committee. Former Greenville resident, now living at Springfield.

A. H. MOUL,
Well known business man.

CHARLES E. COOK,
Attorney at Law, Master in Chancery of Bond County.

W. C. FULLER,
Owner of Greenville Steam Laundry.

DR. L. M. ROSAT,

A native of Switzerland, who came to America in 1881, received her medical education in St. Louis and has been a resident of Greenville for 12 years.

RESIDENCE OF DR. L. M. ROSAT, West Main Avenue.

ually we would succeed and the monument would be built. At this meeting it was decided to call our organization "The Bond County Soldiers' and Sailors' Monument Association." The comrades at this meeting discussed the style and cost of the proposed monument and finally decided that it should not exceed $3,500 and that it be placed on the court house square. Col. Reid and W. W. Lowis were selected

to lay the matter before the Womans' Relief Corps and to solicit their aid in our work. At this first meeting an executive committee was appointed to take charge of matters that would not be practicable to lay before the full committee, to-wit: C. W. Watson, J. B. Reid, W. W. Lowis, J. H. Ladd and Wm. D. Matney.

This committee went to work and kept the ball rolling. They used every means to interest the people in the matter; met all objections and finally reached the point where they saw success crown their efforts

In August 1901, a genera. rally of the friends was held, at which time General John C. Black, National Commander of the G. A. R. was present and delivered a fine address. At this meeting $390 was pledged and the committee began to lay plans to begin work. After advertising, the contract was let to S. O. Sanders of Centralia and early in the spring of 1903, work was begun, and completed August 19, 1903.

The committee decided to unveil the monument September 19, 1903, the fortieth anniversary of the battle of Chickamauga. Saturday Septem-

DR. J. A. WARREN,

President Bond County Medical Society. Ex-Alderman.

MRS. J. A. WARREN.

J. H. ALLIO,

City Attorney of Greenville.

S. VAN DEUSEN,
Supervisor of Central Township.

RESIDENCE OF S. VAN DEUSEN.

ber 19, was a beautiful day and a large concourse of the people of Bond county and of other parts of Illinois was present to listen to the address of Governor Richard Yates, Col. Benson Wood, Lieutenant Governor Northcott and others.

The monument was unveiled and stands today as an object lesson in patriotism and will stand long after the last soldier of the great war has passed away; yes, after all the vast audience that was present at the unveiling have gone to their last rest. As the representative of the old soldiers of Bond county I want to express the thanks of our association to the patriotic citizens of Bond

county who assisted us in our undertaking both financially and in speaking good words for us.

"On Fame's eternal camping ground
Their silent tents are spread
And Glory guards with solemn round
The bivouac of the dead."

Greenville Women's Christian Temperance Union.

By Miss Ella M. Hynes.

"We mean to go straight on in our White Ribbon work; we mean to be as good-natured as sunshine,

but as persistent as fate."

So spoke Frances E. Willard, our peerless leader, whose life and work have just been so signally honored by our state and nation in placing her statue among those of the greatest in our country.

Whether our Greenville Union has always lived up to all the provisions of this declaration is not for us to say, but that we have been "persistent" our record amply testifies. Ours is one of the pioneer organizations of women in the city, having been organized April 1, 1879, with thirty-nine members. The object, as set forth in the constitution, was "to plan and carry forward measures

D. McLEOD,
The Photographer.

MRS. McLEOD.

THOMAS F. CARY,
Chairman of the Board of Supervisors 1903-4.

E. W. MILLER,
Twelve years Deputy Circuit Clerk; now in abstract, real estate, loan and insurance business.

RESIDENCE OF MRS. J. D. TIFFIN, South Third Street.

which will result, with the blessing of God, in the suppression of intemperance in our midst."

The first officers were Mrs. Emily W. Dewey, president; Mrs. Caroline Phelps, corresponding secretary; and Mrs. Elizabeth Colcord, recording secretary. Very few of the charter members are still living, and so far as I can ascertain Miss Lizzie Perryman is the only one living here. Meetings were for some time held monthly in the various churches in turn. The earliest special form of work undertaken was that among the children and youth. In June 1879 a Young Peoples' Temperance Union was formed, its officers being the same as those of the W. C. T. U. This line of work was carried on with great faithfulness and efficiency for many years. Though there were some changes in methods the underlying principles were the same under the name of Band of Hope and later, the Loyal Temperance Legion.

The hearts of the faithful ones, who long persevered in this work in spite of obstacles and discouragements not a few, are frequently cheered in these later days by the testimony of men and women that the good seeds sown in their youthful hearts are now bearing fruit.

As time has gone by and this evil of intemperance—"monster of such hideous mien"—has still defied the earnest efforts of many forces allied against it, our organization has taken up, as conditions demanded them, various lines of reform and humanitarian work, most of them demanded because of the liquor traffic. Thus it was that an aid society, auxiliary to the Union was formed very early in our history, which was a source of help and

J. P. REDMOND,
District Deputy for the Knights of the Modern Maccabees.

COUNTRY RESIDENCE OF H. C. COLEMAN.

R. C. CLARK,

Who was a Greenville business man for several years, now a resident of Anthony, Kans., near which place he owns a section of fine land. He is land and immigration agent for the Missouri Pacific.

comfort to many unfortunate families. This was later combined with the flower mission department and for many years we carried on the beautiful work of ministering so far as possible, to the poor and sick, not only with comforts in the way of food and clothing, but also with flowers. During the last few years we have not been able to do very much on these lines, but on flower mission day, we always distribute flowers with scripture texts attached, to as many as possible of the sick and shut in ones, whatever their

creed, nationality, or circumstances, not forgetting the inmates of alms-house and jail. We also frequently remember in the same way unfortunates in St. Louis, where our floral contributions unite with those from Unions elsewhere, to furnish the means for our workers to perform this mission.

Mention of this work cannot fail to bring to the minds of those who knew her, the sweet face and gentle manner of Mrs. Charles Clark, long since gone to her reward. She was long superintendent of the department of almshouse and jail work, and was untiring in her earnest endeavor to benefit those in both institutions, her loving christian sympathy never failing them. Under her guidance gospel meetings were held, reading matter supplied, and a Sunday School was for some time conducted by her in the old jail building.

Realizing the importance of instilling right ideas in the minds of the children, that they may early learn the dangers of indulgence in intoxicating liquors, we have, through our department of scientific temperance instruction, tried to aid our public school teachers in their compliance with the excellent laws of Illinois on this subject. We have

MRS. R. C. CLARK,

Daughter of Mr. and Mrs. John B. Henninger.

done much by subscribing for journals and distributing other helpful literature, to make this instruction interesting and accurate. One phase of our work is that of nonalcoholic medication, in support of which principles many pages of

REV. A. S. MAXEY AND FAMILY.
Of Hopedale, former residents.

CLARK AND HENNINGER FAMILIES.

Reading from left to right, first row—Trum Henninger, Russel Clark, son of J. J. Clark. Second row—Mrs. Amanda Henninger, Eugene Clark, son of R. C. Clark. Third row—Agnes McAdow, daughter of R. C. Clark; Bessie, daughter of J. J. Clark; William Henninger. Fourth row—Mabel Clark and Lena Mulford, daughters of R. C. Clark; Mrs. Jennie Henninger Clark, Mrs. Trum Henninger, Mrs. R. C. Clark. Top row—John T. Mulford, J. J. Clark, Mrs. J. J. Clark, R. C. Clark, John B. Henninger, W. C. Clark, Shelbina, Mo., brother of R. C. Clark, Virgil Henninger, eldest son of Mr. and Mrs. G. S. Henninger.

This photograph was taken by Simeon Clark, eldest son of Mr. and Mrs. R. C. Clark, the occasion being a family reunion of the Clark and Henninger families.

MR. AND MRS. A. C. CULP AND SON.
Former residents, now living at Hendricksen, Mo.

W. A. ORR,

Who resigned the mayoralty in July 1905, upon removing to Springfield, where he is a member of the law firm of Northcott, Hoff and Orr.

literature have been given out. We have also for many years sent an annual gift box of canned fruits and jellies to the F. E. Willard National Temperance Hospital, Chicago, which is the only strictly non-alcoholic hospital in America. So successful has this treatment been that the anniversary of Miss Willard's death was last year observed by the dedication of a new and commodious building, supplied with all modern conveniences for hospital work. Time fails me to speak, even briefly, of various departments in which more or less work has been done. Beside those already noted, probably most has been done by gospel temperance meetings and medal contests.

No history of Greenville Union should be closed without mention ot a few of the many good women, who have wrought and prayed with us during the twenty-six years of our existence. Among those who have folded their hands and rested from their earthly labors are Mrs. Travis, Mrs. P. C. Reed, Mrs. McConnell, Mrs. Murdock, Mrs. Perry, Mrs. Vest, Mrs. M. V. Denny, Mrs. Dorcas Denny, Mrs. Norman and Mrs. Lundy. The last named served us faithfully as treasurer for fourteen years. In whatever good has been accomplished, our sisterhood feels much credit is due the men, faithful though few, who have as honorary members, given us their support, both moral and financial. Of

these the names of the late Henry Grube, and of F. P. Joy, J. Seaman and Rev. Thomas W. Hynes have been longest enrolled.

Mrs. F. B. Seaman is still our honored president, after seventeen years of continuous intelligent and consecrated service. The other officers at this time are Miss R. Ella Greene, treasurer and Miss Ella Hynes, secretary, with a vice president from each denomination represented in the Union. One of the strong and beautiful features of

J. F. JOHNSTON.
City Clerk.

RESIDENCE OF JOHN H. HAWLEY, West College Avenue.

RESIDENCE OF W. E. DAVIS, East Main Avenue.

DR. J. C. WILSON,
Member of Board of Health and a prominent
practicing physician.

this work is the blending of all denominations into a happy and harmonious fellowship of christian activity, ready to "lend a hand" to push along almost any form of good work.

Since 1884 our regular meetings have been held in the afternoon of the first and third Fridays of each month, with an evangelistic meeting when there is a fifth Friday in the month. All meetings are open to the public, and everyone interested is welcome.

The Killing of Elijah P. Lovejoy
BY AN EYE-WITNESS.

The following account of the killing of Elijah P. Lovejoy, the great abolitionist, at Alton, in 1837, was related to the author of this book on November 7, 1897, by John Wesley Harned, an eye-witness of the tragedy. The account was published in the Greenville Advocate at the time, and was widely copied by the metropolitan press of the United States. Mr. Harned was a wonderful character. He was born in Red River County, Texas, January 26, 1819. He came to Bond county in 1839 and for forty-nine consecutive years voted at Pocahontas, never missing an election. He was the guest of honor

RESIDENCE OF EARL M. DAVIS.

GEORGE GRUBE,
Member of the firm of Grube and
Mange, and a prominent farmer
and grain merchant.

MR. AND MRS. LLOYED P. DAVIS,
Mr. Davis is a member of the firm of Davis and Jackson, druggists.

at the dedication of the Lovejoy Monument at Alton, November 7, 1897, at which time W. A. Northcott, another Greenville man, was the orator. Mr. Harned for many years bore the distinction of being the only surviving witness of the killing of Lovejoy, although James H. White and Mrs. L. K. King, both residents of Greenville, lived in Alton at the time of the killing, although they were children. Mr. Harned who died March 27, 1904, dictated, in November 1897, to the author, the following account of the killing.

"My father, William Harned, ran the Mansion House in Alton. The house was built in 1834, and was first run by Col. Bodkins, then by Louis Kellenberger and then my father took it in 1835. There at that time I met Abraham Lincoln, Stephen A. Douglas, Governor Reynolds, Governor Cole and most of the prominent men of Illinois in that day. It is the only vestige of a hotel now left, that stood at that time. It is still standing and is used for a boarding house. I saw Alton in its infancy, spring up quick and fast. On up to the time

Lovejoy came in 1836, there was but little said about abolition, in that frontier town. It was too unpopular a subject. After Lovejoy came and started his press, you could hear whisperings of discontent against the abolitionists.

"Lovejoy was a mild, pleasant and fine looking gentleman. One night I heard a commotion two blocks away and ran down there to find a mob in his office, breaking up his press and throwing it out of the window, and there in the center of the street, men were breaking it up and throwing it into Piasa Creek.

JOHN W. HARNED,
An eye-witness of the killing of Elijah
P. Lovejoy in 1837.

Residence recently sold by Thomas W. Stewart to Judge C. J. Lindly.

S. W. ROBINSON,
One of Greenville's well known business men.

MRS. S. W. ROBINSON.

J. H. JONES,
Supervisor of this division of the Vandalia Railroad.

DR. FRED C. JONES, Dentist.

J. H. MULFORD,

A member of the firm of Mulford and Monroe, druggists.

J. L. MONROE,

A member of the firm of Mulford and Monroe, druggists.

The second press was taken from Alexander Bodkin's warehouse, where it was deposited, and thrown into the river as soon as it came, a few months later. After the destruction of the second press, the people began to take sides, the great majority against Lovejoy; the minority to defend him and his rights. He was still determined to publish his paper and sent on and got his third press. It was generally understood that the mob would destroy his third press, with threats of violence against Lovejoy. Frequently public meetings were held denouncing Lovejoy, while the more conservative were inclined to dissuade him from publishing his paper.

The third press was purposely landed late at night. After its landing the excitement became intense. The only topic of conversation was Lovejoy's press. Everyone knew that it was coming and understood that a mob was being organized to destroy it as soon as it was landed. A small proportion were in favor of protecting the press, while, as far as I could see, though I was only eighteen years old, there was an element in favor of destroying it at all hazards, even if it took his life. This was common talk on the street. While this element was composed largely of the rougher class of people, I could give the names of ministers of the gospel

who were encouraging the destruction of the press, when by a few words, these same influential men could have settled the matter in Lovejoy's favor.

"On the eve the press was to be landed, each side began to make their preparations. On the evening previous to the arrival of the press there was a consultation held in the Mansion House. There were present Lovejoy, Mayor John M. Krum, A. B. Roff, Royal Weller, Winthrop S. Gillman, my father, William Harned, and others. The question discussed was what was best to be done and how best to proceed. While my recollection of Lovejoy is that he was a mild man, he and others were in favor of defending the press at all hazards. My recollection is that at that meeting Mayor Krum had agreed to furnish what assistance was necessary in defending the press and the meeting adjourned with that understanding. A few days previous a company had been organized under military law, with my father as captain, and had placed themselves at the disposal of the mayor and Lovejoy.

"The next day after the landing of the press, the mob began to collect their forces. The next night the mob gathered early in the evening and began to fill up with whiskey. By 9 o'clock p. m., the crowd numbered about 300. Cap-

tain Harned, Lovejoy and his friends were inside the warehouse of Godfrey and Gillman, in which the press was stored. The building was four stories on the wharf side and three on Second street. I stood watching the crowd, and my recollection of the first demonstration of violence is that the mob threw rocks and broke every window glass in that end of the building. Several shots were also fired into the building. With rocks and sledge hammers they broke the doors open but they were braced on the inside by hogsheads of sugar. The contending forces got near enough to talk to each other and those within warned the mob that if they attempted to come in, they would shoot them.

"Governor Reynolds, a strong pro-slavery man, who has written a history on the subject says that what infuriated the mob was that a man raised a window up-stairs and fired a shot, killing one of the mob. Governor Reynolds is mistaken here for I, as an eye-witness, know that at that time there was not a glass nor a piece of window sash left in the whole side of the building. My father went to the window and asked those in the crowd, who were not taking part in the mob to get out of the way, as the struggle was getting so bitter, something had to be done. A man by the name of Bishop fired at my father, the bullet

J. G. RAY,

Secretary to Gov. W. A. Northcott as Head Consul of the M. W. A. for more than 12 years; now secretary to Head Consul Talbot at Lincoln, Neb.

imbedding itself in the window case by his side. Soon a gun was thrust out of a window by one of Lovejoy's men and Bishop was shot. The mob fell back and left him lying in the street. They soon rallied, picked him up and carried him away. He died a few hours later. That was the first shot fired from the inside of the building. Then the firing became general on both sides. About midnight the mob spliced ladders together and put them up on the east side of the building, where there were no windows and a man, muffled in overcoats, as a protection against the bullets of Lovejoy's men, climbed the ladder with a lighted torch and fired the roof. After it had burned through the sheeting, Bert Loomis punched the fire out and threw water on it, while bullets flew all around him. After they found that the building was on fire, Lovejoy and others went out the south end of the building and turned around the southeast corner to shoot at the men firing the roof. This was repeated several times and about the third time Lovejoy came out to shoot at the man on the roof, he was shot, four buckshot penetrating his breast. I thought he was hit, seeing so many shooting at him but he turned and walked fifteen feet to the door and climbed the flight of stairs. When he reached the head of the stairs, he fell, his feet hanging over the steps. The last and only words he said after he was shot, were: 'I am a dead man.' He and my father were standing side by side when he was shot and John B. Dyo, one of the mob said they could have killed my father just as easy, but Lovejoy was the man they were after.

"I heard my father had been killed and rushed among the first into the building, but found him safe by the dead body of Lovejoy. It was immediately reported outside that Lovejoy was killed. Through the influence of Henry West, the mob then agreed to give up the press and let those inside go peaceably home. They did not keep their promise but hurled rocks and fired upon them. Lovejoy and Bishop, one on each side, were the only ones killed.

"History says that the men, who fired at Lovejoy, lay behind a pile of lumber. If there was any lumber there, I did not see it, but Godfrey and Gillman had the Galena lead trade, and those men were hidden behind piles of pig lead thirty or forty paces below the building. I know the four men who did the shooting and I saw them lying there. I could give their names, but for the sake of their descendants, many of whom are living in this state, I will not do so.

"Lovejoy's body was followed to the grave the next day by but few and the funeral cortege was hooted at by the dead man's enemies. His poor wife was at home in feeble health.

"About the close of the war, Louis Kellenberger, who kept the Mansion House at Alton before my father, came out to visit me. In reviewing the death of Lovejoy, said I, 'Mr. Kellenberger, I reckon it will never be known who killed Lovejoy.' He replied, 'Harned, I am satisfied I know who killed Lovejoy. It was Dr. James Jennings.' He then stated that he (Kellenberger) was the cause of Jennings coming to Alton as the families had been acquainted in Virginia and that Jennings confided in Kellenberger and immediately after the killing wound up his affairs and left Alton. He never wrote back but cut off all communication with his friends and for this and other reasons Kellenberger said he was satisfied that Jennings was the man who killed Lovejoy. Kellenberger said that while Beall, Rock and some others claimed the honor of killing Lovejoy, Jennings had never claimed that. It was a matter that he did not like to talk about."

Some Reminiscences.

By the late Rev. Thomas W. Hynes.

My first visit to Illinois was in 1834, over 70 years ago. It was made on horseback in company with my father, out of Kentucky, through Indiana, and crossing the Wabash at Terre Haute, we spent a week riding through the great prairies. It was my father's long-cherished wish to locate his family on what he thought was the right side of Mason and Dixon's Line. It was then largely unsettled. We often traveled twenty or thirty miles without sight of human being or habitation. Our roads were often

MULFORD AND MONROE'S DRUG STORE.

W. W. HUSSONG,

A prominent merchant. President
of the Hussong Cash Mercantile
Company.

RESIDENCE OF W. W. HUSSONG, South Second Street.

paths or trails. We did not see
Bond county.

My first visit to Greenville was
in 1845. Having an invitation to
visit Hillsboro with a view to
settling there as a minister, and
having friends in this county, who
attended one of the Greenville
churches, I was frequently in Greenville. I moved my family to Hillsboro in March 1846. I was frequently at the church services here
during my residence in Hillsboro.
So that my acquaintance with

Greenville covers the last sixty
years.

In 1845 there were only two
church buildings in Greenville, the
Congregational and Presbyterian,
now happily united. The Baptist
and Methodist Episcopal organizations were both, and for many
years, without houses of worship

and were welcomed to the Presbyterian church for their public worship, at all times, when not in use
by the Presbyterians. This continued till the Methodists built
their first house in 1849 on the lot
now owned by Dr. N. H. Jackson.
Their present brick building was
erected and dedicated in 1877. The

W. E. ROBINSON,

Former County Superintendent of
Schools. Now Supreme Recorder
of the Court of Honor, living at
Springfield.

Harness Shop formerly occupied by Fred Durr.

GEORGE O. MORRIS,
President Board of Education. Real Estate, Loan and Insurance Agent.

MISS VERA MORRIS,
Daughter of Mr. and Mrs. George O. Morris.

MRS. GEORGE O. MORRIS.

first Baptist church was built on Main Street between Third and Fourth Streets in 1854. This was used until they built their present house on South Street.

On the writer's visit to Greenville in 1845, both the church buildings were new—that of the Congregationalists finished nearly, but that of the Presbyterians largely unfinished in the interior. The seats being of plain boards, square and straight-backed, were by no means comfortable. Though the rough-hewed frame was there for a vestibule and gallery, neither was finished and the marks of the

scorer's axe were plainly visible in many places.

The incident heretofore mentioned of the readiness and cordiality with which one Christian church opened its house for other houseless christian churches shows the kindly and fraternal spirit among those who differed on minor and non-essential points.

When the writer removed his family to Greenville as a home in 1854, there were five prayer meetings held on four of the week day evenings. This brought some prayer meeting in conflict with

nearly every lecture of entertainment that might interest or instruct the citizens. The writer made the suggestion that all the prayer-meetings be held on one evening. The suggestion was readily adopted and Thursday evening chosen because two of the five prayer meetings were already held on that evening.

About the same time Father George Donnell suggested that the first prayer meeting in each month be a union meeting. This was also generally agreed to, with especial reference to the young and the Sabbath Schools. For some years

O. E. TIFFANY, A. M., Ph. D.,
Former professor of history and economics in Greenville College.

RESIDENCE OF GEORGE O. MORRIS, South Third Street.

GEORGE H DAVIS,

A Greenville boy who is chief clerk to the General Attorney of the M. W. A., at Rock Island.

RESIDENCE OF JOHN H. DAVIS.

several of the churches united together in the observance of this Thursday prayer service.

Greenville was not a "City of magnificent distances" when the writer first saw it. It was limited by the hills and valleys on the north, the bluff on the west, South Street on the south, and First Street on the east. All east of First Street was in the country, and largely in the farms of Samuel White and Wyatt Stubblefield. This is the reason the next street east of First Street was named

"Prairie"—it was out in the prairie. All the land south of South Street was owned and cultivated as a part of the farm of the Hon. Wm. S. Wait, and was cultivated in corn. The first residence property on this Wait land, as the writer remembers, was the site now occupied by W. W. Hussong. Though not a "churchman" Mr. Wait was a liberal, intelligent, wealthy and public spirited citizen and donated and deeded a piece of land to the Rev. James Stafford, then pastor of the Presbyterian church of Greenville. On this Mr. Stafford erected a two story frame house and occupied it as a residence for many years. It afterwards became the home of Mrs. Sarah Brown and family and was owned

and occupied by her son-in-law, Mr. William Morris who removed the old Stafford frame and erected the more modern and commodious residence now occupied by Mr. Hussong. Mr. Wait deeded this property by metes and bounds as a certain part of Section 10, and so to the present time it is not known as town lots.

The writer well remembers when Mr. J. F. Alexander lived clear out of town, in the house afterward owned by C. D. Harris, and now the home of James Ward. To get there one had to walk all the way from South Street to Mr. Alexander's over a path through the cornfield, or by a much longer distance around the field. All that part of the city now know as "The

PROF. W. DUFF PIERCY.
Former Superintendent of the Greenville Public Schools, now a resident of Mt. Vernon, Ill.

RESIDENCE OF R. W. WILSON.

PROF. J. T. ELLIS,

Former Superintendent of the Greenville Public Schools, now Superintendent of the Department of Training of the Southern Illinois Normal at Carbondale.

South Addition" was then a part of the Wait farm.

The first business in Greenville was in the west part of town, having as a center the intersection of Main and Sixth Streets. When it became a county seat the principal business houses and shops were gradually removed to, and near, the public square.

In my first knowledge of the village of Greenville it had very few and short sidewalks. Indeed, it had none except private walks furnished by the owners of certain places of business for the general public. Around the corner owned by the Morse Brothers, now the lately burned district, were walks, just as far as their buildings extended. So of the corner south of that, known then as the store of the Smith Brothers. At the northwest corner of the square, the residence of Mr. Thomas W. Smith; east of that the residence of E. Gaskins, the store of A. Buie, (Mier's meat market) at the middle of the east side of the square the old hotel; at the southeast corner of the square where Mr. Charles Hoiles did business so long, and in a few other of the most public places there were short sidewalks as the product of private enterprises. But at street crossings and generally through the town you had only mother earth in her natural condition under foot. It rained and it thawed then as well as now and our sub-soil of clay required stilts, boots or paving to pass over it undefiled.

I well remember a service I at-

tended in the decade of the forties, in the old Presbyterian church, less than a block from the public square. I preached to an audience of nine persons—one of whom was a woman. When I expressed to her my surprise that she should come five miles from the country, when her fellow-members living less than a block distant, were unable to attend, she said promptly, "Oh, that is easily explained. We from the country can drive right up to the church door and miss the town mud."

Greenville Bands.

THERE have been several bands in Greenville. One was organized October 10, 1879, and was chartered November 12, 1880, with John A. Elam as leader. Other members were A. D. Albrecht, Ward Reid, Will Robinson, Charles Thraner, Wallace Barr, Will Johnson, Will Donnell, Robert Johnson, Jesse Watson, Walter Powell, Rome Sprague, Jesse Smith, Frank Shaw, Louis Derleth, Frank Boughman and Will White. Many of these were members of various other bands up until the time of organization of the Greenville Concert Band. One of the bands that made quite a reputation was the Head Consul Band, named in honor of Head Consul Northcott, of the Modern Woodmen. Several of the above named musicians were members of this band.

The Greenville Concert Band.

An organization that has done much for the city in the way of furnishing martial music and one that has won laurels at home and abroad is the Greenville Concert Band, which had its inception in the old Schlup building, now used as a livery barn on Third Street, on the evening of October 23, 1896. On this date a number of young men met for the purpose of organizing a band. Frank N. Blanchard was chosen chairman and Will C. Carson, secretary. A committee consisting of E. W. Miller, U. S. DeMoulin and Will C. Carson was appointed to draft a constitution and by-laws, and after a few words of encouragement by Ed DeMoulin, the meeting adjourned to meet October 28, 1896, at which time James Brouse of Mulberry Grove was retained as leader and instructor, and E. W. Miller was elected president, Frank N. Blanchard, vice president and Herbert Mulford secretary and treasurer.

The original members of the band were James Brouse, Frank Blanchard, U. S. DeMoulin, L. P. Davis, Will C. Carson, C. M. Mulford, E. W. Miller, C. P. Blanchard, Vern Norman, Will McAdow, James Mulford, J. G. Ray, G. H. Davis, George Oudyn, W. H. Baughman, Samuel Wallace, W. J. Bruner, A. E. Hill, Don Beedle, John Mulford, F. E. Evans, H. Sieck, I. W. Kesler, J. H. Mulford, Fred Floyd, Charles Sieck, Ernest Trautman, Woodford

F. H. WHEELER'S HARNESS SHOP.

From left to right—F. H. Wheeler, John Sanderson, J. F. Boughman, Louis Staffen.

Interior view of J. M. Hawley's Jewelry Store, on Main Avenue. Mr. Hawley stands behind the counter on the left.

Evans and Owen Seaman. Of these original members only three, U. S. DeMoulin, Charles Breuchaud and George Oudyn are now members.

The band prospered and grew until at one time it had a membership of thirty-six. First prize was won at band contests at Highland and Jacksonville and on each occasion the boys were up against the best bands in the part of the state in which the contests were held. The band has always been very active in campaigns and in local affairs. During the last few years the quantity in membership has been supplanted by quality of tone and the boys have depended entirely on their own resources.

For many months the band was composed of George M. Oudyn, Clarence Davis, Clarence Hair, U. S. DeMoulin, H. C. Diehl, Charles Breuchaud, Erastus DeMoulin, Fred C. Jones and A. M. Keith, but in May, 1905, the band was re-organized. Ed DeMoulin of this city being a new member with three Mulberry Grove men, who will play in the band.

Clark Lodge No. 3, I. O. O. F.

By R. K. Dewey.

Clark Lodge No. 3, I. O. O. F., was chartered January 10, 1839. A report made by Past Grand Sire

Thomas Wildey, the father of Odd Fellowship in the United States, who had been made the traveling agent of the Right Worthy Grand Lodge of the United States, made at the October session of the Right Worthy Grand Lodge of the United States held at Baltimore, says:

"At Greenville in July, 1838, in the state of Illinois, I met with a number of brethren, among whom was Past Grand James Clark, formerly of Harper's Ferry, Md. They were desirous of organizing a lodge and presented a petition in due form for a lodge to be located at Greenville and called Clark Lodge No. 3. The charter was granted and the brethren instructed in the work of the order."

On the same western trip of Past Grand Sire Wildey, he granted the petition for a charter for the Grand Lodge of Illinois, which was instituted in October 1838, and at its first session in 1839, it granted the charter of Clark Lodge No. 3, so that the charter came through the Grand Lodge of Illinois, instead of from the Right Worthy Lodge of the United States.

It has been claimed by our members that Clark Lodge No. 3 is the oldest continuous working lodge in the state of Illinois, and in proof thereof I find that at the session of the Grand Lodge held at Springfield August 23, 1842, a proposition was presented to require the surrender

of the charters of Western Star Lodge No. 1 and Alton Lodge No. 2, both of Alton, if they were not re-organized before the next regular session of said Grand Lodge.

On May 23, 1843, the following resolution was adopted:

"Resolved—That the Grand Secretary be and is hereby instructed to demand and receive the charters, books, papers and furniture of said lodges Nos. 1 and 2 for the violation of Section 1, Article XI of the constitution of the Grand Lodge of Illinois." On November 29, 1843, the lodges were suspended as shown by the Grand Secretary's Report of above date, but after a time were reinstated, viz.: August 26, 1848. Alton Lodge No. 2 was instituted upon petition from members of old numbers 1 and 2.

Clark Lodge No. 3 was instituted by Past Grand David P. Berry of Greenville and Past Grand James E. Starr of Alton on the tenth day of January 1839. The charter members were James Clark, D. P. Berry, Thomas Dakin, Patrick O'Byrne, Daniel Ward, A. W. Cheneworth and James E. Starr, the last named being from Alton. The following were the first officers: James Clark, Noble Grand.; Patrick O'Byrne, Vice Grand; James Bradford, Secretary; Robert F. White, Treasurer; Thomas M. White, Warden and Conductor; Thomas Dakin, Inner Guardian; Officers,

PEPIN'S SHOP.

J. P. PEPIN,
For 16 years a leading blacksmith and horseshoer.

second quarter—Patrick O'Byrne, N. G.; T. M. White, Secretary. Officers, third quarter—R. F. White, N. G.; Seth Fuller, Secretary; Officers, fourth quarter—T. M. White, N. G.; R. F. White, Secretary.

The lodge had no seal. One was ordered October 12, 1850, and received October 26, 1850.

The lodge met for several years in the second story of the James Clark building at the northwest corner of Main and Fifth Streets. After many years, say about 1855, the lodge moved to the second story of the frame building standing on the east side of the court house square about where S. M. Harnetiaux's restaurant now stands, from which place it moved to the third story of the Sprague Block, which

it occupied for a long time. Finally M. B. Chittenden built a two story frame building on the ground where Watson's drug store now stands and the second story was rented by Clark Lodge, owing to some trouble in renting room in the Sprague Block. After occupying that room for some time the building was removed to make room for the two brick buildings and the First National Bank building, when the Lodge moved to the third story of the First National Bank, being the Mansard roof part, but that room being so hot in summer and so cold in winter, the lodge again removed to the Sprague Block where it remained until April 1903, when it moved to the northwest corner of

Main and Third, second story, where it had a very fine room and banquet room. The lodge was holding its meetings there at the time of the fire of October 27, 1904, which burned everything belonging to the lodge, valued at over $1,000, with $500 insurance. The loss of our old records was more deeply deplored than anything else, as we are the oldest continuous working lodge in the state of Illinois.

This record is made up by the writer hereof from personal knowledge of over fifty years in attendance on said lodge and from private notes in his possession. The following is a list of the members of said lodge in the years 1858 and 1859. On account of the loss of

PHILIP STOUT,
Constable of Central Township for several years.

The old Travis blacksmith shop, at one time Mt. Gilead church. This shop stood on the site of the present J. P. Pepin blacksmith, carriage and repair shop.

our records by fire I cannot give date of initiation or time of death:

Myron Ostrom, Thomas Chamberlain, Joel Elam, S. B. Holcomb, James M. Fergus, Joseph Campbell, Alex Kelsoe, W. S. Colcord, C. W. Holden, Adolph Hefter, Wm. Bell, J. E. Travis, David H. Winans, D. H. Phillips, D. D. Robbins, Theo. Smith, P. G. Vawter, Richard Stowe, J. B. Hunter, L. M. White, S. W. Marston, Williamson Plant, J. K. McLean, M. B. Chittenden, R. C. Sprague, Anson Sprague, George Laws, John T. Barr, Jacob Koonce, Daniel Jett, J. H. Birge, L. P. Littlefield, David Able, E. Gaskins, Thos. W. Smith, M. G. Dale, D. P. Hagee, John B. Reid, John F. Laws, A. G. Morgan, Wm. Scott, S. R. Perry, W. A. Libbey, C. T. Floyd, O. B. Colcord, E. A. Floyd, T. W. Floyd, G. W. Hill, Hance Corsby, H. W. White, S. H. Croker, Alex Buie, E. Francisco, J. F. Alexander, George Gibson, Cyrus Birge, Rufus Elam, J. A. Combs, J. Mattinly, D. Wilkins, Robert Thompson, Wm. McGuire, Geo. W. Moffat, J. T. Fouke, Edwin Birge, J. L. Lester, S. B. Gower, R. K. Dewey, D. B. Sturgis, John Melone, G. W. Miller, J. H. Murdock, C. B. Hamilton, J. H. Moss, J. P. Paulding, C. E. Stearns, M. V. Denny, Henry H. Wood, Alex Calahan, Thomas Metcalf, Lemuel Adams, F. A. Sabin, S. H. Wise, E. B. Smith, John T. Castle, F. M. Eakin, Ralph Wilds, A. L. Doud, Thos. J. Purnell, A. Sellers, J. J. Mathews, L. J. Seagraves, M. Klump, R. L. George, C. M. Hamilton.

In looking over this list of mem-

MR. AND MRS. R. W. HASTINGS AND CHILDREN, HAZEL AND BYRL.

HENRY D. JACKSON,

Bookkeeper for a large coal company at Portland, Oregon, and a rising young attorney.

PROF. A. H. JACKSON,

Born and raised near Greenville, a teacher for 29 years. Ten years President of Bond County Teachers' Association.

MRS. A. H. JACKSON,

A Bond County Teacher for seventeen years.

F. E. MIER,
Proprietor of Mier's meat market.

F. E. MIER'S MEAT MARKET, North Second Street.

bers I find but ten are still living and only one is still a member of the lodge and that one is R. K. Dewey, who is the oldest Odd Fellow belonging to the lodge, and there are but very few, if any, in the state older in the order. There have been over 415 members initiated in this lodge since its organization. The present membership is 110. There are now thirty-six past grands belonging to the lodge. Our membership is steadily increasing, some six or ten having been initiated, advanced and exalted since the fire of October last.

Although Clark Lodge is the oldest working lodge in the state she has never had a permanent home until a few months ago. The lodge has purchased the drug store and grounds at the northwest corner of the public square, and are having it remodeled so as to use the second story for a home for the old lodge. The price paid was $7,000, which at present advanced prices of real estate within the city, is considered a good bargain.

Greenville Lodge No. 245, A. F. and A. M.

By Joseph H. McHenry.

Greenville Lodge No. 245 A. F. and A. M. was instituted under dispensation October 28, 1856. The dispensation was granted on petition of William M. Bell, W. H. Collins, P. W. Hutchinson, J. B.

H. A. DURRE,
A well known business man.

Mr. and Mrs. F. B. Sells and Daughter, Mrs. H. A. Durre. Mr. Sells is an insurance agent.

SAGER HARRALSON,
One of Greenville's young business men.

Lansing, Isaac Minor, Neely Mc-Neill and W. F. White. W. B. Herrick, Grand Master of the Grand Lodge of Illinois, granted the dispensation and appointed as officers: W. H. Collins, W. M.; P. W. Hutchinson, S. W.; J. D. Lansing, J. W. The first man made a Mason by the lodge was Dr. W. A. Allen, who was given the Master Mason's degree on January 15, 1857.

The lodge continued under dispensation for nearly a year, until a charter was issued by the Grand Lodge at Springfield October 7, 1857. It was signed by J. H. Hibbard, Grand Master, and the charter members were: W. H. Collins, W. M.; P. W. Hutchinson, S. W.; W. P. White, J. W.; John Burchsted, W. A. Allen and Neely McNeill.

At the first meeting after the charter was issued, McKenzy Turner, acting as proxy for the Grand Master, instituted Greenville Lodge No. 245, under its charter, in due form.

The first election of officers by the lodge was held November 23, 1857, and the following were elected: S. Stevenson, W. M.; W. A.

Allen, S. W.; C. W. Holden, J. W.; J. H Birge, Secretary; John Burchsted, Treasurer; E. H. Blanchard, S. D.; T. D. White, J. D.; C. A.

Darlington, Tyler; J. D. Lansing and W. A. Allen, Stewarts.

The following is a list of the Masters of the lodge since its first organization and the term or terms during which they served: W. H. Collins, 1856-57; S. Stevenson, 1858-59; E. H. Blanchard, 1860; T. D. White, 1861; J. H. Birge, 1862; S. Stevenson, 1863; T. D. White, 1864-65; J. F. Alexander, 1866-69; E. T. King, 1870; J. B. Reid, 1871; J. C. Gerichs, 1872-74; L. Adams, 1875; P. C. Reed, 1876; J. C. Gerichs, 1877; I. Norman, 1878; J. C. Gerichs, 1879; Dr. James Gordon, 1880; I. Norman, 1881; J. B. Reid, 1882-83; I. Norman, 1884-87; C. F. Thraner, 1888; G. C. Scipio, 1889; C. J. Lindly, 1890; C. F. Thraner, 1891; E. Baumberger, 1892-94; A. L. Hord, 1895; W. B. Bradsby, 1896; Ned C. Sherburne, 1897; W. T. Easley, 1899-1900; E. E. Wise, 1901-2; E. E. Cox, 1903; Joseph H. McHenry, 1904; E. S. Titus, 1905-6.

The present officers are E. S. Titus, W. M.; E. W. Miller, S. W.; J. K. Murdock, J. W.; F. Thraner, Treasurer; J A. Scott, Secretary; E. E. Cox, S. D.; Thomas Biggs, J. D.; Ed McGraw, Tyler; J. H. McHenry, and H. W. Park, Stewarts; Rev. J. G. Wright, Chaplain.

There are now on the rolls of the lodge 90 members in good standing, and since the first organization a total of 284 names have been enrolled. W. H. Williams, who died January 1, 1906, was up to that time the oldest member of the lodge, he having become a member May 25, 1866. F. Thraner follows in point of seniority, dating his membership from October 1867.

The lodge was instituted in the

RESIDENCE OF MRS. ELIZABETH McGINNESS.

J. V. Dixon and Son, E. Bliss Dixon.

J. V. Dixon was born and raised in Bond County and has been in the hardware business since 1898. Is a member of the Board of Education.

Integrity Lodge No. 72, A. O. U. W.

By J. T. Fouke.

Integrity Lodge No. 72, A. O. U. W. was instituted April 28, 1877, with the following officers, S. M. Inglis, P. W. M.; George S. Phelps, W. M.; Henry Howard, F.; William Ballard, O.; Cyrus Birge, Recorder; George C. Scipio, Financier; M. V. Denny, Receiver; C. W. Holden, G.; Samuel Werner, I. G.; S. M. Tabor, O. W. Henry Howard was the first representative to the meeting of the Grand Lodge at Ottawa, Ill., in February 1878.

The present membership is 28. The present officers are: John B. Reid, P. W. M.; Ed McGraw, M. W.; James Kingon, Foreman; Joseph L. Koonce, Overseer; Joseph T. Fouke, Recorder; Frederick Thraner, Financier; C. K. Denny, Receiver; Sylvanus Hutchinson, I. W.; Thos. D. Stevenson, O. W.

The lodge has paid out $42,000 benefits on the death of twenty-one members.

Independent Order Mutual Aid.

The Independent Order of Mutual Aid was organized September 20, 1880, with the following officers: J. J. Clarkson, P.; C. W. Seawell, P. P.; John Kingsbury, V. P.; Henry Rammel, R. S.; J. M. McAdams, F. S.; H. T. Powell, T.; E. C. Stearns, J. J. Clarkson and H. T. Powell, Trustees; A. T. Reed, C.; C. H. Beatty, I. G.; O. L. Lupton, O. G.

Odd Fellows hall, and continued as renters of Clark Lodge until 1896, when the lodge room, now owned by the Masons was completed. This is one of the handsomest lodge rooms in the state, comprising the third story of a large brick building on the northeast corner of Main Avenue and Second Street.

The first action by the lodge looking to the erection of a lodge room was taken January 25, 1893, when George M. Tatham moved that a committee be appointed to consider the advisability of building. George M. Tatham, C. F. Thraner and G. C. Scipio were appointed as such committee. The matter was kept before the lodge through the summer of 1893, a number of committees being appointed and many conferences held, but no progress was made toward getting the work started and at a meeting held November 22 of the same year, the matter was postponed till spring and was not revived again in the lodge till February 26, 1896. On that date C. J. Lindly, Ned C. Sherburne and J. F. Watts were appointed a committee to confer with J. H. Livingston in regard to the matter of building in connection with him. On April 22 Ned C. Sherburne, Dr. W. T. Easley and C. E. Davidson were appointed a building committee and instructed to proceed with the erection of a building in connection with Mr. Livingston. The hall was completed and the first meeting held therein Wednesday evening, March 3, 1897. Ned C. Sherburne presiding as Worshipful Master. The second meeting held in the new lodge room was a lodge of sorrows to pay a last tribute of affection to the memory of Brother T. D. White, who at the time of his death, was the oldest member of the lodge. His remains were carried to the beautiful new temple and the Masonic funeral services were held there April 2, 1897. This is the only instance of a funeral having been conducted in a lodge room in this city.

The Masons have as tenants for their hall the Woodmen, Royal Neighbors and Knights of Pythias.

J. V. Dixon's Hardware Store.

FRANCIS BLAKELEY,

Well known business man, proprietor of Blakeley's Furniture Store.

275. Meetings are held twice a month in Masonic Temple.

The camp has been signally honored in that one of its members, Hon. W. A. Northcott, was for about thirteen years the Head Consul of the order, building it up from a weak little band to the largest fraternal order in the world.

The present officers are: Venerable Consul, George Hines; Worthy Adviser, John Cole; Banker, Fred Floyd; Clerk, Albert Plog; Escort, S. Harralson, Wachman, John Wilson; Sentry, Joseph Hochdaffer; Physicians, Dr. W. T. Easley and Dr. B. F. Coop; Managers, Philip Diehl, E. W. Dressor and W. C. Presgrove.

Browning Lodge No. 238 Knights of Pythias.

Browning Lodge No. 238, Knights of Pythias is a representative young men's lodge of Greenville. The lodge was instituted February 15th, 1890, by Ben Hur Lodge No. 203 of Vandalia, Ill., when the following first officers were installed: C. E. Cook, C. C.; H. J. Ravold, V. C.; J. G. Wright, P.; J. E. Groves, K. of R. & S.; N. H. Jackson, M. F.; J. S. Bradford, M. E.; W. T. Easley, M. A.; Ed DeMoulin, I. G.; M. C Heuter, O. G.

Since its organization, the lodge has enjoyed a steady growth and has at present a good working membership of sixty-two members. Browing Lodge has quarters in Masonic Temple which is noted for being one of the finest lodge rooms in Illinois.

The present officers for 1906 are.

The society has paid out in Greenville for ten deaths $23,000. The present officers are: President, L. L. Tice; Financial Secretary, S. Wannamaugher; Secretary and Treasurer, E. D. Wallace. The lodge has a membership of fifteen.

Victory Camp, No. 452, M. W. A.

By George Grube.

Victory Camp No. 452, Modern Woodmen of America, which is now the largest lodge in Bond county, was organized November 2, 1887, in Masonic Hall by R. T. Court, Deputy Head Consul. There were twenty-four charter members as follows:

L. D. Blanchard, W. A. Brown, T. S. Dewey, W. E. Davis, John H. Davis, Philip Diehl, Ed DeMoulin, H. C. Travis, Wm. T. Easley, U. E. Follett, J. E. Groves, Wm. Gerkin, W. O. Holdzkom, E. F. Johnson, Wm. M. Klump, E. B. Wise, W. A. McLain, Vance McLain, W. J. Murdock, I. Norman, Wm. G. Pervoe, Ward Reid, Charles Stewart and J. W. Wise.

The first officers of the camp were: Venerable Consul, I. Norman; Clerk, Ward Reid; Worthy Adviser, E. B. Wise; Excellent Banker, W. O. Holdzkom; Escort,

W. E. Davis; Watchman, L. D. Blanchard; Sentry, Ed DeMoulin; Physician, Wm. T. Easley; Managers, E. B. Wise; J. E. Groves, W. A. McLain.

The camp has had a steady growth from the first until the present membership numbers about

RESIDENCE OF FRANCIS BLAKELEY.

WASHINGTON SHERMAN AND FAMILY.
When they came to Greenville in 1897.

PRESENT RESIDENCE OF WASHINGTON SHERMAN,
At No. 301, East Spring Avenue.

WASHINGTON SHERMAN AND FAMILY, at the present time.

H. C. Diehl, C. C.; Sager Harralson, V. C. C.; John Floyd, Prelate; George V. Weise, K. of R. and S.; E. E. Wise, M. at A; C. E. Cook, M. of F.; F. N. Blanchard, M. of E.; James Boughman, M. of W.; F. E. Watson, I. G.; Thomas Biggs, O. G.; C. E. Cook, Representative to the Grand Lodge.

Greenville Court of Honor.

By Frank N. Blanchard.

Greenville Court of Honor No. 3, was organized in the office of W. E. Robinson in the court house and the first officers elected were Dr. W. T. Easley, President, Pro Tem; R. C. Morris, Secretary and C. J. Lindly delegate to the Supreme Court at Springfield, Ill., which meeting was held July 19, 1895. At the Supreme Court a few years later W. E. Robinson, of Greenville, was elected Supreme Recorder,

which position he still holds.

Permanent organization of Greenville Court was not effected until August 3, 1895, at which time the following officers were elected: Worthy Chancellor, W. E. Robinson; Vice Chancellor, Stella M. Reid; Past Chancellor, W. V. Weise; Recorder, R. C. Morris; Treasurer, Clara A. Robinson; Chaplain, Rev. J. G. Wright; Conductor, Ned C. Sherburne; Guard, Dicie Miller; Sentinel, J. H. Davis; Medical Examiner, Dr. W. T. Easley; Directors, W. W. Lowis, J. Seaman and A. L. Hord.

Meetings are now held in old Odd Fellows' hall and the court has a membership of 130. The present officers are:

Worthy Chancellor, E. R. Gum; Vice Chancellor, J. F. Akins; Recorder, F. N. Blanchard; Conductor, Ward Reid; Chaplain, Nellie A. Wheeler; Guard, E. W. Miller; Sentinel, Robin Reid; Medical Examiner, Dr. W. T. Easley and J. E. Groves; Directors, E. E. Brice, Mrs. W. A. Leidel and P. H. Tate.

Melrose Rebekah Lodge.

By Mrs. Laura Hair.

On February 16, 1897, twenty members, who had taken withdrawal cards from Memento Rebekah Lodge No. 125, I. O. O. F., of Vandalia, Ill., met in the hall of Clark Lodge No. 3, I. O. O. F., in Greenville, for the purpose of instituting a Rebekah Lodge. Mrs. May D. Stone, President of the state association acted as Grand Master of the occasion and a lodge was duly organized, with sixteen charter members. On March 31, of the same year, forty-three new members were initiated, making in all fifty-nine members. At one time Melrose Lodge had one hundred members enrolled. The first elected officers were as follows:

N. G., Mrs. Lizzie Dressor; V. G., Mrs. Kate Gullick; Recording Secretary, Mrs. Lizzie Dewey; Financial Secretary, Mrs. Jennie A. Scott; Treasurer, Mrs. Nancy Miles. The

A. F. RICKFELDER,
A leading horseshoer and blacksmith of Greenville.

A. F. RICKFELDER'S BLACKSMITH SHOP, South Second Street.

following were the first appointed officers: R. S. N. G., R. K. Dewey; L. S. N. G., James Scott; Warden, Mrs. Sarah Boughman; Chaplain, Mrs. Alice Lindly; O. G., A. L. Bone; I. G., John Miles; R. S. V. G., J. H. Boughman; L. S. V. G., E. W. Dressor.

Like all other orders of its kind Melrose has increased in membership but it has also decreased, and at present has but forty-four members. In October of 1904, when the Odd Fellows hall was burned, we suffered a great loss, all our regalia, rituals and seal being burned, in fact nothing being saved but our lodge records and constitution. Luckily, however, an insurance was carried and we received $150 for our loss. The present officers are: N. G., Miss Myrtle Loggins; V. G., Miss Carrie Thraner; Recording Secretary, Mrs. Laura Hair; Financial Secretary, Mrs. Maude Scheske; Treasurer, Mrs. Emma Leidel; Warden, Mrs. Carrie Loggins; Conductor, Mrs. Jennie Scott; I. G., Mrs. Nancy Dowell; O. G., G. L. Loggins; Chaplain, John Boughman; R. S. N. G., J. A. Scott; L. S. N. G., Mrs. Lizzie Dressor; R. S. V. G., Mrs. Mary Plog; L. S. V. G., Mrs. Nellie Wheeler.

The Rebekahs are a sociable band of people and will do all in their power for their fellow men and any member who needs aid in time of sickness may depend on their Rebekah sisters. The door is always open to new members and any one wishing to join a social order should not fail to consider the advantages the Rebekahs offer.

Ada Camp No. 598, R. N. of A.

By Mrs. Mary Gerkin.

A camp of Royal Neighbors of America, auxiliary to the Modern Woodmen, was organized in this city by Mrs. Lizzie Grist, deputy supreme oracle, on March 27, 1897, with twenty-five charter members. The officers elected were as follows: Mrs. Frances M. Ross, Oracle; Mrs. C. H. DeMoulin, Vice Oracle; Miss C. H. Ogden, Recorder; Mrs. M. Gerkin, Receiver; Mrs. M. Maynard, Chancellor; Mrs. Dora Hastings, Marshal; Dr. B. F. Coop, Physician; Mrs. Bertha Johnson, Outer Sentinel; Mrs. L. O. Dixon, Inner Sentinel; Mr. Ed DeMoulin, Mr. A. D. Ross and Mrs. Mary Kingsbury, Board of Managers.

Oracle Ross appointed Mrs. Ada Northcott as past oracle. The name selected for this camp was Ada, in honor of Neighbor Ada Northcott. Although Ada Camp began its life with so few members they all went to work with a will to get new members. The next month, April, seventeen were taken into the order.

Death has robbed us of six mem-

HUFFMAN AND PRESGROVE DRAYS.
Reading from left to right are Frank Dowell, James Wiles, Bert McLain, Wm. C. Presgrove and John Huffman.

A. D. Ross.

MRS. A. D. ROSS AND SONS.

bers, Charles Kingsbury, Mrs. C. H. DeMoulin, Mrs. Lawrence Ross, Mrs. Robert Sample, Miss Emma Boughman and Mrs. Frank Trost. There are now eighty-one beneficiary and sixteen social members in good standing. The officers for 1906 are:

Mrs. Leona DeMoulin, Oracle; Mrs. Mabel Buscher, Vice Oracle; Mrs. Laura Hair, Past Oracle; Mrs. Bertha Johnson, Chancellor; Mrs. Mary Plog, Recorder; Mrs. Maude Scheske, Receiver; Mrs. Dora Hastings, Marshal; Mrs. Anna Streiff, Inner Sentinel; Mrs. Katherine Rickfelder, Outer Sentinel; Mrs. Lucinda McCutcheon, Mrs. M. A. Riedemann and E. S. Frey, Managers; Dr. Wm. T. Easley and Dr. B. F. Coop, Physicians.

Mrs. Dora Hastings has the honor of having held her office of Marshal ever since the camp was organized in 1897. The Royal Neighbors are noted for their kindness and help in time of trouble and sickness. I will further say: "By their works ye shall know them."

Mutual Protective League.

By Lloyd P. Davis.

Security Council No. 156 of the Mutual Protective League was organized in this city April 3, 1899, by H. L. Tripod, who was then state deputy of the order. At the organization of the council E. E. Burson, Supreme Vice President of the order, was present and gave instructions in the secret work. The charter membership of the council was fifteen and it has had a steady

increase in membership up to the present time, and now has enrolled about sixty members. The officers elected at the time of the organization were:

Rev. C. D. Shumard, President; Mrs. J. L. Bunch, Vice President; Lloyd P. Davis, Secretary and Treasurer; B. F. Coop, M. D., Medical Examiner; all of whom still hold these respective offices, being re-elected at each term.

This council is in a very flourishing condition, having its regular monthly meetings. Until recently the meetings were held in Odd Fellows Hall. While this lodge is not the largest in the city it is considered by its members as one of the safest and surest on life insurance lines.

Royal Americans.

By Earl M. Davis.

The Fraternal Army of America, which was organized in Greenville July 18, 1901, and the Loyal Americans, which order was organized in 1903, were merged on September 15, 1903, and took the name of the Loyal Americans. The first officers of the Loyal Americans were George Alderman, President and Ollie Dixon, Secretary. The first officers of the Fraternal Army were Sam Plant, President and E. M. Davis, Secretary. These last named are the present officers. There are at present twenty-six members en-

RESIDENCE OF A. D. ROSS, East College Avenue.

MR. AND MRS. BENJ. BAITS AND DAUGHTERS.

MRS. AMANDA M. BAITS, *Deceased.*
An early settler of this county.

rolled. There is no regular place of meeting.

Knights of the Modern Maccabees

By J. P. Redmond.

Bancroft Tent No. 1035 Knights of Modern Maccabees was organized by J. E. Bancroft, January 22, 1903. The charter closed February 13, 1903, with 163 members. The first officers of this tent were as follows: Past Commander, A. L. Bone; Commander, J. L. McCracken; Lieutenant Commander, Will Lucas; Record Keeper, Will C. Wright; Finance Keeper, W. E. Jackson; Chaplain, T. F. Chamberlain; Physician, Dr. C. C. Gordon; Sergeant, George Hines; Master at Arms, E. J. Clarkson; 1st Master of the Guards, Wm. Dewey; 2nd Master of the Guards, Louis Lucas; Sentry, Harry Keesecker; Picket, John B. Floyd.

The local branch of Maccabees has been prosperous from its organization, holding regular meetings and has, the past year, grown materially in membership of such high character as to insure its growth for years to come. It has been honored with the presence of Great Commander N. S. Boynton and other distinguished head officers. J. P. Redmond was chosen to represent the tent at its Grand Review, in Battle Creek, Mich., June 4, 1904.

The financial standing of the tent was good until October 27, 1904, when fire destroyed the building in which the tent held its meetings and the tent lost regalia and records valued at $200.

The present officers of the tent are: Past Commander, W. C. Ful-

ler; Commander, R. W. Wilson; Lieutenant Commander, Alvin Watson; Record Keeper, L. L. Lucas; Finance Keeper, J. F. Johnston; Chaplain, M. B. Hawley; Physicians, Dr. W. T. Easley and Dr. J. E. Groves; Sergeant, G. B. Carr; Master at Arms, Edward Skates; First Master of the Guards, Charles Watson; Second Master of the Guards, Levi Rule; Sentinel, R. F. Stubblefield; Picket, Martin Willman.

The Modern Maccabees is one of the largest and strongest fraternal beneficiary organizations in the world today, doing business in all the healthy states of the Union on six assessments a year. The average age of all members admitted in the year 1903 was 29 years.

Greenville Hive No. 878, L. of M. M.

By Mrs. Lucy M. Cable.

Greenville Hive No. 878, Ladies of Modern Maccabees was organized July 10, 1903, with the following charter members: Dr. Lina M. Rosat, Dr. Marie L. Ravold, Eilia A. Hall, Dora F. Lutz, Lucy M. Cable, Martha Palmer, Sara J. Stubblefield, Carrie Wasem, Philopine Dever, Lena Clementz, Anna DeMoulin, Emma DeMoulin, Cordia

BAITS' BROS. MACHINE SHOP.

ANTON PLOG,
A member of the firm of Plog and White, restauranters.

A. Harper, Eliza Hair, Victoria Hair, Birdie Noe, Florence A. Jackson, Dora Palmer, Emma Wannamaugher. The following were the first officers of the lodge: Commander, Carrie Wasem; Past Commander, Marie L. Ravold; Record Keeper, Dora F. Lutz; Finance Keeper, Eilia Hall; Chaplain, Lucy M. Cable; Sergeant, Anna DeMoulin; Mistress at Arms, Birdie Noe; Sentinel, Martha Palmer; Picket, Lena Clementz; Physician, Dr. Lina M. Rosat.

The hive at present has a membership of thirty-five and the following are the officers: Commander, Laura Hair; Past Commander, Parilee Mueller; Lieutenant Commander, Emma Wannamaugher; Record Keeper, Carrie Wasem; Finance Keeper, Kate Murdock; Chaplain, Lucy M. Cable; Sergeant, Mrs. Matilda Susenbach; Mistress at Arms, Bessie Betterton; Sentinel, Jane Near; Picket, Hannah C. Davis; Physicians, Dr. L. M. Ravold and Dr. L. M. Rosat.

Banker's fraternal Union.

By J. H. Allio.

Greenville Council, No. 110, Bankers' Fraternal Union, was organized in Masonic Temple, December 18, 1903, by W. A. Northcott, Supreme Organizer. The first officers of the council were Past President, C. J. Lindly; President, E. E. Cox; Vice President, M. M. Sharp; Financial Secretary, J. H. Allio; Corresponding Secretary, G. L. Meyer; Banker, George V. Weise; Associate Editor, Will C. Wright; Sergeant at Arms, G. M. Oudyn; Conductor, Oscar Wafer; Inside Guard, Will McAdow; Outer Guard, G. G. Davis; Trustee, Ward Reid; Musical Director, Ed DeMoulin; Medical Examiners, Dr. W. T. Easley and Dr. B. F. Coop. The same officers are still in office. The present membership is 33.

MRS. ANTON PLOG.

Colby Post No. 301, 6. H. R.

By J. H. Ladd.

Colby Post No. 301, G. A. R. was mustered in by Captain Henry D. Hull on July 2, 1883, with the following named charter members: J. B. Reid, C. W. Watson, R. K. Dewey, *E. B. Wise, *John Losch, Wm. Nagle, John H. Boughman, *Wm. H. H. Beeson, *Rev. J. B. White, *D. B. Evans, *U. B. Bowers, S. M.

FORMER COUNTY TREASURER H. W. BLIZZARD, MRS. BLIZZARD, SON AND DAUGHTER.

WM. A. LEIDEL,
Manager of Leidel Ice Company.

LEIDEL ICE COMPANY'S ICE HOUSE, at Rankins Park.

Tabor, John H Hawley, Joseph T. Fouke, *T. B. Wood, Wm. T. Pointer, Geo. H. Follett, J. W. Reed, *Lemuel Adams, B. A. Harbine, Thomas K. Ridgway, Wm. Ingels, *David W. Merry, *James Stack, Lewis J. Myers, James C. Sanderson, *August Breuning, Thomas S. Vaughn, *Henry Voate, *Wm. A. Allen, *Fred Merry, *Geo. C. McCord, *John Schlup, Joseph N. Harned.

Those marked with a * are the deceased charter members.

Colby Post was named by the first captain of Co. F 130th. Ill. Volunteers in honor of Captain W. M. Colby, who was mortally wounded in the charge at Vicksburg, May 22nd, 1863 and who died May 23rd, 1863.

The first officers of the Post were: Post Commander, J. B. Reid; Senior Vice, C. W. Watson; Junior Vice, R. K. Dewey; Adjutant, U. B. Bowers; Quartermaster, E. B. Wise; Surgeon, W. H. H. Beeson; Chaplain, J. B. White; Officer of the Day, John Losch; Officer of the Guard, Wm. Nagel; Sargeant Major, D. B. Evans; Quartermaster Sergeant, J. F. Boughman.

From this time on the Post commanders have been: J. B. Reid, 1884; R. K. Dewey, 1885; J. H. Hawley, 1886; Lemuel Adams, 1887; J. C. Sanderson, 1888; J. T. Buchanan, 1889; J. B. Reid, 1890-91; D. B. Evans, 1892; R. K. Dewey, 1893; J. B. Reid, 1894; W. W. Lowis, 1895; J. B. Reid, 1896-98; J. T. Buchanan, 1899-1900; C. K. Denny, 1901; H. H. Staub, 1902; A. C. Jett, 1903; J. H. Ladd, 1904-5.

The officers of the Post for 1905, were as follows: J. H. Ladd, Commander; J. W. Daniels, Senior Vice Commander; Wm. T. Pointer, Junior Vice Commander; Dr. D. Wilkins, Surgeon; Rev. O. Hockett, Chaplain; J. T. Buchanan, Officer of the Day; George Johnson, Officer of the Guard; W. W. Lowis, Adjutant; C. K. Denny, Quartermaster; J. H. Hawley, Quartermaster Sergeant; J. B. Reid, Sergeant Major.

The 1906 officers are: Commander, J. F. Boughman; Senior Vice Commander, J. L. Koonce; Junior Vice Commander, Ransom Pope; Surgeon, Dr. W. D. Matney; Chaplain, Rev. O. Hockett; Quartermaster, C. K. Denny; Officer of the Day, J. T. Buchanan; Officer of the Guard, George Ewing; Adjutant, W.

W. Lowis; Quartermaster Sergeant, Wm. M. Goad; Sergeant Major, John H. Hawley.

One half the charter membership has answered the last roll call.

Colby Relief Corps.

By Mrs. C. K. Denny.

Colby Relief Corps was organized April 7, 1894, and Mrs. J. B. White with twenty-five other ladies signed the petition for the charter. The same was received April 21st, and the first meeting called on that date.

STORE OF W. A. AND R. F. STUBBLEFIELD.

CYCLONE HOSE COMPANY NO. 1.
View taken in front of the Post Office Building.
Reading from left to right—G. L. Loggins, James G. Mulford, E. M. Davis, Charles Sapp, George Price, A. Near, C. F. Thraner, Secretary and Treasurer; J. L. McCracken, Harry Baumberger, Lee Loyd, Thomas Stevenson, J. E. Buscher, J. A. Scott, Adolph Wirz, Philip Diehl, A. Chamberlain, Robert White, Louis Senn, L. E. Derleth, Chief.

Mrs. Julia Remann, President of McIllwain Corps No. 221, of Vandalia, Ill., installed the following officers: President, Mrs. Julia Watson; Senior Vice President, Mrs. Ella Evans; Junior Vice President, Mrs. Lucy Ingels; Treasurer, Mrs. Juliette Hoiles; Chaplain, Mrs. Mary Preston; Conductor, Mrs. Louisa Wood; Guard, Mrs. Ellen Wheeler; Assistant Conductor, Mrs. Ada Northcott; Assistant Guard, Mrs. Lydia Norman. The president Mrs. Julia Watson, appointed Mrs. Mary Lowis, secretary.

Thirty-nine members signed the roll. Since the organization of the Corps we have lost by death five members. The 1905 officers of the Corps were: President, Mrs. Ellen Wheeler; Senior Vice President, Mrs. Melvina Matney; Junior Vice President, Mrs. Kate Wise; Treasurer, Mrs. Stella Reid; Secretary, Mrs. Emma Denny; Chaplain, Mrs. Maria Wilkins; Conductor, Mrs. Agnes Mulford; Guard, Mrs. Jennie Staub; Assistant Conductor, Mrs. Louisa Wood; Assistant Guard, Mrs. Alpha Bunch.

The 1906 officers are President. Mrs. Agnes J. Mulford; Senior Vice President, Mrs. Melvina Matney;

Junior Vice President, Mrs. Lizzie Dressor; Treasurer, Mrs. Ward Reid; Secretary, Mrs. C. K. Denny; Chaplain, Mrs. Maria Wilkins; Conductor, Mrs. Louisa Wood; Guard, Mrs. Jennie Staub; Assistant Conductor, Mrs. Nellie Wheeler; Assistant Guard, Mrs. J. G. Wright.

Sons of Veterans.

Two Sons of Veterans Camps have been organized in Greenville, but both have been disbanded. The first, John H. Hawley Camp No. 291, was mustered November 25, 1889, with eighteen members. The camp flourished for several years and then disbanded.

The second camp, D. B. Evans Camp No. 130 was organized July 10, 1901, by Captain F. T. Reid. The camp surrendered its charter on June 15, 1903, although it still turns out on Decoration Day with the members of Colby Post.

The Shakespeare Club.

By One of the Members.

The Shakespeare Club was orga-

nized in the year 1888 with the following officers and members: Mrs. W. A. Northcott, President; Miss Victoria Allen (now Mrs. Benstein) Secretary; Miss Belle Tiffin, (Mrs. Harold, deceased) critic; Mrs. K. M. Bennett, Mrs. N. R. Bradford, Mrs. C. W. Watson, Mrs. W. V. Weise, and Mrs. Mary R. Broker.

Primarily, the object was mutual aid and inspiration in literary work, and the cultivation of the higher types of social entertainment. For several years the Plays of Shakespeare were read and studied. Later history, either ancient or modern, American or European, formed the basis of work, and a few years have been spent in the study of art. About fifty ladies, in all, have held membership in the club, the yearly limit being fifteen. Five have died, Miss Tiffin, (Mrs. Harold), Mrs. I. Norman, Mrs. W. V. Weise, Mrs. C. W. Watson and Mrs. Dorcas Denny.

The following compose the present officers and members: Mrs. F. P. Joy, President; Mrs. N. R. Bradford, Vice President; Mrs. Wait-Mitchell, Secretary and Treasurer; Mesdames, K. M. Bennett, N. E. Daniels, Ella E. McLain, George Colcord, W. A. McNeill, E. G. Bur-

THE MILLIONAIRES CLUB.

Top Row—Left to right, E. W. Miller, Sam M. Seawell.
Middle Row—A. Owen Seaman, K. E. Grigg, Will C. Wright, Fred E. Evans, Aleck Biggs.
Bottom Row—Thomas Biggs, Will Baumberger, H. W. Park, R. S. Denny, Abe McNeill, Jr.

ritt, O. E. Jackson, C. J. Lindly, W. A. Northcott, C. D. Hoiles, M. D. Bevan, Walter Joy and Miss Eula Carson.

Considerable work of a philanthropic and charitable nature has been accomplished in a quiet way, from year to year, yet the best results have been realized to the members, themselves, along the line of literary research and culture.

The Pierian Club.

By Mrs. C. F. Thraner.

The Pierian Club was organized in 1891 by Mesdames J. S. Bradford and L. E. Bennett. The first officers were, President, Mrs. J. S. Bradford; Vice President, Mrs. L. E. Bennett; Secretary and Treasurer, Miss Ione Wait. The Club federated in 1896.

The present officers of the club are: President, Mrs. C. F. Thraner; Vice President, Mrs. W. D. Donnell; secretary and Treasurer, Mrs. E. E.

Wise; Corresponding Secretary, Mrs. E. E. Cox; Critic, Mrs. A. L. Hord; Members, Mesdames, E. B. Brooks, F. N. Blanchard, G. F. Casey, E. E. Cox, W. D. Donnell, A. L. Hord, W. W. Lowis, E. W. Miller S. M. Thomas, C. F. Thraner, E. E. Wise, George Von Weise, Dr. Marie Louise Ravold, Misses Maude Watts and Mabel Wait.

The deceased members are Miss Carrie L. Barr, 1894; Miss Ione C. Wait, 1894; Miss Ellen Donnell, 1901; and Mrs. John Breuchaud, 1904. The club colors are green and white.

The Monday Club.

By Miss Adele Wait.

The Monday Club was organized in the spring of the year 1895. The first president was Mrs. Alexander Armstrong and the first secretary and Treasurer was Miss Jessie Allen. There were seventeen charter members. During the ten years

the Monday Club has been in existence it has entertained extensively, beside having spent a year each in the study of Emerson and English Literature, two years in the study of Shakespeare, and three years in the study of art. This was in anticipation of the Louisiana Exposition at St. Louis in 1904.

The club has been called upon to mourn the loss of two of its members, Mrs. Wilhelmina C. Hoiles and Mrs. Carrie McLain. The present officers are President, Mrs. C. K. Denny; First Vice President, Mrs. J. F. Carroll; Second Vice President, Mrs. K. E. Grigg; Secretary and Treasurer, Mrs. H. A. Hubbard; Quiz, Miss Adele Wait.

The purpose of the Monday Club is for mutual improvement intellectually and socially.

The charter members were Mesdames: W. A. McLain, Willie Hoiles, Daise Hoiles, J. F. Carroll, C. K. Denny, L. E. Derleth, A. L. Hord, E. Baumberger, H. A. Hubbard, Alexander Armstrong, Misses Ethel A. Reed, Jessie Allen, Ethel Allen,

A. H. KRAUSE'S JEWELRY STORE.
Mr. Krause is the central figure at the desk.

Dana Grigg, Lillian, Wait, Isabel Brown—sixteen in all—to which number the membership was at first limited. Later it was extended to twenty. Blue Monday was selected for the day of meeting from the fact that fewer outside matters occur to interfere with regular attendance on the first day of the week. A number of names were suggested but the one by which the club is known was chosen from the day on which the meetings were held. As the organization was not effected until some time in the spring a regular course of study was not decided upon until the beginning of the next reading year. The few months were spent in reading from the standard poets.

The Browning Circle.

By Mrs. J. E. Wafer.

The Browning Circle was organized in January 1897, with twenty members. Eight of the original members continue members at the present time. There has been but one death in the circle, that of Mrs. M. Ella Harris. Two other members are now living in California, one in Arkansas, one in Vandalia, Ill., and one in Indiana.

The first officers were: President, Miss Alice Birge; Vice President, Miss Lizzie Colcord; Secretary, Mrs. Estella Holdzkom; Treasurer, Mrs. Teressa Wafer.

The present officers are: President, Mrs. Wafer; Vice President,

Mrs. Lillie McNeill; Secretary, Mrs. E. E. Elliott; Treasurer, Mrs. Dell Albrecht.

The Ranger's Adventure.

(This account of the escapade of Tom Higgins, a Bond county pioneer is taken from "Historical Collections of the Great West" published by Henry Howe in 1852. The book has for fifty years been in the family of Mr. George Perryman of Greenville.)

Thomas Higgins a native Kentuckian, in the late war (Mexican War) enlisted in a company of rangers, and was stationed in the summer of 1814, in a block house or station, eight miles south of Greenville in what is now Bond county, Illinois. On the evening of the 30th of August a small party of Indians having been seen prowling about the station, Lieutenant Journay with all his men, twelve only in number, sallied forth the next morning just before daylight in pursuit of them. They had not proceeded far on the border of the prairie, before they were in an ambuscade of seventy or eighty savages. At the first fire the Lieutenant and three of his men were killed. Six fled to the fort under cover of the smoke, for the morning was sultry, and the air being damp, the smoke from the guns hung like a cloud over the scene; but Higgins remained behind to have "one more pull at the enemy" and avenge the death of his companions.

He sprang behind a small elm, scarcely sufficient to protect his body, when the smoke partly rising, discovered to him a number of Indians, upon which he fired, and shot down the foremost one.

Concealed still by the smoke, Higgins re-loaded, mounted his horse, and turned to fly, when a voice, apparently from the grass, hailed him with: "Tom, you won't leave me, will you?" He turned immediately around and seeing a fellow soldier, by the name of Burgess, lying on the ground wounded and gasping for breath, replied: "No, I'll not leave you, come along."

MR. AND MRS. JOHN HINDEN,
Now deceased, who came to Greenville in 1856.

"I can't come," said Burgess, "my leg is all smashed to pieces." Higgins dismounted and taking up his friend, whose ankle had been broken, was about to lift him on his horse, when the animal taking fright, darted off in an instant and left them both behind.

"This is too bad," said Higgins, "but don't fear; you hop off on your three legs, and I'll stay behind between you and the Indians and keep them off. Get into the tallest grass and crawl as near the ground as possible." Burgess did so and escaped.

The smoke, which had hitherto concealed Higgins, now cleared away and he resolved, if possible, to retreat. To follow the track of Burgess was most expedient. It would, however, endanger his friend. He determined therefore, to venture boldly forward, and, if discovered, to secure his own safety by the rapidity of his flight. On leaving a small thicket, in which he had sought refuge, he discovered a tall, portly savage near by and two others in a direction between him and the fort. He paused for a moment and thought if he could separate and fight them singly, his case was not so desperate. He started, therefore, for a little rivulet near but found one of his limbs failing him—it having been struck by a ball in the first encounter, of which, till now, he was scarcely conscious. The largest Indian pressed close upon him and Higgins turned round two or three times in order to fire. The Indian halted and danced about to prevent his taking aim. He saw it was unsafe to fire at random, and perceiving two others approaching, he knew he must be overpowered in a moment, unless he could dispose of the forward Indian first. He resolved, therefore, to halt and receive his fire. The Indian raised his rifle, and Higgins watching his eye, turned suddenly, as his finger pressed the trigger, and received the ball in his thigh. He fell, but rose immediately and ran. The foremost Indian, now certain of his prey, loaded again and with the other two pressed on. They overtook him—he fell again, and as he rose, the whole three fired and he received all their balls. He now fell and rose a third time; and the Indians, throwing away their guns, advanced upon him with spears and knives. As he presented his gun at one or the other, each fell back. At last the largest Indian, supposing his gun to be empty, from his fire having been thus reserved,

advanced boldly to the charge. Higgins fired and the savage fell.

He had now four bullets in his body, an empty gun in his hand, two Indians unharmed, as yet, before him, and a whole tribe but a few yards distant. Any other man would have despaired. Not so with him. He had slain the most dangerous of the three; and having little to fear from the others, began to load his rifle. They raised a savage whoop and rushed to the encounter. A bloody conflict now ensued. The Indians stabbed him in several places. Their spears, however, were but thin poles, hastily prepared, and bent whenever they struck a rib or muscle. The wounds they made were not, therefore, deep, though numerous.

At last one of them threw his tomahawk. It struck him upon the cheek, severed his ear, laid bare his skull to the back of his head, and stretched him upon the prairie. The Indians again rushed on, but Higgins recovering his self-posession kept them off with his feet and hands. Grasping, at length, one of their spears, the Indians, in attempting to pull it from him, raised Higgins up; who, taking his rifle, dashed out the brains of the nearest savage. In doing so, however, it broke, the barrel only remaining in his hand. The other Indian, who had heretofore fought with caution came now manfully into the battle. His character as a warrior was in jeopardy. To have fled from a man, thus wounded and disarmed, or to have suffered his victim to escape, would have tarnished his fame forever. Uttering a terrific yell, he rushed on and attempted to stab the exhausted ranger, but the latter warded off his blow with one hand and brandished his rifle-barrel with the other. The Indian was, as yet, unharmed, and under existing circumstances, by far the most powerful man. Higgins' courage, however, was unexhausted and inexhaustible. The savage, at last, began to retreat from the glare of his untamed eye to the spot where he dropped his rifle. Higgins knew that if he recovered that, his own case was desperate. Throwing his rifle barrel aside and drawing his hunting knife, he rushed upon his foe. A desperate strife ensued— deep gashes were inflicted on both sides. Higgins, fatigued and exhausted by the loss of blood, was no longer a match for the savage. The latter succeeded in throwing his adversary from him, and went immediately in pursuit of his rifle. Higgins, at this time rose and sought the gun of the other Indian.

Both, therefore, bleeding and out of breath were in search of arms to renew the combat.

The smoke had now passed away and a large number of Indians were in view. Nothing, it would seem, could now save the gallant ranger. There was however, an eye to pity and an arm to save—and that arm was a woman's!

The little garrison had witnessed the whole combat. It consisted of six men and one woman. That woman, however, was a host, a Mrs. Pursley. When she saw Higgins contending, single-handed, with a whole tribe of savages, she urged the rangers to attempt his rescue. The rangers objected as the Indians were ten to one. Mrs. Pursley, therefore, snatched a rifle from her husband's hand and declaring that "so fine a fellow as Tom Higgins should not be lost for want of help" mounted a horse and sallied forth to his recue. The men, unwilling to be outdone by a woman, followed at full gallop—reached the spot where Higgins fainted and fell before the Indians came up, and while the savage, with whom he had been engaged, was looking for his rifle, his friends lifted the wounded ranger up, and throwing him across a horse before one of the party, reached the fort in safety.

Higgins was insensible for several days and his life was preserved by continual care. His friends extracted two of the balls from his thigh, two, however, yet remained— one of which gave him a good deal of pain. Hearing afterward that a physician had settled within a day's ride of him, he determined to go and see him. The physician asked him fifty dollars for the operation. This Higgins flatly refused, saying it was more than a half year's pension. On reaching home he found the exercise of riding had made the ball discernible. He requested his wife to hand him his razor. With her assistance he laid open his thigh until the edge of the razor touched the bullet; then inserting his two thumbs in the gash, he "flirted it out" as he used to say, "without costing him a cent." The other ball remained and gave him but little pain and he carried it with him to the grave. Higgins died in Fayette county, Illinois, a few years since. He was the most perfect specimen of frontier man in his day and was once assistant doorkeeper of the Illinois House of Representatives. The facts above stated are familiar to many, to whom Higgins was personally known, and there is no doubt of their correctness.

A LIST OF COUNTY OFFICERS
From 1817 To Date.

Sheriffs.

Samuel G. Morse, 1817; Samuel Houston, 1819; Hosea T. Camp, 1824; L. H. Robinson, 1828; Sloss McAdams, 1830; W. K. Martin, 1846; S. H. Crocker, 1848; Richard Bentley, 1850; Jacob Koonce, 1852; Williamson Plant, 1854; Josiah F. Sugg, 1856; S. H. Crocker, 1858; Wm. Watkins, 1860; Williamson, Plant, 1862; James L. Buchanan, 1864; John Fisher, 1866; John F. Wafer, 1868; Williamson Plant, 1870; A. J. Gullick, 1872; John McCasland, 1879; A. J. Gullick, 1880; Samuel Brown, 1882; Joseph F. Watts, 1886; Joseph C. Wright, 1890; John McAlister, 1894; Joseph E. Wright, 1898; W. L. Floyd, 1902 and present incumbent.

County Treasurers.

Francis Travis, 1819; James Galloway, 1820; James Durley, 1821; Felix Margrave, 1824; Leonard Goss, 1825; Thomas S. Waddle, 1827; John Gillmore, 1829; James Bradford, 1831; Peter Hubbard, 1836; Peter Larrabee, 1845; John M. Smith, 1851; J. F. Sugg, 1853; J. F. Alexander, 1854; J. K. McLean, 1856; J. S. Denny, 1858; Milton Mills, 1864; Cyrus Birge, 1866; R. L. Mudd, 1873; M. M. Sharp, 1876; J. M. McAdams, 1880; A. J. Utiger, 1882; John T. Buchanan, 1886; Everett E. Mitchell, 1890; Joseph F. Watts, 1894; H. W. Blizzard, 1898; John H. Ladd, 1902 and present incumbent.

County Judges.

Thomas Kirkpatrick, 1821; Benjamin Mills, 1822; John Gilmore, 1823; John B. White, 1837; M. G. Dale, 1839; John F. Draper, 1852; S. N. McAdow, 1855; S. P. Moore, 1860; E. Gaskins, 1865; James Bradford, 1873; A. G. Henry, 1877; Cicero J. Lindly, 1886; Salmon A. Phelps, 1890; John F. Harris, 1894; Joseph Story, 1898 to present time.

State's Attorneys.

Wm. H. Dawdy, 1872; Wm. H. Dawdy, 1876; George S. Phelps, 1880; W. A. Northcott, 1882; .W A. Northcott, 1884; F. W. Fritz, 1892; G. L. Meyer, 1904.

County Clerks.

Daniel Converse, 1817; Thomas Helms, 1819; James Jones, 1820; J. H. Pugh, 1822; Green P. Rice, 1822; James M. Robinson, 1823; Asahel Enloe, 1825; Joseph M. Nelson, 1827; Isaac Murphy, 1829; James E. Rankin, 1829; James Durley, 1830; Willard Twiss, 1831; James Bradford, 1836; Enrico Gaskins, 1846; J. S. Denny, 1865; R. L. Mudd, 1877; M. V. Denny, 1882 Lemuel Adams, 1886; Alfred Adams, 1890; Wm. D. Matney, 1894 and present incumbent.

Surveyors.

R. O. White, 1869; John Kingsbury, 1879; R. K. Dewey, 1884 to date.

Circuit Clerks.

James Jones, 1819; John M. Johnson, 1821; David Nowlin, 1825; Thomas Morgan 1823; James Bradford, 1836; Alexander Kelsoe, 1848; John B. Reid, 1860; J. A. Cooper, 1868; George S. Phelps, 1872; T. P. Morey, 1876; D. B. Evans, 1884; Ward Reid, 1892; John L. Bunch, 1904, and present incumbent.

County Superintendents of Schools.

Benjamin Johnson, 1839; Wm. S. Smith, 1844; Samuel N. McAdow, 1850; Rev. Thomas W. Hynes, 1855; M. V. Denny, 1877; P. C. Reed, 1882; T. P. Morey, 1885; J. C. Blizzard, 1890; W. E. Robinson, 1894; W. T. Harlan, 1898 and present incumbent.

Coroners.

———Floyd, 1852; ———Senn, 1862; Robert Mackey, 1866; C. H. Stephens, 1868; J. I. McCulley, 1870; C. H. Stephens, 1872; James McCracken, 1874; M. B. Chittenden, 1876; James Gordon, 1880; Wm. P. Brown, 1882; Wm. H. H. Beeson, 1884; G. T. Kirkham, 1886; Wm. T. Easley, 1892; C. C. Gordon, 1900; Don V. Poindexter, 1904.

Location Guide for buildings pictured in the
1905 Historical Souvenir of Greenville

Introduction

For this bicentennial history, the committee decided to identify as many of the sites as could be found in the 1905 Historical Souvenir. Most have been found by using the 1875 and 1900 plat books, a1928 Sanborn Insurance map, an 1893 city directory, and the 1915 Greenville Advocate Centennial Edition. I would also like to acknowledge several past members who have helped me with this over the past thirty years: Doug and Sue Hoiles, Mary Jane Sandifer, Roger Reidemann, Frank Joy, Bob Wilson and Bill Donnell. John Coleman and Lester Harnetiaux have proof read and added corrections. Of the 132 photos identified, only 50 of these structures remain as of 2014.

Kevin J. Kaegy

Bond Co. Historical Society

Page 2 and 3: This bird's eye view of Greenville was taken from the roof of a home located on Eastern Avenue at Cooper Street looking west. In the left view, the central house with the barns is at Ladue and Durley. The right view is actually the corner of Cooper and McAdams. Many of these homes including the three in the foreground still exist.

Page 3: The Greenville Carnegie Library on the southwest corner of Main at Fourth had just been completed when the original edition of this book came out. It still stands and is on the National Register of historic places.

Page 4: The Civil War Monument on the courthouse lawn, unveiled in 1903, was also new at the time and still stands on the lawn.

Page 7: The Samuel White home stood on the southwest corner of Main at Sixth. It was probably built in the 1830's and was the early home of Ansel Birge. It was torn down about 1900.

Page 8: The Cox Monument, maintained by Robinson Cemetery Association, is located two miles north of Pocahontas and one mile east of Pokey road on Cox Monument Avenue.

Page 11: The Drake House was built in the early 1830's and dismantled in 1905. It stood on the northeast corner of Main and Sixth streets.

Page 14: Home of Mrs. Adele Wait stood on the northwest corner of Washington and Third St. Dismantled in the late 1920's. Two homes, facing Third Street, sit on this site today.

Page 15: The residence of Mrs. Louisa Ravold, known as Linden Grove, was built in 1865 and still stands on 1215 East Vine Street.

Page 17: The old mill at the foot of Mill Hill was built about 1850, and in early years operated by Lansing and Ostrum. The Streuber family operated it for many years, and it was dismantled about 1913. Route 127 crosses the site at 702 Mill Hill Road.

Page 18: The State Bank of Hoiles & Sons. This original building was erected in 1859 and called the Sprague Block. It was torn down to clear the site for a new bank erected in 1919. This was on the southwest corner of Main and Second St.

Page 19: Built in 1892 by C. D. Hoiles this grand home passed into the possession of the Bass-Mollett family, who ran a funeral home here and later their publishing company. It stood on the northwest corner of Beaumont and First Street until it was razed in 2011. It was the largest home in Greenville.

Page 20: The residence of Judge S. A. Phelps stood on the east side of Third Street North of Oak St. Drastically altered and converted to apartments in the late forties, it was taken down about 1990.

Page 20: The Hotel Eureka, better known as the Franklin House. Lincoln stayed here when he visited on September 13, 1858. It was built about 1838 on the northeast corner of College and Third. Developer James Moss purchased it and had it dismantled in 1892. The timber frame structure still exists within the walls of the home on the southwest corner of College Ave at Stephens Street. Moss then built the brick structure on the square that became Weise's Department Store.

Page 24: The original portion of the Bradford Bank on the Second Street side of the square. The stone façade was added to this and the building south of it in 1914. The combined building served this bank until 1967, and still exists.

Page 25: The John Bradford home at 315 East College was built in 1895. It served as a music studio and dorm rooms for Greenville College's students. It was on the northeast corner of College and Prairie and was razed in 2001.

Page 25: The Samuel Bradford residence stood on the southeast corner of College and First Street. This home was taken down in 1967 to clear the site for the new Bradford Bank. Ornamental porch railings from this home are actually on the cupola of the bank today.

Page 26: View of the south side of the square on Main Street in 1892 looking east from Third Street. Watson's Drug Store, then in the center building, now fills all three buildings shown here. The third flood mansard roof section was removed after a storm damaged it about 1900. Built in 1868 and 1869, these three buildings still stand.

Page 28: The suburban residence of James F. Carroll was built about 1875 and still stands just southwest of the city limits at 706 Hillview Ave.

Page 29: The E. V. Gaskins home was built in the 1890's on the northwest corner of Spring and Prairie facing South. It was torn down shortly after WWII and replaced with a smaller home, which was torn down in the 1990's. It is now a parking lot.

Page 31: The third Bond County jail at 215 S. Third Street was built in 1859 and served until 1897. Peter Peppin remodeled this structure in 1934 by adding a stone entry and porch. Today it continues to serve as a retail site.

Page 32: The 1854 courthouse stood on the same square as it does today. This photo was taken during the fire that gutted the building in 1883.

Page 32: The fourth jail at 609 West College Ave. was built in 1897 and served until 1974. It is now a residence at the top of Mill Hill.

Page 41: Laying of the cornerstone of the present courthouse by the Masons took place June 4, 1884. This view is from College Avenue looking southwest across the courthouse site.

Page 41: The courthouse built in 1884 continues to serve Bond County. The cupola, dormers and ornamental chimney caps were removed around 1948

Page 42: The one story school was on the south side of the block along Spring Street and Second.

Page 42: The Old High School, built in 1859, was in the center of the block between Second, First, Spring, and Winter Streets and facing Second.

Page 42: The Old Public School building was on the northeast corner of the above block at Winter and First Streets.

Page 43: All three of the old public schools were taken down to clear the block for Central School in 1894.   Central served until 1970 when students were transferred to the new elementary school on Dewey Street. It was taken down shortly after, and apartments built on the block.

Page 45: Greenville College, built as Almira College in 1855, this structure was originally known as "Old Main". In 1892, it was purchased by the Central Illinois Conference of the Free Methodist Church and renamed Hogue Hall. It faced College Avenue between Spruce and Elm, and was razed in 2008.

Page 51: The Methodist Church, northwest corner of Second at Summer was built in 1877 and replaced in 1907 with a larger church, which burned down January 1, 1973.

Page 53: The Presbyterian Church on the southwest corner of Main at Prairie was built in 1902 and 1903. It served until 1969. It then became The Church of Christ until about 1990, when it was sold and razed.

Page 53: The old Presbyterian Church was located on the northwest corner of Third and South Street. It was built in 1845 and burned in 1897. The Congregational Church invited the Presbyterians to meet with them. In 1898 both congregations merged and built what became the Presbyterian Church on Main Street in 1902-1903.

Page 54: The old Congregational Church was built in 1839 and dismantled in 1903 to clear the site for the Carnegie Library. The timber frame of the church was rebuilt as a barn on the old Lindley farm on Airport Avenue, west of Rt.127. The barn was torn down about 1990.

Page 55: The second structure to serve the Baptist congregation was built at 218 East South Street in 1902 and burned in 1951. The new church was built on the site that continues to serve today.

Page 55: The Old Baptist Church was built in 1854 and served its congregation until 1902. It was on the north side of Main St. between Third and Fourth Street. This structure was moved to a different location in 1905. It is the same building as the Baits Bros. Machine Shop photo on page 147. See the description of that photo on page 169 for more information.

Page 57: The original St. Lawrence Church on Prairie Street was built in 1877 and replaced in August of 1911. A third structure, built in 1993, is on the site today.

Page 57: Grace Episcopal Church was built in 1882 on the northeast corner of Third and Spring, it closed in 1952. It was sold to the Central Christian congregation and moved to the southwest corner of Prairie and South Streets in 1963. It is still in use today.

Page 58: The Christian Church was built in 1891 on the northwest corner of Prairie and Main. The congregation moved in 1962 to a new structure and this one was razed. This is now a parking lot for Young Funeral Home.

Page 58: Rutschly's Hall on the north side of College Avenue between Second and First Street. The Plymouth Brethren met here until about 1920 when they moved one block north. Drastically remodeled in the 1930's, this is now a flat roofed structure.

Page 59: The Free Methodist Church was built on the southwest corner of College and Elm in 1899. It was razed to clear the site for the 1960 structure that sits here today.

Page 60: The African Methodist Church was built in 1881 at 410 South Prairie Street. It recently closed and was converted to a home in 2000.

Page 60: The second Baptist church was organized in 1890. They met in an old store front on the west side of Prairie south of Harris Avenue. In later years, it was known as True Vine Baptist Church and closed in the 1950's, it has been torn down.

Page 62: The Advocate office was located on the south side of College Avenue between the alley and Third Street from 1901 to 1911. It then moved to Second and South. In 1913, this building burned down along with the DeMoulin Block.

Page 62: The W.W. Lowis residence still stands on the northwest corner of Third at Oak Street. He was Editor of the Advocate from 1895 to 1908

Page 63: The Greenville Sun was located in the middle of the east side of the square on Second street. Originally called the Bond County Democrat, it was published from 1876 to about 1920. The building still stands.

Page 64: The residence of George Perryman was on the south side of Beaumont between the alley and Spruce Street. It was razed in 1920 to clear a site for the Carrie Burritt Dorm. She was the wife of college president Eldon Burritt.

Page 65: The residence of Abraham McNeil was on the east side of Fourth St. at Alice Ave, it was razed in about 1940.

Page 68: The Charles Davidson residence was originally built in the 1880's. The Victorian turret and wrap-around porch were added about 1900. It still stands on the northwest corner of Fourth and Washington.

Page 68: The pressed brick plant of Greenville Lumber stood on the southwest corner of Franklin Ave. and West St., and was brand new in this photo. The dome shaped structures in the foreground were the kilns. It was probably demolished in the 1920's.

Page 69: The residence of William Northcott on the northwest corner of College and Prairie. Northcott served as Lieutenant Governor of Illinois from 1896 to 1904. It still stands.

Page 72: The former law office of W.A. Northcott still stands on Second Street but is now attached to the First Bank building and contains the drive-up windows. The front has been covered with stucco and has a painted mural.

Page 73: The original Vandalia Line Depot burned down June 22, 1884 at 7:30 pm. It was rebuilt on the same site at Franklin and Third.

Page 74: The Vandalia Line built the second and best-remembered depot in 1884. The Vandalia Line merged into the Pennsylvania Railroad in 1917. The last regular passenger stop was about 1958. Most of this structure burned in 1974. A freight room, built in the 1920's, survived the fire and remains as the Shank Real Estate office.

Page 75: The residence of J. Seaman still stands on the southwest corner of College and Prairie. Built in the 1870's it was extensively remodeled in the 1950's by the Dewey funeral business. In the 1970's Phil Schildnecht added the two-story front porch that exist today. It is now known as the Young Funeral Home.

Page 77: The residence of Dr. N. H. Jackson stood south of College between Forth and Fifth Street. It was razed about 1955, and a duplex was built on this site.

Page 78: The residence of T.P. Morey still stands on the southwest corner of Main at Elm Street. It has been very well maintained and the only thing changed has been the removal of the picket fence.

Page 79: The residence of Mrs. E. A. Gullick still stands on the southeast corner of Main at Fourth. Located just west of the post office, it has served as a bed and breakfast in recent years.

Page 80: The residence of E.M. Gullick stood on the southeast corner of College at Fifth Street. The wrap-around porches were removed many years ago. This home recently suffered fire damage and was razed in 2014.

Page 81: The Thomas House hotel was established in 1880 in the old Hoiles home. The front portion was added to the structure about 1895. It continued to operate through the 1950's when it became a resident care home for elderly men. It was located on the southwest corner of Second and South and was razed about 1984.

Page 82: The Residence of Dr. Wm. T. Easley was located on the northwest corner of College and Fourth Street. It was razed about 1960. The site now contains Dr. Logullo's dentist office.

Page 82: The Residence of Prof. W.E. Milliken was on the west side of Elm, just north of Durley. It was razed about 1990 to clear site for Crum Recreation Center. It its last years it was known as Strahl-Tidball house and served as dorm space.

Page 83: The residence of C.W. Seawell still stands on the southeast corner of College and Elm. Now known as the Watson Tidball Alumni House for Greenville College.

Page 83: The residence of J. E. Hills stood on the southeast corner of College and Spruce Street. It was razed in 2014.

162

Page 84: The residence of Sherriff Joseph Watts stood on the north side of College Avenue between Prairie and Spruce. Razed in 2001 for construction of the Ellen Mannoia Dorm.

Page 84: The residence of K. E. Grigg still stands on the northeast corner of College at Fifth Street. This home was extensively remodeled in the 1920's with brick veneer and a sunroom added to the front and east side.

Page 85: The residence of Frank Abrams may have been on lots he owned on Ward Street east of Charles but this has not been confirmed.

Page 86: Weise and Bradford's Greenville Store still stands on the corner of College and Third Street.   Today it is now the Hibachi buffet. It was built in 1892 by James Moss.

Page 86: The George Von Weise Home was built in 1893 and still stands on the northwest corner of Oak and Second Street. Donnell Funeral home has operated here since the mid 1950's.

Page 87: The Ward Reid home was on the northwest corner of College and Spruce. For many years, it was the college president's home. It was razed in 1959 for the Sims Student Union building.

Page 88: Residence of F.P. Joy, southwest corner of Spruce and College. Still known as Joy House, this was the college president's home from 1960 through 2013. It is now an admission office.

Page 89: The residence of Walter Joy still stands on the northwest corner of Spruce and Main Street.

Page 89: The F.P. Joy and Company Store still stands on the northeast corner of College and Second Street. It is Lisa's Antiques and Mario's Pizza today. In the 1930's, the front façade was altered and the third floor window removed.

Page 90: The F.P. Joy and Company Annex was their men's division location on the Second street side of the square. Today it is Joe's Pizza.

Page 91: The residence of Mrs. Eliza Jett still stands on the southwest corner of College and Fourth Street. The porch has been enclosed.

Page 94: The DeMoulin block stood on the southwest corner of Third at College. It was built in 1899 and burned in 1913.

Page 94: The Post office was in the corner of the DeMoulin block, under the north turret, on the southwest corner of Third and College.

Page 95: The residence of W.D. Donnell was built about 1898 and was owned many years by the Whitlock family. It still stands at 333 N. Third Street in the Piety Hill neighborhood.

Page 95: The store of W.D. Donnell and Wise, Cox and Titus, was built about 1890 on the northwest corner of College and Second Street. The Donnell Funeral Home has moved a couple of times and is still in business. Raymond Genre established his men's clothing store on this corner in 1939. The structure burned in 1978. Genre's built the new structure on the site and it has served as a courthouse annex since the early 1990's.

Page 97: The residence of Mayor Edmund DeMoulin was built in the 1890's on the southwest corner of Third and Washington. It had a rather unusual partial turret along the north wall. It was purchased by Greenville Lumber Company and torn down in the mid 1970's. Greenville Lumber occupied all of that city block until 1987.

Page 98: The residence of U.S. DeMoulin was built in 1900 and still stands on the southwest corner of Fourth at Winter. It has been extensively remodeled and preserved by the Bowmans, Baumhoeggers and Walters families.

Page 100: The original DeMoulin factory was built in 1896 and had several major additions added over the next ten years. The entire complex was destroyed by fire in 1907. The company rebuilt on the same site where it stands today on South Fourth at the railroad tracks.

Page 101: The residence of Philip Diehl was built in 1902 and still stands at 406 South Fifth Street. It has been well preserved over the years.

Page 101: The residence of Erastus DeMoulin was built in the 1800's and still stands on the northeast corner of Washington Ave. at Fourth Street. It was the Chester Pierce home for many years as well.

Page 102 and 103: The Helvetia Milk Condensing Plant was built in 1899 south of the Greenville railroad depot. More commonly known as Pet Milk, the company's buildings were added to and removed from the site through the 1980's. Most of the original production buildings were torn down in 1992 prior to Malinkrodt Chemical purchasing the site.

Page 104: This view of Helvetia Milk condensing Plant was taken on the south side of the plant along Latzer Drive at South Third Street.

Page 105: This view of Helvetia Milk condensing plant was taken on the southeastern corner of the plant site along Latzer Drive at south Second Street.

Page 106: The Greenville Milk Condensing Plant was in business from about 1902 thru 1920. It was on the north side of Franklin Avenue between Third and Fourth Street.

Page 106: L.D. Blanchard's Union Roller Mill was, according to an early directory, located at 615 East Vine Street and no longer exists. Around 1895, the Jacksonville-Southeastern railroad built a spur into Greenville. The depot was on Vine Street near Hena and Blanchard's mill and a brickyard were the only known businesses in this otherwise residential area. By 1910, the railroad spur was taken out.

Page 107: This photo is of the south half of the west side of the Greenville town square. The main floor businesses were the Hussong General Mercantile, George Morris Real Estate and Loans, and J. Seaman Hardware Company. These buildings burned in October of 1904.

Page 110: The residence of John Ladd still stands at 416 S. Fifth St. between Winter and Spring. This home has not been changed and retains its ornamental porch and trim.

Page 110: The country residence of A.J. Sherburne still stands southwest of Greenville. It is the Marti family dairy farm that overlooks Route 40, I-70 and the Millersburg Road interchange. It was built in 1875 by Asa Sherborne who was an engineer on the St. Louis Vandalia and Terre Haute Railroad.

Page 113: Mrs. John Bunch's millinery store was just behind the DeMoulin block and faced College Avenue between the alley and Third Street. It was lost in 1913 when the DeMoulin Block burned down.

Page 116: The F.W. Fritz home was built about 1900 on the northeast corner of Main at Spruce. Due to extensive termite damage it was taken down about 1990 and the site is now a parking lot. Shortly after this photo was taken, a very unusual free-floating sunbonnet porch was added to the west and south sides of this house.

Page 116: F.W. Fritz had his law office on College Ave. on the north side of the square in the east end of the Posch Building.

Page 117: The Dr. B.F. Coop residence was built about 1895 on the northeast corner of College at Fourth Street. It was later owned by Dr. Cartmell for many years. After WWII, the front yard was sold and a service station was built in front of it. This large home was always kept painted and maintained although it stood unoccupied for many years. It was razed about 1980 for a municipal parking lot.

Page 118: H. H. Wirz cigar store and factory was on the south side of the square on the west side of the alley. Built by George Hill for his Fashion Emporium in 1840, the building was purchased by Wirz in 1878. This was the last frame building on the south side of the square and was razed to clear the site for the Firestone building in about 1940. It was located at 210 West Main Street.

Page 118: The Charles Thraner residence stood on east Main Street. The exact location is not known but this was probably on the south side between First and Prairie.

Page 119: The J.E. Wright home still stands extensively remodeled on the southeast corner of Locust at St. John. The third floor is now a loft and a fourth floor cupola has been added by the Sanders family.

Page 120: The Frank E. Watson home was built in 1901 at 314 East College Ave. It was lived in by two generations of the family. The college purchased this site for future growth and the home was razed about 2004.

Page 120: Watson Drug Store has been an anchor on the south side of the square since 1881. Watson's started business in the center of three buildings erected by W.S. Smith in 1868 and 1869. Throughout the past years, they have come to occupy all three stores fronts.

Page 121: The Caroline Idler home stood on the east side of what is now the corner of Idler Lane and Vine St. It was likely demolished in the 1950's when a new home was built there.

Page 122: The residence of Dr. L.M. Rosat was on the northeast corner of Main Street at Fourth Street. In later years, it contained several apartments and, although well maintained, was razed by Midland State Bank for a parking lot about 1996.

Page 123: The S. Van Deusen Residence was on the southeast corner of Fourth at Harris Avenue. It was originally built by the Hoiles family and was razed in 1968 for the construction of the Kroger store. It is now the Hospital Auxiliary thrift store.

Page 124: The Mrs. J.D. Tiffen home on south Third Street. This home was on the southwest corner of Third at Winter and was razed by Erastus DeMoulin in the early 20's so that he could build a new home on that site, which still stands today.

Page 124: The H.C. Coleman home stood on the north side of East Vine Street at the top of the hill. It was replaced by a three-story home in 1915, that was later owned by Ed Essenpries. The third floor was removed after it was damaged in a storm about 1950. The entire structure was torn down after an extensive fire did damage in 2010.

Page 126: The residence of John H. Hawley is on West College Avenue on the southwest corner of Fifth Street. The bay window and porch have been removed.

Page 127: The residence of W. E. Davis was on east Main Street. It was the second house west of Elm Street and it was torn down about 1970 for construction of the education wing of the Free Methodist Church.

Page 127: The Earl Davis residence still stands at the northeast corner of Cooper and McAdams. This home also appears in the bird's-eye-view photo on page 3.

Page 128: The Judge Cicero Lindley home originally faced Third Street from the south part of the Dairy Queen lot. In the mid 1970's it was moved to the back of the block to face north at Oak and Fourth. It was razed in the 1980's for a municipal parking.

Page 131: Mulford and Monroe Drug store was built on the northwest corner of Third Street at College Avenue about 1870. It was built by Charles Bennett who also operated a drug store. It was later known as O'Neal's drug store and it is now owned by Wall Real Estate.

Page 132: The residence of W.W. Hussong was on the east side of Second Street, south of Harris Avenue. It was razed about 1995. It was owned by the John Dierkes family who operated the Zephyr Gas Station next door to it.

Page 132: Fred Durr's Harness shop was on the Second Street side of the square. Durr's occupied the first floor and The Item newspaper office was upstairs. About 1914, Bradford Bank purchased this building south of their facility and remodeled both structures into the building that exists today on the east side of the square.

Page 133: The George Morris home was on the southeast corner of Third at Winter. In the 1950's, Southwestern Electric built their new office here and in the early 1970's sold it to the city of Greenville for a municipal building.

Page 134: The residence of John H. Davis at 319 North Prairie. This home is still standing, although greatly altered. The turret-type porch has been removed and an addition added to the left.

Page 134: The R.W. Wilson Home. It is thought that this home was on north Spruce Street and was removed when Greenville College built the new Armington Center in the 1980's.

Page 135: F. H. Wheelers Harness Shop occupied the western half of the Posch bulding on the north side of the square

Page 136: Hawley's Jewelry Store was on Main Street but the exact location is not yet known. After the DeMoulin Block burned in 1913, Hawley's did build a small building on that site which was the Baumberger-Whitlock insurance office for many years.

Page 137: The Peppin blacksmith shop stood on the north side of Summer Avenue, between the alley and Fourth Street. This building was torn down after WWII.

Page 137: The old Travis blacksmith shop was purchased by Peppin and torn down about 1890 when he built his new shop along Summer Avenue.

Page 139: F.E. Mier's Meat Market was in the north building on the east side of the square. This building still exists, and from the 1940's through the 1990's contained a jewelry store.

Page 140: The Lawrence and Elizabeth McGinniss home was built in the 1870's and still exists on the northeast corner of Oak at Elm Street. It has been owned by Greenville College for many years. The McGinniss family were devout Irish Catholics and helped found the St. Lawrence Parish in 1868.

Page 141: J. V. Dixon's Hardware Store still exists on the southeast corner of Second and Main Streets. The porch and one porthole have been removed. This building contained a furniture store for many years, and is now the Green Door Antique Shop.

Page 142: The location of the Francis Blakeley was the northeast corner of Elm and Durley Streets. This house was purchased shortly after this photo by Dr. Katherine Luzader, the county's first female physician. She did major remodeling about 1912, including adding a wrap around porch. This house was torn down about 2005, and is now a parking lot for Greenville College.

Page 143: The residence of Washington Sherman faced Raspberry Alley but had a Spring Street address. This beautiful home had all of its trim stripped off and contained run-down apartments for many years. It was torn down in 1993 when the St. Lawrence Congregation built their new church on this site.

Page 145: A. F. Rickfelder's blacksmith shop was on the southwest corner of Second and Spring Streets. It was torn down in the 1930's, and a large metal warehouse was later built by U & E Farm Supply, which remains on the site today.

Page 145: Huffman and Presgrove Dray was a delivery service. At the time most freight was brought to town by train. Dray services kept busy hauling merchandise, supplies, and passengers from the depot, uptown to the business district. The exact location of this buisness is not known, but the photo appears to have been along Second Street.

Page 146: The residence of A.D. Ross still stands at 515 East College Avenue on the north side of the street, east of Locust.

Page 147: Baits Brother's Machine Shop was originally the old Baptist Church. In 1905 it was moved to the southeast corner of Summer and Third, where this photo was taken. It was moved again in the 1920's to College Ave. where Harold Gaffner later added a car dealership building in the front, and used this building as a garage. It was demolished in 1966 for construction of the current Bradford National Bank.

Page 149: Leidel Ice Company appears to have had different locations over the years, one of which was on Vine Street. In 1898 the company purchased land just east of Stubblefield which had a lake on the site, probably for the purpose of cutting ice in the winter. This photo was likely taken there. Their locations in town were possibly storage sites for ice that they used during the summer months.

Page 149: Stubblefield Grocery was in the eastern end of the three Smith buildings on Main Street. Hughey Hardware was in that building many years. Since the 1990's, Watson drug store has occupied the site.

Page 150: The Cyclone Hose Company is posed on North Third Street in front of the DeMoulin Building. This building burned down in 1913; its predecessor had burned in 1899. Some of these men fought both fires.

Page 152: A. H. Krause Jewelry store was on the south side of the square just west of the First National Bank building on Main Street. The east half of this building was removed in 1919 when the "new" bank was built. The west half remains between the bank the new west wing of the bank.

Name Index